The Houses of Louis Kahn

The Houses of Louis Kahn

George H. Marcus and William Whitaker

Yale University Press
New Haven and London

Published with assistance from the Graham Foundation for Advanced Studies in the Fine Arts.

Copyright © 2013 by George H. Marcus and William Whitaker.
All rights reserved.
This book may not be reproduced, in whole or in part, including illustrations, in any form (beyond that copying permitted by Sections 107 and 108 of the U.S. Copyright Law and except by reviewers for the public press), without written permission from the publishers.

The drawings, photographs, documents, and models in the Louis I. Kahn Collection of the Architectural Archives of the University of Pennsylvania reside in the Harvey and Irwin Kroiz Gallery. Since 1981 the generous support of Harvey and Irwin Kroiz has made possible the study, conservation, expansion, and sharing of the Kahn collection.

yalebooks.com/art

Designed by Miko McGinty
Set in Marat Sans type by Tina Henderson
Printed in Italy by Graphicom

Frontispiece: Margaret Esherick House, Chestnut Hill, Philadelphia, 1959–62. Chimney, seen through a living-room window. Photograph 1990

Jacket illustrations: (*front*) Steven and Toby Korman House (detail, fig. 91); (*back*) Louis Kahn inspecting completed millwork at the Norman and Doris Fisher House, Hatboro. Photograph summer 1966 by Norman Fisher. AAUP, by the gift of Norman and Doris Fisher.

Library of Congress Cataloging-in-Publication Data

Marcus, George H.
 The houses of Louis Kahn / George H. Marcus and William Whitaker.
    pages cm
 Includes bibliographical references and index.
 ISBN 978-0-300-17118-1 (cloth : alk. paper) 1. Kahn, Louis I., 1901–1974—Criticism and interpretation. 2. Architecture, Domestic—History—20th century. I. Whitaker, William. II. Title.
 NA737.K32M35 2013
 728'.37092—dc23   2012051171

A catalogue record for this book is available from the British Library.

This paper meets the requirements of ANSI/NISO Z39.48–1992 (Permanence of Paper).

10 9 8 7 6 5 4 3 2

When I first was introduced to modern architecture, the books were being burned. The books that I care for a great deal somehow did not look as bright as the pages of Le Corbusier's explorations, his drawings, his speculations, his point of view. I even learned that a simple house, which was never a consideration in my training, became something of importance.

—Louis Kahn, "The White Light and the Black Shadow," 1968

Contents

Preface	viii
Note to the Reader	x
Prologue	2
Home	4
Houses	18
Furnishings	74
Epilogue	94
Jesse and Ruth Oser House	96
Philip and Jocelyn Roche House	108
Morton and Lenore Weiss House	116
Samuel and Ruth Genel House	128
Fred and Elaine Clever House	150
Bernard and Norma Shapiro House	158
Margaret Esherick House	170
Norman and Doris Fisher House	194
Steven and Toby Korman House	220
Notes	251
Bibliography	261
Index	263
Illustration Credits	269

PREFACE

One can learn a lot by visiting the houses of Louis Kahn, seeing the way in which natural light is handled and admiring the beauty of his materials and how they are put together, but to understand how he conceived and developed his designs, one must visit the Louis I. Kahn Collection in the Architectural Archives at the University of Pennsylvania. The collection chronicles his entire engagement with the design of dwellings, from his earliest known independent drawing of a house, which was done in 1930 and appears on the letterhead of his first partnership, to his final design, put down on paper within weeks of his death in 1974. Its documentation of Kahn's career includes some thirty-six thousand drawings and numerous models, photographs, correspondence files, datebooks, and office records containing the nitty-gritty of his architectural practice. In preparing this study we reviewed all of this material as it pertained to Kahn's houses, and with the riches we found there (along with the memories of those who witnessed his design firsthand) we have been able to present a new and unexpected understanding of Kahn's creative activity.

The first comprehensive look at the architect's work was the groundbreaking exhibition Louis I. Kahn: In the Realm of Architecture, which opened at the Philadelphia Museum of Art in September 1991. While this retrospective became the foundation for later research and scholarship on Kahn, it also "stirred up a lot of trouble" for the owners of a number of Kahn's houses, as Doris Fisher slyly noted. The dribs and drabs of admiring students and architects who had appeared on their doorsteps in years past increased in great numbers and were supplemented by busloads of institutional supporters and architectural tour groups (a situation exacerbated by the release of the documentary film *My Architect*, in 2003). For assistance in organizing access to the houses, these same groups began to contact the Architectural Archives. This initiated a process that brought the archives staff, first Julia Moore Converse, its director, and then William Whitaker, who succeeded her, in closer contact with the owners, as well as their houses. Eventually it was the staff of the archives who gave the tours, and in doing so, took on the houses as an area of special expertise. Out of this decades-long context of engagement with the houses came another collaboration using the resources of the archives, a curatorial seminar and exhibition at Penn in 2008–9 on Kahn's interiors and furniture. This was led by George H. Marcus and brought the narrative of Kahn's houses into sharp focus. At the same time, Whitaker led another seminar on the preservation of Kahn's buildings, concentrating on the Fisher house. These involvements spurred the two of us to undertake additional research on Kahn's houses, their furnishings, and his clients, which became the cornerstone of this study.

We gained an invaluable understanding of Kahn's working process through discussions with his clients and their families, who shared their experiences, gave access to their documentation, and, in some cases, helped to correct the historical record, especially with respect to projects that were not built: Lynne Adler, Fred and Elaine Clever, Liliane Clever, Weber DeVore, Jr., and Eleanor (DeVore) Sayre, Lisa Esherick, Norman and Doris Fisher, Nina Fisher and Claudia (Fisher) Gohl, Jill (Fleisher) Bonovitz, Barbara Fruchter, Rick Genel and Nancy (Genel) Levanoni, Mitzi (Goldenberg) Marks, Tony Goldenberg, Steven Kitnick, Steven Korman and Toby (Korman) Davidov, Margy Meyerson, Wendy Oser and Julie (Oser) McLeod, Bernard and Norma Shapiro, Helen Stern, and Morton and Lenore Weiss. Later owners of the houses also provided us with insights as well as access, especially for newly commissioned photography: Charles Firmin-Didot and Bianca Sforni, Robert and Lynn Gallagher, Andrew and Leigh Gustine, Roy Hemmann, Marlyn Ivory, Mark and Maggie Robinson, Samuel and Rosanne Spear, Caryl Wolf, and particularly Larry and Korin Korman, whose enthusiasm and support added greatly to this book.

While trying to understand the experience of building and living in Kahn houses was an objective of ours, so too was documenting the discussions and decisions that occurred in Kahn's drafting room and in the studios he taught at the University of Pennsylvania. The extensive reminiscences of David C. S. Polk and Anne Griswold Tyng were of particular value. William Huff, David Reinhardt, Robert Venturi, and Thomas R. Vreeland, key members of Kahn's staff during the mid-1950s, offered important nuances about the development of a series of unbuilt houses, while David G. De Long, Nick Gianopolus, David Karp, Harriet Pattison, Vincent Luis Rivera, Roy Vollmer, and Henry Wilcots contributed significantly to our knowledge of other projects.

Many scholars provided support, sharing their thoughts and their viewpoints as well as their research: David B. Brownlee, Urs Büttiker, Jeffrey Cohen, Julia Moore Converse, Emily T. Cooperman, Lindsay Falck, Michael J. Lewis, Ralph Lieberman, Richard Longstreth, Shilpa Mehta, Peter Reed, Susan Solomon, and George E. Thomas.

Others helped in countless ways: Mansfield Bascomb, Suzanne Binswanger, Pierson Booher, Aubin Clever, Robert Cohn, Taryn D'Ambrogi, David Dillard, Kenta Fukunishi, Gwen Gain, Paul Galloway, Michael Gohl, Caitlin Kramer, Vincent Leung, David McLeod, Nancy Miller, Grant Mudford, Janet Parks, Anandaroop Roy, Vincent Saldutti, Jr., Miranda Saylor, Michael Shoriak, Caitlin Smith, Angela Spadoni, Melissa Steely, Marilyn Jordan Taylor, Edward Teitelman, Matt Wargo, and especially Nancy Thorne, whose devotion to the Kahn Collection and the Architectural Archives is exemplary.

Publishing this book with Yale University Press has been a most satisfying experience. Miko McGinty's spare design has most elegantly enhanced the story of Kahn's work that we set out to tell. From our first encounters with Patricia Fidler, publisher, art and architecture, and Michelle Komie, senior editor, art and architecture, to the last proofs we checked, overseen by Heidi Downey, senior manuscript editor, and Mary Mayer, art book production manager, the entire process was handled smoothly and effectively. The acquisition of images, both new photography and rights to earlier photographs, was supported by the Graham Foundation for Advanced Studies in the Fine Arts.

Finally, any research into the life and work of Louis Kahn, and especially a project focused on his design of private houses, benefits immensely from the involvement of his three children, Sue Ann Kahn, Alexandra Tyng, and Nathaniel Kahn, to whom we are most grateful.

G. H. M. and W. W.

NOTE TO THE READER

Unless otherwise noted, all works illustrated are by Louis Kahn, and all houses and projects are located in Pennsylvania.

The following abbreviations are used in the captions and notes:

AAUP	Architectural Archives, University of Pennsylvania
AGT	Anne Griswold Tyng
EIK	Esther Israeli Kahn
GHM	George H. Marcus
Kahn Collection	Louis I. Kahn Collection, University of Pennsylvania and the Pennsylvania Historical and Museum Commission
LIK	Louis I. Kahn
WW	William Whitaker

Fig. 1 Norman and Doris Fisher House, Hatboro, 1960–67. Living room from entry. Photograph 1990

PROLOGUE

Louis Kahn completed nine houses and designed some two dozen more, eight of which were developed enough to go out to bid. This is not a large amount, but neither is it narrow in its reach: houses spanned almost his entire career, and they spoke, often before his larger commissions did, to many of the issues that stirred him as an architect and made him a singularly revered figure in the history of modern design. And yet, almost no in-depth scholarly attention has been paid to them, even though the design of houses was every bit as compelling for him, and as pivotal for his work, as the design of his other buildings.

Kahn's houses are difficult to grasp at once, for they were designed not as architectural manifestos but as buildings that express the circumstances of their creation. Possibly this is why it has taken so long for them to achieve the reputation they deserve. Kahn's houses can be brilliant, but they are not demonstrative. The Fisher house is perhaps the most reticent—a house that keeps its secrets but repays the effort to make sense of its genius (see figs. 199, 217–26). Its canted façade hides its face from the street; the door is set deep within the entranceway. Its two cypress-clad cubes intersect elegantly, but this is hidden, a surprise that is not revealed until you begin to walk around the site. Only as you ramble down to the creek does the house open up with great windows in a composition of inspired serenity. Within, all is reversed: whereas the outside is calm, the inside is animated. As you enter, a large window draws you to the landscape beyond, but an angled opening pulls you aside, toward a monumental stone chimney. Tall inset windows, standing like confessionals, join with chimney and kitchen walls to define the boundaries of the living room, inglenook, and dining room. It is here, as you confront the stonework, the rough plaster surfaces, the traditional woodwork, the views, and, especially, the light, that Kahn's vision is resolved in great intimacy (fig. 1).

Kahn's houses have been overshadowed by the almost universal attention paid to his monumental buildings based on a heroic narrative established in the first monograph on his work, written by his great champion and Yale colleague Vincent Scully, Jr., and published in 1962. The narrative follows the young Russian-Jewish immigrant as he grew up in extreme poverty in Philadelphia, was recognized for his talents as an artist and a musician, went to the University of Pennsylvania to study architecture with Paul Cret, and surely would have made an immediate name for himself had it not been for the Great Depression and the Second World War. Before the early 1950s, Kahn was little known and "had built almost nothing," according to Scully, although he had already served on several local and national planning commissions, completed a synagogue, two hospitals, four private houses, thousands of dwelling units in several large government housing projects, and various other undertakings.[1] He came into his own only at the age of fifty, the myth continues, after his stay at the American Academy in Rome in the winter of 1950–51 when, with the design of his Yale University Art Gallery (1951–53), he began to rethink the tenets of orthodox modernism and "reintroduced the antique notion of mass," as David G. De Long, a scholar and student of Kahn's, described it. "Beginning with aspects of mass," De Long explained, "he later examined aspects of spatial division, of openings, of interior and exterior correspondence, so that in the end nothing remained the same."[2]

Architects in the early 1950s would have been mystified by Scully's assessment that Kahn was little known, for as one of the organizers, vice president, and later president of the short-lived American Society of Planners and Architects (1943–48), Kahn belonged to a group that, according to the architectural historian Andrew Shanken, "sheltered virtually every self-styled modernist architect and progressive planner on the East Coast," including Marcel Breuer, Serge Chermayeff, Walter Gropius, Wallace K. Harrison, George Howe, Philip Johnson, and José Luis Sert.[3] Both his mass housing and his private dwellings had attracted considerable renown: housing was what brought him some of his earliest publications, his earliest participation in architectural exhibitions, and his first professional prizes. His Weiss house, constructed from 1947 to 1950, brought Kahn the Chapter Medal from the Philadelphia chapter of the American Institute of Architects (AIA) in 1950, and his early career was capped two years later when he was awarded the Medal of Achievement from the New York chapter of the AIA; had he built almost nothing and been little known, this award for "distinguished work and high professional standing" would not have come to him.[4]

Little changed in the appreciation of Kahn's houses over the decades following the publication of Scully's book, except in Japan, where his sense of detail and attention to craft and material have been of continuous fascination.[5] Elsewhere, his influence had been restricted largely to the pavilion plans he devised in the mid-1950s for the Adler and DeVore houses, which inspired a line of distinguished architects, including Charles Moore, John Hejduk, and Peter Eisenman, to follow him in the reconsideration of modern domestic spaces.[6] The focus shifted with the landmark retrospective of 1991, In the Realm of Architecture, in which Kahn's houses were given a broader and more respectful treatment as important works in their own right, even though none was among the twenty projects scrutinized in its catalogue.[7] No significant academic interest in Kahn's houses followed, and they have remained remarkably unstudied.

In writing about Kahn's houses, scholars have relied principally on his poetic statements, such as the one that appeared in his essay "Form and Design" in 1960: "Reflect then on what characterizes abstractly House, a house, home. House is the abstract characteristic of spaces good to live in. House is the form, in the mind of wonder it should be there without shape or dimension. *A* house is a conditional interpretation of these spaces. This is design. In my opinion the greatness of the architect depends on his powers of realization of that which is House, rather than his design of *a* house which is a circumstantial act. Home is the house and the occupants. Home becomes different with each occupant."[8] While such statements illuminate Kahn's perspective and demand serious consideration, they do little to shed light on his concrete experiences in designing houses. They say nothing about how he was inspired by his clients, how he transmuted their aspirations into built form, or how he completed many of his commissions with designs for their interiors and furnishings. Nor do they say anything about his process of invention, which, because of the small scale of these projects, can be followed in vivid detail. In this study, his earliest architectural endeavors have been brought to surprising light, his creative influences revealed, and his youthful method uncovered. This method continued to enrich his vocabulary as his houses evolved, often before these new ideas were explored in his monumental works, and he developed them over a period of more than forty years into one of the most remarkable expressions of the American private house.

HOME

In reflecting on the factors that Louis Kahn brought to the design of his houses, one cannot overstate the importance of his sense of home (fig. 2). For sixty-eight of his seventy-three years he lived in the city of Philadelphia, but it was the Baltic island of Ösel (now Saaremaa), where he spent two years of his early youth, that he would consider his birthplace.[1] While Kahn was, in fact, born on the western fringe of the Russian Empire in 1901, it was not Ösel but the mainland port town of Pernow (now Pärnu, Estonia), where his father was stationed as a paymaster in the tsar's army, that can claim his birth. Still, Kahn always thought of his birthplace as Ösel (he did not know otherwise), and he would speak of the idyllic island, with its low, traditional houses and medieval castle by the sea, as if it were out of a fairytale.[2]

Kahn's family was poor, and like so many eastern European Jews at that time, they sought the promise of a better life in America. Times were difficult, perhaps even desperate, for when his father, Leopold, made the passage to Philadelphia in June 1904, he left behind his two children and his wife, Bertha, pregnant with a third. Following her husband's departure, Kahn's mother moved with the children to Ösel and its main town of Arensburg (now Kuressaare), a summer resort where her family operated a small guesthouse. After spending two years on this mild and wooded island, Kahn, then five and a half years old, his mother, and his two siblings sailed for the United States to join Leopold in the teeming metropolis of Philadelphia.[3]

The rural world the children had known on the Baltic island was replaced by the blackened, brick row houses in the Northern Liberties, an area of the city swelling with an immigrant population but falling on tough times. Trapped, it would seem, in a cycle of insecurity and degradation, the family, as Kahn later recalled, "spent the next 10 years moving constantly," never living long enough in any one place to feel it was their own.[4] The family would slowly move up to the predominantly Jewish neighborhood of Strawberry Mansion, where they eventually bought a house with the help of their sons' earnings. Kahn and his wife, Esther, after their marriage in 1930, moved to the more prosperous area of West Philadelphia for what they expected would be a temporary stay in the house of her parents, but they ended up living there for thirty-seven years.[5] It was not until 1963 that they bought a house of their own, at 921 Clinton Street in the center of the city, but they did not move in until alterations were completed in 1967.[6]

Owning a house did not bring them a home, in any case. Home was elusive; it had to do with people, not architecture, and Kahn's own unconventional family arrangements—he had three children with three different women—made it impossible for him to experience this however much he might have longed for it.[7] His daughter Sue Ann recalled that she once asked him, "'Daddy, why don't you ever design us a house?' and he answered: 'You have to understand, what I think of Home is not this home. I could never build myself a house.'" Sue Ann explained: "He had the feeling that his personal life at home never lived up to his romantic ideal of what a home was." To him, home was remote. It meant that "if an outsider were looking in (through a window with many

Fig. 2 Louis Kahn in his office, 138 South 20th Street, Philadelphia, October 1952. Kahn Collection

Fig. 3   Lenore and "Bubby" Weiss in their house in East Norriton Township, April 1991

mullions) he could see a woman cooking over a stove, a happy family with the light glowing," but this was not his family.[8] Kahn was very precise about what he meant by home. It "can only exist when people are in it," he explained. "They are the creators of *home*. You don't build a home. You build a house. At best, if you build a house, there comes out of it a sense of a way of life, a reflection of a way of life which inspires your own way of living."[9]

Kahn sensed that in the act of building houses, the relationships he forged with his clients and his ability to create spaces that would reflect their way of living would determine how successful these enterprises would be. Each house he designed was completely different because each client and each client's desires were different, and clients were what made his houses exceptional. He was attentive to their needs and relentless in trying to accommodate them as his own architectural attitudes evolved. When he got it right, their lives were brightened, as Lenore Weiss acknowledged in a letter to him in 1953, a few years after their house near Norristown was completed: "As far as we're concerned it grows more beautiful all the time and we enjoy it more and more"—and they continued to do so for another half century (fig. 3).[10] When he got it wrong, he would try again and again and again to get it right.

Kahn's patrons were mainly successful young businesspeople and professionals, many from his own progressive Philadelphia milieu. And quite a few, but far from all, were Jewish, like him. Initially, in the aftermath of the Depression, clients were difficult to come by, and Kahn had to struggle to get enough work.[11] Several of his earliest clients came as friends wanting additions and renovations or, like the Osers and the Genels, new houses (fig. 4). Others came through Esther. Her family was acquainted with the Broudos, for whom Kahn designed a house for a site adjacent to the Osers' in Elkins Park, but it was never built because of wartime restrictions. She herself was a good friend of Kit Sherman, who, with her husband, Jacob, wanted to build in Merion, but nothing came of the commission.[12] She also met the Finkelsteins, two radiologists, when she was working as a research assistant at the University of Pennsylvania. They wanted a new wing for their house in Ardmore, but after much discussion and redesign over a period of three years, the plan was scuttled.[13] As Kahn became better known and more successful, a number of his clients emerged from the world of archi-

Fig. 4 Ruth and Samuel Genel in their house in Wynnewood, September 1951. Collection of Rick Genel

tecture and planning: Fred Clever, for whom Kahn was to complete a house in Cherry Hill, New Jersey, was executive director of the Citizens' Council on City Planning in Philadelphia when Kahn joined its regional committee, while Marty Adler, whose hopes for a house in Chestnut Hill were dashed, was on its Penn Center committee.[14] Other clients came through publicity and magazine articles (the Hoopers, a wealthy Baltimore couple who wanted an addition to their traditional house, read about the Oser house in *Architectural Forum*[15]) but some came by chance (Ida Jaffe happened to spy the Genel house as she drove by on Lancaster Pike in Wynnewood[16]). And at least one couple, the Fishers, found Kahn with the help of the Yellow Pages.

All of Kahn's houses are located in the Philadelphia suburbs, but his clients were not new to the suburban lifestyle (fig. 5). Most already lived in garden communities in Philadelphia or the surrounding townships, although not necessarily in houses that they themselves owned. They came to him because they dreamed of houses that were modern, putting them in the vanguard of those who were engaging architects to design residences for themselves. They chose remaining building lots among the older traditional houses in the privileged communities of Chestnut Hill and the Main Line, or in

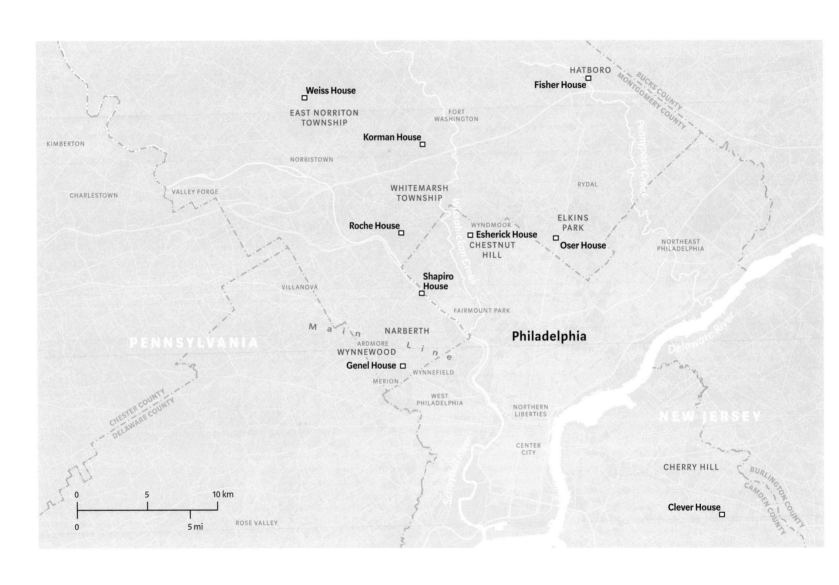

Fig. 5 Philadelphia region with the houses of Louis Kahn

Fig. 6 Margaret Esherick at Fort Point, San Francisco, June 1957. Collection of Lisa Esherick

subdivisions on land that had formerly belonged to country estates. Modern houses were still unusual, especially in these locales, and being able to build them could be a challenge for both architect and client. At times, financial impediments were raised: the Federal Housing Authority (FHA) would not guarantee the mortgage for the Oser house because it was modern,[17] and, ironically, the Philadelphia Savings Fund Society (PSFS), with its landmark International Style headquarters towering over Philadelphia, rejected Fred Clever's mortgage application because as an advanced, modern structure the house was not considered "marketable."[18] At other times design changes were required before a house could be started. A number of modern houses had already been built in Chestnut Hill, but the Woodwards (who had developed this Philadelphia garden suburb in the early twentieth century and maintained some design control over new construction) pressed Kahn to soften the façade of the house he was designing for Margaret Esherick "to make the appearance less controversial," much as they required Robert Venturi to alter the design of his nearby Mother's House (fig. 6).[19]

Many of Kahn's clients were socially and politically engaged, bearing a commitment to improving people's lives that ran parallel to what had been one of the goals of modern design since the nineteenth century. They championed a wide range of social causes, but none were quite so far left as Jesse and Ruth Oser; she was an organizer for the Philadelphia teachers union, and although the couple never joined the Communist Party, they were fellow travelers and had visited the Soviet Union during the early 1930s (fig. 7).[20] Others were outspoken in expressing their humanitarian concerns: Fred Clever was instrumental in founding the New Jersey chapter of the American Civil Liberties Union; Philip Q. Roche spoke out publicly for penal reform when he left his post as head psychiatrist at the Eastern State Penitentiary in Philadelphia; and Philip and Helen (Leni) Stern, wealthy figures in Washington, D.C., political circles, compiled a book espousing voting rights in the District of Columbia and exposing the contradictions between the city's public face and its impoverished citizens.[21] Kahn too had been a social and political activist through his work as housing advocate during the 1930s and 1940s, but except for a short period in the late 1940s, when he took up the cause of world government and supported the candidacy of Henry Wallace for president of the United States, this did not carry over into his personal life.[22] He continued to admire liberal motives, however, and was especially in awe of the Sterns, who taught him how the design of a house, even a luxurious one, can embody the egalitarian values of its owners.

Fig. 7 Ruth and Jesse Oser performing with the Hollywood Peasants folk-dance group they organized in 1945. Collection of Julie Oser McLeod

Kahn was a charismatic figure; one has only to listen to him address an audience in recordings or watch him on film to understand how dazzling he could be. A single meeting with him could hook a prospective client, as it did Alice Seiver. "Inspired" after her first encounter, and frustrated by his busy schedule and lack of response to her entreaties, she shamelessly pursued him to design an addition to her house in Villanova. "What nerve I show to write this letter to you," she admitted in December 1959, "after you have had one from me last August (plus a phone call last October)! But, again at the risk of being considered so big a nuisance, I shall write, if only to say at this time that I am here waiting—and if 'wait' for you I must—*that* I shall. You probably do not remember the evening at our place last July for any reason other than that it was so gosh-awfully hot. I, and Larry, on the other hand, remember it to be a most enchanting few hours of a lecture you gave us. Your lecture was terrific. We've thought of it, and spoken together about it so much since. Really—please think of our desire to have you design an addition. The fact that we *need* it more and more as the time passes is beside the point. The point is: we want *you* to do it, and we'll wait for you."[23] While the Seivers waited in vain, Steven Korman, a real-estate developer, had more luck. He too pursued Kahn, stopping into his Walnut Street office frequently until the architect agreed to design a country house for him and his family in Whitemarsh Township. They then met on weekends (when Kahn would be free of other involvements) and, as Korman recalled, talked about "how we wanted to live our lives" so that Kahn could design a house that was appropriate for them.[24] Some of Kahn's other clients also seemed to anticipate the excitement of a personal as well as an architectural adventure. "We enjoyed our afternoon with you on our mutual wave-length," Philip Stern wrote soon after their first meeting, "and look forward to both a blossoming house and a blossoming friendship."[25] After design conflicts within the subdivision in Chestnut Hill ruled out construction of her house, Marty Adler lamented, "I can't tell you how distressed I am about our change of plans. I had been looking forward so much to living in a Lou Kahn house and to the fun of building it with you."[26]

Kahn was inspirational, as more than one client noted. Yet it could go both ways, and he was generous in acknowledging the contributions of his clients (considerably less so those of his associates).[27] After Lawrence Morris, a Wall Street lawyer and Vanderbilt descendant, and his wife, Ruth,

Fig. 8   Doris and Norman Fisher, c. 1995. Collection of Doris and Norman Fisher Family

decided not to proceed with the house he designed for them in Armonk, New York, Kahn expressed his gratitude for their participation in the process: "It is seldom that an architect meets a client who proves a collaborator in the development of his ideas. Our relationship has helped me create new approaches to the problems of house and its architecture."[28] Jonas Salk, too, became a "collaborator," as well as a friend.[29] Just as he spurred Kahn to achieve a remarkable solution for his biological laboratory in California, Norman and Doris Fisher and Philip and Helen Stern became close to Kahn and challenged him to create designs for them that were also exceptional. These relationships developed even though Kahn may have seen the Sterns and Fishers only sporadically over the long periods he was working on their houses. His description of Salk—"He respects the realm you are working in. He doesn't try to invade, but inspires"—might equally have been applied to them.[30]

The Fishers respected Kahn's approach but held him in check as he worked with them to design a compact house in Hatboro for their family (fig. 8). They were modest, cognizant of their own needs and preferences, as well as their budget, and very attentive to the ramifications of each suggestion he made. Kahn listened too. "He was most accepting of our input," they remembered, "and, when not, was careful to explain why not."³¹ They were also very patient as he designed and redesigned their house, preparing four distinct schemes over a period of four years until he got it right for them and for himself. When finally they moved in and found that he had not gotten it quite right, he redesigned once more, adding a large window in the dining room, where he had thought they would prefer an intimate, inwardly focused space.

A later conversation between Kahn and Doris Fisher reveals the depth of friendship and mutual understanding that had developed over some seven years of work:

> LIK: There wasn't a thing in this house, Doris, that was a restraint. Not a thing.... All I had to be is more frugal in making what I had to make. It was pared down to having less in number, not less in the quality of the central idea. So you don't know you've gotten one window less or so forth, you see? After all, you were a pretty good policeman in that respect. You didn't allow anything to happen unless you could justify the expense and that helped me a tremendous amount, don't forget! Because as an architect you can want things, you see, which are really unessential and when a person, the client, does not feel the same wants, you have to then drop it....
>
> DF: This is unusual and this is one of the qualities that I think endeared you to us when we first met you. I mean that very seriously. We spoke to lesser men who were very adamant in their approach—not aesthetic—but about certain things they thought had to be done with no consideration for our needs and we didn't feel you would think that way... although you were very stubborn!
>
> LIK: You had marvelous judgment as to the validity of things.... I'm sure that if there were other ideas which would cause you to spend even more money... if you thought it was valid you would never have given up. It was a sense of validity. Not so much "needs" and "how much" and "how many." It was the beauty of beauty which has a sense of validity in it. If it is valid, it transcends all knowledge.... If it's valid, and it has not been put forth, it just simply kills you not to have it. That's why it's no loss to have been more frugal in the design of your house.³²

The Sterns—she an artist, he a journalist, publisher, and sometime deputy assistant secretary of state—also became friends with Kahn, as from the very start Philip anticipated they would (fig. 9). Kahn visited them in Washington, bringing art supplies for their young daughters (who thanked him with pictures and poems). They invited each other to their

Fig. 9 Helen and Philip Stern, from *O Say Can You See "By Dawn's Urban Blight,"* 1968. Collection of Helen Stern

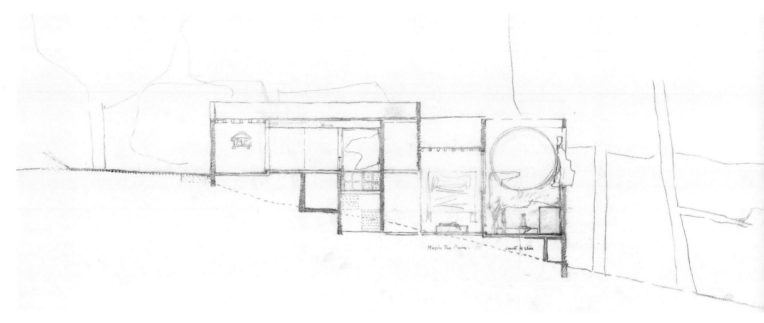

Fig. 10   Philip and Helen Stern House, Washington, D.C., 1966–70. Section with "court to stars" adjacent to master bedroom. Louis Kahn, c. October 1967. Kahn Collection

Fig. 11   Philip and Helen Stern House. Site plan. Louis Kahn. Dated October 26, 1968. Kahn Collection

celebrations, and even when the Sterns had to relinquish their building plans for unforeseen reasons, Kahn was sympathetic and remained close to them. Unlike the Fishers, the Sterns gave Kahn a free hand. "You invited us to tell you all about our ideas," Philip responded by mail after an early meeting with the architect, "so that you could know all our dreams and fantasies and include them in your own conception." And indeed, they had a wealth of dreams and fantasies. Some were "zany" suggestions: "Wouldn't it be wonderful on a clear and starry night to be able to lie in bed and look up at the sky? We think so. . . . Is it conceivable that the bedroom ceiling could be a large clear dome, under (or over) which there would be a many-bladed diaphragm that would open and close like the lens opening of a camera?"[33] (Kahn never acquiesced on the dome, but in one version of his designs, he added a terrace for stargazing adjoining the master bedroom; fig. 10.) The Sterns' desires constantly changed. They wanted a "tree house," a "gallery," and a "dancing room"; they asked for a small, separate building for their five children to sleep in (which they called the "piccolo"), and then they rethought it completely as a "place for doing/creating things."[34] Kahn indulged their whims, pulling out all stops in envisioning exceptional spaces for them (see figs. 88–89).

The Sterns responded excitedly, eager to build what they saw as they reviewed each of Kahn's successive presentations. But they put their foot down when it came to an atrium, because as Kahn told it, this seemed undemocratic to them (fig. 11): "A plan . . . I had in which anyone who came to visit was faced by a kind of atrium—an outside garden which is captured in the very middle of the house—and you had to go to one side to a living room and to one side to a dining room. This they fought very much, although they loved it very much. . . . They fought it because it appeared to be a preferential thing—like you could stop at the entrance, you could sit near a fireplace, you could go into the garden, but you don't come into the house. . . . They had great pain giving the atrium up. But now they feel utter joy in being able to give up something which is terribly attractive. . . . They would rather have it infinitely less, you see, because the house now has this direct sense of invitation."[35]

Kahn's other clients were not wealthy like the Sterns, and their budgets were generally limited. Staying within budget was a constant problem, and it frustrated him, as he told Norma Shapiro in exasperation at her Narberth house one day: "I'll never work again on a job where money is an issue" (but, of course, he continued to do so).[36] He designed for his clients' aspirations and reacted later if the clients received bids that were over the anticipated costs. He had no reluctance about redesigning entire houses to cut down on their scale, and thus their expense. He frequently put more of his, and his staff's, design and drafting time into a house than he was ever able to recover, which is evident when one tallies existing time sheets and billing records. Ida Jaffe must have heard of Kahn's reputation for incessant redesign, for she tried to head this off in an early letter to him as she anticipated building a house on the Main Line: "Mr. Jaffe and I would be very happy if we succeeded in conveying to you our desire for a compact, easy-to-maintain dwelling plus the charm and individuality with which we know you can endow it. . . . We are eager to avoid the necessity for numerous re-figurings and hasten to convey this message in writing in order to clarify our position to you and to ourselves."[37]

While it is sometimes thought that Kahn did not build many houses because his designs were too expensive, his clients often had other reasons for not going through with their plans, sometimes even when money was given as the pretext. "Achingly," the Sterns wrote to tell Kahn that a new, unexpectedly high estimate made them reconsider building their "dream house," but this turned out to be a front. Philip, who had been diagnosed with cancer, did not want anyone to know about his illness, and the Sterns realized they could not proceed with the project.[38] Morton and Mitzi Goldenberg also kept Kahn in the dark when they canceled their house in Rydal without explanation just as they were about to break ground (the couple had decided to divorce).[39] Kahn became bitter over this, expressing his irritation in a letter to their lawyer over a dispute about his fee. "For reasons we do not know, Mr. Goldenberg abandoned the project. He probably reconsidered his financial situation and desires regarding the house. We are unhappy about this considering how much effort was put into what we believed would have been a significant addition to architecture. We know also that the biggest loss is Mr. Goldenberg's, because he has no house—only paper plans" (see fig. 76).[40] And when Kahn did have a chance to build, things did not always go smoothly; Jocelyn Roche remembered that building their house in Whitemarsh Township was "a two-years' trip to hell" (see fig. 133).[41]

Fig. 12 Louis Magaziner, Louis Kahn, and Henry Klumb, associated architects. Prefabricated House Studies, 1937–38. Elevation of Prefabricated House 5D. Louis Kahn. Kahn Collection

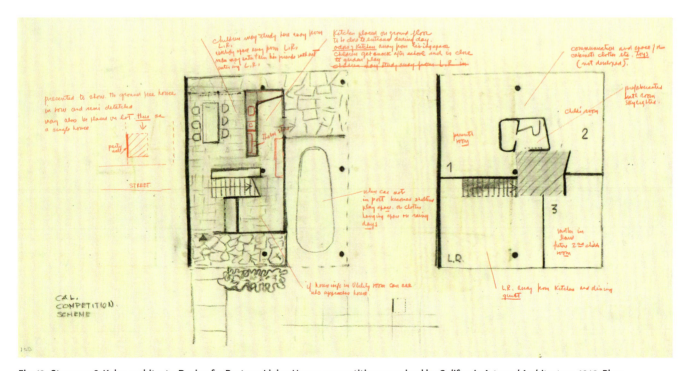

Fig. 13 Stonorov & Kahn, architects. Design for Postwar Living House, competition organized by *California Arts and Architecture,* 1943. Plan. Louis Kahn. Kahn Collection

The effort Kahn put into developing schemes for his houses was not just architectural, it was also psychological. As a designer, he was thinking about houses, he was thinking about the idea of house, but he must also have been thinking about home, however little he said an architect could do about that. How else can we understand his insistence on the centrality of the family, on designing evocative, sheltered spaces for his clients to dine in and enveloping hearths where they could gather (see fig. 201)? An urge to come to terms with the life of buildings and to envision them as homes emerged even in his early architectural drawings. The row house Kahn designed with Henry Klumb and Louis Magaziner in 1937–38 for steel prefabrication required efficiency of interior arrangement and simplicity of assembly, but he made an attempt to humanize the cold uniformity of factory housing in his rendering of the structure (fig. 12). To the stark white building he added animating elements, a colored tile front and a lively arrangement of potted plants on the ground level, a little horse in relief on the façade, and a small window drawn open, which allowed his own empathy for the imaginary inhabitants to come forth. He even brought empathy to a simple plan, his submission to the Design for Postwar Living House competition organized by California Arts and Architecture in 1943 (fig. 13). With the explanatory texts he scrawled across the sheet, he created a narrative of home as he envisioned the dynamics of a family living in the house: "man may entertain his friends without entering L.R. [Living Room]," "housewife in utility room can see who approaches house," "children get snack after school," "children may study here." In his drawings, he reinforced these narratives with the depiction of fully furnished interiors, such as an unidentified kitchen with a bevy of furniture and decorations that became his artistic hallmarks (see fig. 92) or the Roche house, which has all the fittings of a stable home, from the silver and ceramics on the dining-room shelves to the sprightly toy bunny on the child's bed (see fig. 135).

These drawings were not just about describing Kahn's architectural intents, they were about engagement, like sharing the unbounded joy of the airy couple dancing in the garden room at right in a drawing of the Fleisher house (fig. 14).

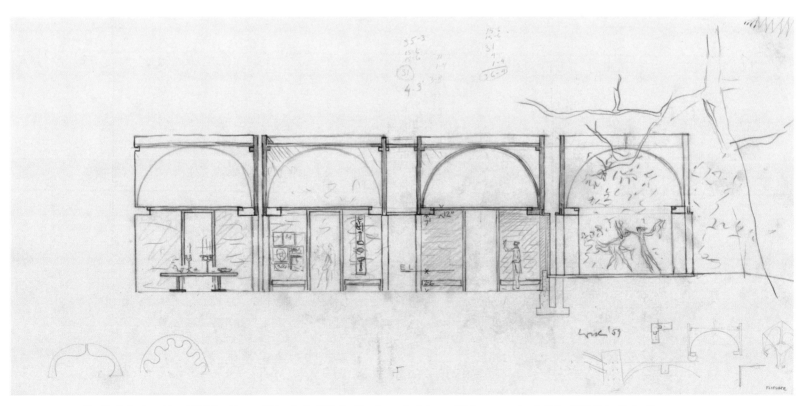

Fig. 14 Robert and Janet Fleisher House, Elkins Park, 1959. Section through dining and living rooms. Louis Kahn, 1959. Kahn Collection

Fig. 15   The Korman family at their compound in Whitemarsh Township, c. 1973.
Collection of Larry Korman

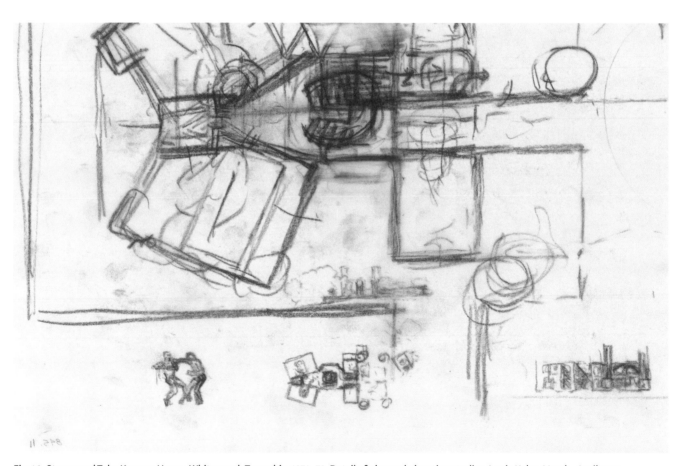

Fig. 16   Steven and Toby Korman House, Whitemarsh Township, 1971–73. Detail of plan and elevation studies. Louis Kahn. March–April 1972.
Kahn Collection

Fig. 17 Leonard and Barbara Fruchter House, Wynnefield, Philadelphia, 1951–52. Perspectives of living room. Louis Kahn. Kahn Collection

Moreover, they reveal Kahn's fascination with family interactions. As he was thinking of the nature of the house he was designing for the Kormans, he must have been imagining the nature of the family that would live there (fig. 15) and the nature of the activities that would take place there, in this case, the roughhousing between father and sons that was characteristic of their lifestyle (for he placed two figures boxing at the edge of one of his sheets of drawings for the house; fig. 16).[42] Even more explicit, and poignant, is the altercation that appears in paired views of the living and dining rooms of the Fruchter house, which was to have been built in Wynnefield (fig. 17). As a mother stands scolding her son, the boy sticks out a red tongue at her—the only color note on the sheet, and an exclamation point to demonstrate that this house would be functioning as a home.

Home was what an architect—any architect, according to Kahn—would want to enable in designing a house. "The house," he wrote, "must always be as good, must be so good, that the one who will live in it after the person who ordered it, would feel comfortable in it.... It's a confirmation that a house ... has a sense [of] agreement about it. An agreement means a sense of commonness, a sense of a prevalence, which is a prevalence of harmony, a kind of rapport with the next person."[43] It would be nearly impossible, however, for an architect to gauge if or when this ideal state of home had been attained, and if the house he had designed for one person had had a kind of rapport with the next. Thus he must have been stunned (in addition to being "touched and grateful") when out of the blue in 1959 he received a letter from a Mrs. Paul Silver, who had just moved into the Oser house almost two decades after it was built (see figs. 122–25, 129–32). "Dear Mr. Kahn," she penned on stationery not yet bearing her new address:

> I have been wanting to write you a note for several months now to tell you that we are living in a house that you designed, "Stonebridge," Stetson road, and loving it.
>
> I understand that you built it for the Oser's, and then the Leidner's lived in it, and we feel that somehow deep in your subconscious, you had us in mind and designed it for our needs....
>
> I had always dreamed of a house designed by an architect to function just for us, and this house of yours is just that. It is quite an achievement, or is it just what good design is supposed to do, for a house to live, breathe, and expand with the needs of its owners....
>
> We have four children ranging in age from sixteen years, ten years, four years and one year old. Our house gives us beauty, privacy, and convenience to raise this varied family.... At the present, we cannot afford to do much, but the furnishings are not important in this house, it has a beauty of design in its structure, unfurnished.
>
> This is my first experience in writing a "fan" letter but I must tell you how I feel or I will bust! Thank you for being such an artist and for designing a house for us.[44]

HOUSES

In the fall of 1930, in spite of having been recently let go from his job as a designer in the office of his mentor Paul Cret, Louis Kahn must have felt optimistic. He was about to embark on an independent career and enter into an architectural design partnership with another of Cret's laid-off workers, Solis Daniel Kopelan.[1] Turning away from the French Beaux-Arts classicism that Cret favored, Kahn and Kopelan charted a different course: their architectural work would be modern. Using the smooth, reverse side of one of the hundreds of picture postcards he had amassed on his travels through Europe in 1928–29, Kahn drew the essence of a modern house, a strong graphic image that would be reproduced on the firm's letterhead (fig. 18). This abstracted, stark white building with two chimneys, sheltered balcony, and large expanses of glass announced the firm's commitment to modernism and signaled an expectation that the design of houses might become a cornerstone of Kahn's career.

Fig. 18 Kahn & Kopelan, architects. Study for partnership logo. Louis Kahn, October 1930. Collection of Sue Ann Kahn

This was a bold move for Kahn. The house he drew was unlike almost anything that had been built in the Philadelphia area, and it would have been a radical statement for even the most advanced architects in the United States at that time.[2] It seems to demonstrate an awareness of recent French design, particularly the white cubic forms found in the houses of André Lurçat and Robert Mallet-Stevens, although here the asymmetry of those buildings has been subdued.[3] While Kahn's European travels had taken him to France, there is no indication that he had seen the buildings of these architects on his trip. His own explorations of contemporary architecture, which he called "modern work,"[4] had led him north, to the Dutch modernists, specifically Hendrik Berlage, Willem Dudok, and J. F. Staal; to the work of Fritz Schumacher in Hamburg and Eliel Saarinen in Helsinki; and to Ragnar Östberg's Stockholm city hall. These architects were not known for their private houses, however, and their approach to design was quite different from that of the French architects.[5]

To create the firm's logo Kahn fell back on his Beaux-Arts training, which held that precedents could be used as touch points for design even as the goal was to reinterpret them. In his paper "Styles—Archaeology," Paul Cret had explained this: "We know better, thanks to photographs, to the multiplicity of books, to travel, what the architecture of past centuries was and also what distortions it requires to be applicable to our modern problems. We must recognize that what we are borrowing from the past is always a form void of spirit and that it is our task to give it new life."[6] At the University of Pennsylvania, Kahn had been trained to refer to publications of the great buildings of the past, but when it came to modern architecture he had had no grounding. "Before," he would later explain, "I was always full of references, and here the references were lost. I didn't know references. I started from zero."[7] Starting from zero was probably not so difficult for someone working in Cret's office, however. A host of references were available in the numerous architectural journals that Cret subscribed to, many of them international, which were eventually clipped and kept in extensive files for use in his architectural practice.[8] One can picture the somewhat bewildered young architect sitting in the office library and thumbing through journals as they arrived, educating himself about modern buildings and, when the time came, just as he was finishing up in Cret's employ, finding inspiration in them for a logo.

What must have caught Kahn's eye was a perspective drawing and a photograph of a white house with chimneys on either side in the newly received October 1930 issue of *Architectural Record* (fig. 19). This house, which might be understood as an example of French modern architecture seen through English eyes, was located at Silver End, a corporate housing estate in Essex, England, designed by Thomas S. Tait of John Burnett and Partners in 1926–27.[9] Ignoring its ornamental details, Kahn borrowed elements from both illustrations for his logo: from the photograph he drew the central doorway, balcony with its cantilevered roof and small windows at its side, and dark shadows that emphasize the central setback at top, while from the drawing he took the flanking chimneys and the strongly cast shadow under the balcony. Compared to the logo, however, the Silver End house is too broad and lacks the gridded surface of floor-to-ceiling windows at its base. Kahn must have taken inspiration for the tightened silhouette and the windows, as well as the frontal view, from the illustration of Le Corbusier's Maison Planeix in Paris (1926–27) that had been published in the previous month's *L'Architecte,* a French journal that Cret also received (fig. 20).[10] Allowing for the lapse in time required for mail from France, it probably arrived and was on the library tables at the same time as the October *Architectural Record* with its

Fig. 19 Thomas S. Tait of John Burnett and Partners, architects. Silver End Garden Village, Essex, England, 1926–27. From *Architectural Record,* October 1930

Fig. 20 Le Corbusier and Pierre Jeanneret, architects. Maison Planeix, Paris, 1926–27. From *L'Architecte,* September 1930

Fig. 21 Child's room, 1930. Watercolor and pencil on paper. Collection of Sue Ann Kahn

Fig. 22 Bernhard Pfau, architect. Playroom, Düsseldorf, 1929. From *Moderne Bauformen,* March 1930. Paul Cret Clipping Files, AAUP

Fig. 23 Howe & Lescaze, architects. Classroom, Oak Lane Country Day School, Philadelphia, 1929. From *Architectural Record,* April 1930. Paul Cret Clipping Files, AAUP

images of Silver End. It was in this way that Kahn was able to draw on the most advanced design of his day to project an image of up-to-date modernity for the firm.

In a watercolor most likely done earlier in the spring, an interior of a child's playroom, Kahn had already used this method for composing an image (fig. 21).[11] The design of domestic spaces was not something that had been part of his training, and since he had had little personal experience to help him in creating them, even in his imagination, again he had to search for sources. "At that time I didn't have any children," Kahn told the architectural historian Jan Hochstim in 1972 in describing this drawing. "I was probably leafing through books and being acquainted with the human scale as it relates to everyday life—houses, schools, things that we didn't bother with at the Beaux-Arts. . . . In a way this drawing is sort of a beginning in which I try to take pieces and parts out of what were images not understood very well, but very much believed in. And this drawing is really a very key drawing. Everything in a way that I do now is not very far from this, even providing for things on window sills and the things of that nature."[12]

These pieces and parts, revealing Kahn's awakening to disparate strands in modern architecture, came once again from the pictorial sources found in Cret's office: illustrations in the March 1930 issue of the German periodical *Moderne Bauformen* and the April 1930 issue of *Architectural Record,* which probably would also have arrived at the library simultaneously. "I would say this really comes out of my fascination with the early-modern Bauhaus work," Kahn told Hochstim, "with the kind of bareness and the new lighting fixtures and the unstructured entrance—the openness." These were inspired by the photograph in *Moderne Bauformen* of a playroom in Düsseldorf designed in 1929 by the German architect Bernhard Pfau (fig. 22),[13] but his source for the child's chair and the toys on the floor and windowsill was much closer to home: the photograph of a classroom in Howe and Lescaze's Oak Lane Country Day School in Philadelphia (1929), the first International Style building in the region, from *Architectural Record* (fig. 23).[14] Kahn went so far as to copy such features as the curve of the string of the toy wagon and the curious swag of the light cord, leaving little of the composition to his own imagination. Even the naive stick figure on the blackboard, which he told Hochstim was the "child's room symbolism," closely resembles one in the photograph. Kahn completed his image with a view through a picture window to a pastoral landscape, a theme he would explore in a group of watercolors from this period, including his *Coming Storm.*

By working out the origins of these two compositions we see with clarity how Kahn filtered ideas and images during his initial engagement with modernism. Shocking as it

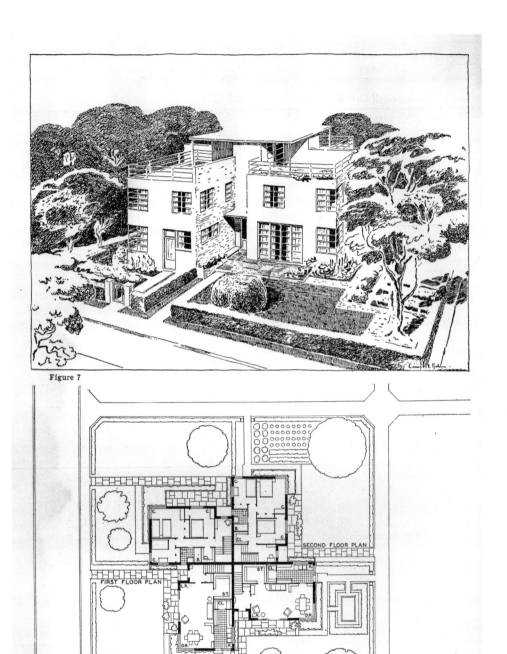

Fig. 25 Henry Wright, architect. Swastika Cottages, 1921. From *Journal of the American Institute of Architects,* October 1921

Fig. 24 Louis Kahn, for Architectural Research Group, associated with Magaziner & Eberhard, architects. Northeast Philadelphia Housing Corporation Project, 1933. Bird's-eye perspective and plan of Windmill unit. From *Housing in Philadelphia,* 1933

may seem, Kahn's method is, as he himself suggested, fundamental to understanding his work, a process of observation and reflection that opened up new avenues of awareness developed through the act of creation itself.[15] "We should not imitate when our intention is to create—to improvise," he wrote, echoing Paul Cret, in his 1931 essay "The Value and Aim in Sketching." "We can never think clearly in terms of another's reactions; we must learn to see things for ourselves, in order to develop a language of self-expression. The capacity to see comes from persistently analyzing our reactions to what we look at, and their significance as far as we are concerned. The more one looks, the more one will come to see."[16] And look Kahn did, developing his intuitive sense by turning to references that were close at hand.[17]

If at first Kahn's architectural focus was on the single-family house, during the Depression years his attention was reoriented toward mass housing, where he would explore the important issues of community and collective identity. In 1933, working in association with the architects Magaziner & Eberhard and acting through the Architectural Research Group, which he had founded in March 1932 to provide activity for a group of unemployed Philadelphia architects, Kahn prepared the general development plan for a 54-acre site in a sparsely settled section of the city on behalf of the Northeast Philadelphia Housing Corporation. This proposal was submitted to the newly launched housing subsidy program of the Public Works Administration but was never acted upon.[18] The project included a series of novel cluster configurations of semidetached housing types, among them the so-called Windmill plan (fig. 24). Kahn singled out the Garden City–inspired planning of Radburn, New Jersey, designed by Henry Wright and Clarence Stein, as a significant influence on his work at the time and on the plan for this development in particular.[19] As now might be expected, the youthful Kahn turned to published sources for his Windmill design, in this case, Wright's prolific writings on the subject of Garden Cities and on prototypes for and alternatives to American housing forms. What Kahn must have drawn from was Wright's Swastika Cottages, which had been published in the *Journal of the American Institute of Architects* in 1921 (fig. 25) and then in a revised form in *Architectural Record* in March 1930.[20] Kahn reflected on the advantages he saw in it: "The arrangement of four houses in this manner offers unbroken garden area for each house," providing "those amenities which rightfully belong to every home occupant, open-air living space, a place to grow a tree, ample sunlight, cross ventilation," and in a nod toward efficiency and convenience, "modern equipment."[21] The first-floor plan, a demonstration of Kahn's interest in "openness," featured a combined living and dining room along with the kitchen, laundry, and storage. The second floor had three bedrooms and a bath, and on the rooftop was a space he described as a garden.

With its use of ordinary brick, steel casement windows, and common construction methods, the Windmill house adhered to aspects of the Silver End precedent, but it also reveals Kahn's continuing interest in Le Corbusier, in this case, his housing estate in Pessac (1923–25), which had been illustrated in the March 1932 issue of *Architectural Forum* (fig. 26).[22] Kahn, drawing directly from the buildings in France, borrowed the roof garden from a building in Pessac and set it down on one of his own projects in Philadelphia. Kahn also adopted Pessac's square columns, parapet wall, and pipe railing for the roof garden, one component of Le Corbusier's "Five Points of

Fig. 26 Le Corbusier and Pierre Jeanneret, architects. Housing estate, Pessac, France, 1923–25. From *Architectural Forum,* March 1932

HOUSES

Architecture," but he bypassed many other elements that are closely associated with his buildings, in particular, the *pilotis,* or columns, on which his houses stand, and his horizontal strip windows.

Increasingly, Kahn was absorbing a more nuanced understanding of European modernism, which he fully expressed between 1935 and 1937 in his work on the Jersey Homesteads project. This was a greenbelt housing development near Hightstown, New Jersey, built for the government's Resettlement Administration and supported by the International Ladies Garment Workers Union. Kahn was assistant principal architect of the project under Alfred Kastner, a German émigré who had arrived in the United States in 1924 and was well versed in contemporary European intellectual currents. This was Kahn's earliest opportunity to collaborate with someone with that depth of knowledge of international modernism, and these were his first single-family houses that were built. Kahn spent more than a year in Washington, D.C., working with Kastner and a group of collaborating architects on the Jersey Homesteads, designing twelve different types of houses, some minimally attached, others in freestanding units. Economical construction was a significant priority for the architects, who chose to use concrete slabs for roofs and floors, and concrete blocks, painted white, for walls. These basic materials, along with the absence of ornament, gave the houses an austere, abstract quality, as seen in a photograph of a rendering that Kahn kept in a scrapbook of his work of the 1930s (fig. 27). While Kahn's increasing knowledge of Le Corbusier was evident in his proposals for the Jersey Homesteads school and community building, a work that explored the use of free planning within a columnar structural system defined by slender pilotis, his concern for the everyday life of the community was equally developed, indicated by his adaptation of the American front porch for some of these houses.

In its near total adherence to the austerity of the International Style, Kahn's Jersey Homesteads lacked any response to local traditions. But with his Jesse and Ruth Oser House, built only a few years later, between 1940 and 1942, he was fully engaged with them: he employed naturally treated wood, detailed according to longstanding traditions; chose locally quarried stone for construction; and related the house carefully to its site (fig. 28). John Ebstel, Kahn's preferred photographer, captured this sensibility during the winter of

Fig. 27 Alfred Kastner, principal architect, with Louis Kahn, assistant principal architect. Jersey Homesteads, Roosevelt, New Jersey, 1935–37. Perspective of Type-B house. Archival photograph of lost original, c. 1935. AAUP, by the gift of Sue Ann Kahn

Fig. 28　Jesse and Ruth Oser House, Elkins Park, 1940–42. From northeast. Photograph 1943. Kahn Collection

Fig. 29 Jesse and Ruth Oser House. Fireplace. Photograph 1943. Kahn Collection

1943 (fig. 29). The afternoon sun streams into the inglenook, vividly revealing the variegated texture and tones of the tiled fireplace wall. Here, in a close variant of his drawings of interiors, Mercer tile (which was made nearby and retained a strong connection to the American Arts and Crafts Movement) and Pennsylvania folk art (in this case local red ware) are juxtaposed with a mechanistic composition by Fernand Léger on the cover of *Fortune,* European ceramics possibly brought back by Kahn from his travels, and laminated furniture by Alvar Aalto, demonstrating Kahn's new, dual interests.

The period between 1937 and 1942 had reshaped Kahn's thinking profoundly as he found in the buildings of Philadelphia architects, many of whom he knew and worked with, a new understanding of modernism that responded to the specifics of place. Kahn's Philadelphia colleagues believed that local building traditions were essential to producing a modern work. Among them was Kenneth Day, who saw a "direct acceptance of customary local methods of construction and materials, and site considerations, as something to be welcomed as helping when honestly expressed, to produce a truly functional result" rather than as something to be avoided "in an effort to make the work look like some European structure produced under different conditions."[23] Day and Kahn were in active association by 1938, working together on large-scale housing projects for the Philadelphia Housing Authority, and as Kahn confronted his first design for a private house, Day was someone to whom he would have turned as he honed his own approach.[24] Day's Marshall Cole House, in New Hope, built from 1934 to 1936 on the site of an old stone quarry, has, like the Oser house, simple massing and no ornamentation, but it is larger in scale and more luxurious (fig. 30). It shares an open plan, modern efficiency, and steel casements, providing large expanses of glass and corner windows, but it also combines naturally finished wood siding, laid vertically and flush to the frame (perhaps in an effort to maintain a geometric purity, a pursuit that would engage many other American architects by the end of the decade), with local stone. Philadelphia architects took pride in being able to take stone from the very site on which a house was to be built, and this is something Day was able to do in New Hope.

Day's sensitivity to local building traditions was not a singular one. As early as 1912, in the October issue of *Architectural Record,* the influential critic Montgomery Schuyler pointed to developments in the Philadelphia suburbs as models for suburban architecture elsewhere: "Of all buildings, one would say, homes ought to be the least pretentious . . . the most straightforward, vernacular, idiomatic, expressive." He found these qualities best expressed in the fieldstone country houses of Philadelphia architects in particular, who took "all the hints with which the older buildings of the same material provided them, the farm houses and the barns of colonial Pennsylvania, which give the older settlements of that style an aspect of stability and duration almost or quite unequalled elsewhere in our country."[25] A related article in the same issue featuring the recent work of a group of young Philadelphians (including Walter Mellor, Arthur I. Meigs, and H. Louis Duhring) elaborated on the evolution of "a type of country house which, quite unlike most American work, is a logical development—a type in which there is more local than borrowed precedent, and in which local materials are frankly expressed in terms of honest craftsmanship."[26] As these logical developments continued into the late 1920s, historian George Edgell affirmed their enduring quality, noting that "perhaps the most charming and successful examples we have of the tasteful use of local materials occur in or near Philadelphia, where a group of brilliant designers have made a study of the use of the attractive local limestone. . . . It muddles our conception of the work, however, to

Fig. 30 Kenneth Mackenzie Day, architect. Marshall Cole House, New Hope, 1934–36. From *Architectural Record,* July 1938

HOUSES   27

try and associate it with any historic style. It is straightforward building and honest design, with an eye to fine proportion, picturesque composition, and the use of the full possibilities of the material."[27]

Edgell singled out a group of Philadelphians, including Duhring, Edmund Gilchrist, Robert Rhodes McGoodwin (Kahn's design critic during the 1921–22 school year), the firm of Mellor, Meigs & Howe, and Edmund Purvis (Kenneth Day's partner). Among these men, George Howe would have the most profound influence on Kahn and on the translation of the region's earlier mannerisms into modern form.[28] Howe, who was some fifteen years older than Day and Kahn, had studied at the Ecole des Beaux-Arts in Paris, and had come to be regarded along with his partners, Mellor and Meigs, as among the leading American designers of country houses during the 1910s and 1920s.[29] Paul Cret had admired their work and had written an appreciation of High Hollow, Howe's own house in Chestnut Hill, in 1920, noting that the setting "is so skillfully selected that one forgets that it has been created in the last two or three years. It seems just as integral a part of the hill as the terraces and houses of Amalfi are of the cliff over the bay. The greatest achievement of art is to make itself inconspicuous. The terrace wall curves along to follow the contours, just as do those stone walls which retain the scarce loam of the vineyards.... These walls, built shortly before the war, seem to be old. A careful selection of their material (an old quarry was reopened to secure it) and a still more interesting workmanship have contributed to this result" (fig. 31).[30] While the suave eclecticism of the firm's houses, later dismissively characterized by Howe as Wall Street Pastorale, draw much from a consideration of the specifics of site, in addition to the celebration of craftsmanship, it also allowed him to develop his interest in simplification and explore use of new materials (concrete). In the end, however, the pastoral sensibility developed in these houses amounted to the creation of fantasy landscapes that in Howe's mind denied the realities of their own time.

In the late 1920s, Howe made a radical break, joining in partnership with William Lescaze, who had brought knowledge of European modernism with him when he emigrated from Switzerland in 1920. Howe and Lescaze were leading promoters of the type of advanced design popular abroad, seen most forcefully in their PSFS building, Philadelphia's iconic modernist structure.[31] It was completed in 1932, the

Fig. 31 George Howe, architect. High Hollow, George Howe House, Chestnut Hill, Philadelphia, 1914–16. Photograph December 1984

Fig. 32 George Howe, architect. Square Shadows, William Stix Wasserman House, Whitemarsh Township, 1932–34. From west. Photograph 1936. AAUP, by the Gift of Louis E. McAllister

year Howe resumed design work on the William Stix Wasserman House in Whitemarsh Township, known as Square Shadows (fig. 32). This house was conceived along International Style lines before the 1929 stock market crash, but after Howe and Lescaze effectively ended their collaboration later that year (the partnership would endure on paper for another three years), Howe drew on aspects of his earlier design sensibility to complete the commission differently, giving the house a distinct site specificity not seen in the preliminary scheme. Howe emphasized the clarity of structure through a frank expression of how the building was put together. Stone, and the use of stone, became the expression for load-bearing walls. Where the wall was providing enclosure only, Howe switched to brick, and the stone abruptly gives way to red brick in logical but unexpected areas, such as on the parapets and in the brick balcony, which takes on a rhythmic pattern. Cast-in-place concrete slabs supported on Lally columns completed the material palette of the house. Square Shadows derives its power not only from modernist conceptions of space and art but also from the very facts of its structure and construction. In its simple cubic massing, use of local stone and construction techniques, corner windows, and steel sashes, it, like Day's Cole house, is a formal precedent for the Oser house.

Kahn met Howe in 1930 and followed his work closely throughout the decade.[32] Kahn's expertise in mass housing led to his first collaboration with Howe: in March 1938, Howe recruited Kahn, along with Kenneth Day, Oscar Stonorov, and others, to enter the Glenwood Low-Cost Housing Competition for the newly organized Philadelphia Housing Authority, ultimately preparing designs for two redevelopment sites.[33] During these years, 1938–39, Howe was completing construction drawings for Fortune Rock, a summer house on Somes Sound in Maine commissioned by Clara Fargo Thomas and built by Maine craftsmen (fig. 33).[34] The oiled cedar clapboards, the silver-gray shingles, and the stone used for the chimney and base walls (gleaned from the site itself) merge seamlessly with the natural surroundings. Like the vernacular fishermen's houses that cling to the coast, Fortune Rock is positioned at the edge of the sound, but with the benefit of modern structural techniques it is dramatically cantilevered over the shoreline. On the interior, the 6-by-6-inch timber frame is exposed, and a variety of plywood laminates, finished with spar varnish, are used for wall surfaces. The subtle

Fig. 33 George Howe, architect. Fortune Rock, Clara Fargo Thomas House, Mount Desert Island, Maine, 1937–39. Living room wing, from east with Howe on balcony. Photograph 1939. AAUP, by the Gift of Louis E. McAllister

Fig. 34   Fishermen's houses, Percé, Quebec, 1937. Tempera on paper. Collection of Sue Ann Kahn

choice of natural colors for the exterior is brought to the interior, emphasized by the use of a pale gray-blue for the ceiling and eaves—blending reflections of water and sky with the horizon to create a remarkably serene setting.

Fortune Rock was being detailed and finalized while Kahn was working with his then partners Howe and Day, perhaps even in the same room with Louis E. McAllister, Howe's draftsman on the project, whom he had known since his school days.[35] Kahn would have been very much aware of how Fortune Rock reflected the building traditions of New England and the Canadian coast, which he himself had seen on road trips in past summers and had captured in many drawings and watercolors, such as his view of Percé done in 1937 (fig. 34). Kahn's travels helped to shape his feeling for vernacular architecture, as his sketches of the Amalfi Coast of 1929 also attest.[36] His extended trip in 1937, in which he and Esther drove with their friends Kit and Jay Sherman through Maine to the Gaspé Peninsula and along the St. Lawrence, took him into an area that was largely untouched by tourism; it was just being discovered by artists who were seeking ways to express a modern art rooted in the American landscape. Paul Strand, among other prominent artists, photographed in Percé (in 1929 and 1936), and Kahn spent perhaps a week there, making dozens of sketches and creating wonderfully expressive paintings that are not just images of the buildings or the landscape but composite pictures of the life lived there. These were not literal depictions but improvised renderings through which he tried to capture a feeling for these places, from the tectonics of the earth and how the great forces of nature shape a landscape, to the way in which the inhabitants respond to those conditions. In this composite view, one of five or six studies he made of the locale along the north beach of Percé with its clapboard buildings and the rocky headland in the distance (a feature that, in reality, was out of sight from this vantage point), he captured not only the sense of "agreement," as he would later call it, of the simple settlement but also the manner in which the structures accommodated the topography through the simple practice of adding to and extending a building in a staggered, or telescoped, fashion.[37] This is a direct approach to construction, with no sense of ostentation, a quality that Kahn would search for in his own work.

While Fortune Rock presents a more developed expression of the vernacular than the Oser house, the community building group at the Pine Ford Acres housing project in Middletown, designed in 1941–42 by Kahn, then in partnership with Howe, provides a specific example of Kahn's drawing from these traditions (fig. 35). Following the example of the vernacular buildings he depicted in Percé, Kahn chose the simplest and most direct means to group the masses of the

Fig. 35 Howe & Kahn, architects. Pine Ford Acres, Middletown, 1941–43. Community Building. Bird's-eye perspective. Archival photograph of lost original. Louis Kahn. Kahn Collection

Fig. 36 Pine Ford Acres. Community Building. Photograph September 25, 1945

structure, stepping them down the hill gently, and with the final one, where the playschool was to be, extending the roof out to provide a broad porch where the mothers could gather in the shade while their children played (fig. 36). A similar impulse is felt in his drawings for the unbuilt Louis and Rae Broudo House, designed at the time Kahn was working on Pine Ford Acres (fig. 37). Kahn rarely used a gabled roof, but one appears here, stepped back to allow for an arbor-covered seating area. The house would have been built of the same materials as the neighboring Oser house.

Despite his intimate knowledge of the contributions of George Howe, Kenneth Day, and other area architects from the mid-1930s, Kahn would later give his then-partner Oscar Stonorov credit for first bringing natural materials into a modern architectural context in the Philadelphia area. In recommending Stonorov for fellowship in the American Institute of Architects in 1955, Kahn noted: "In Stonorov's early modern houses he pioneered indigenous materials before others. For this he deserves marked credit considering that these houses were built in the midst of general adherence to the so-called International Style."[38] Stonorov, who had been born and raised in Frankfurt and immigrated to the United States in 1929, was co-editor of the first volume of the catalogue raisonné of Le Corbusier's work, published in 1929.[39] He must have been aware that Le Corbusier was heading in new directions at that time, beginning to embrace the primitive (what Kahn characterized as the "peasant"[40]), to incorporate local materials into his architecture, and to move beyond the Machine Age into something new, but these experiments of Le Corbusier do not appear to have affected Stonorov's work until later in the 1930s, well after Howe's and Day's works were completed.[41]

What Kahn must have found so seductive was the way that Stonorov had used early Pennsylvania farmhouses and other vernacular structures as the core of a number of houses he designed to accommodate a modern lifestyle. He created

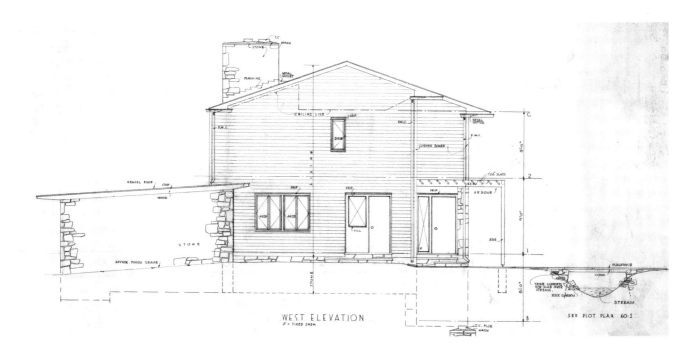

Fig. 37 Louis and Rae Broudo House, Elkins Park, 1941–42. West elevation (detail). Louis Kahn. Dated December 5, 1941. Kahn Collection

HOUSES   33

Fig. 38 Oscar Stonorov, architect. Avon Lea Farm, Oscar and Betty Stonorov House, Charlestown, 1938–40. From east. Photograph 1941. The farmhouse core is the whitewashed-brick section in the center. AAUP, by the Gift of Tina Daly, Andrea Foster, Derek Stonorov, and Tasha Stonorov

a beautiful rural enclave in Charlestown Township in Chester County, which included Avon Lea Farm, built for his family in 1938–40 (fig. 38). To a stone-walled farmhouse core, which he whitewashed, Stonorov added a series of wings that provided living spaces both indoors and out, a kitchen area, and a studio. He was especially progressive in the importance he gave to the kitchen, understanding that the kitchen would become an increasingly central aspect of house planning in the United States, something in which Kahn would have little interest. In 1945–46, Stonorov, in partnership with Kahn, designed another addition, a few miles away, this one to a log-cabin vacation house for Bernard and Reba Bernard (fig. 39). It provided for a light-filled living space (a common alteration in updating early farmhouse forms), as well as bedroom spaces on the upper floor. While Kahn was involved in the design, it seems that the overall responsibility was Stonorov's, reflected most clearly in the way the second floor is supported on tapered posts (identical to those at Avon Lea Farm) (fig. 40).[42]

Fig. 39 Stonorov & Kahn, architects. Bernard and Reba Bernard House, Kimberton, 1945–46. From east. The original log-cabin vacation house is in the foreground. Photograph c. 1948. Collection of Estelle Solomon

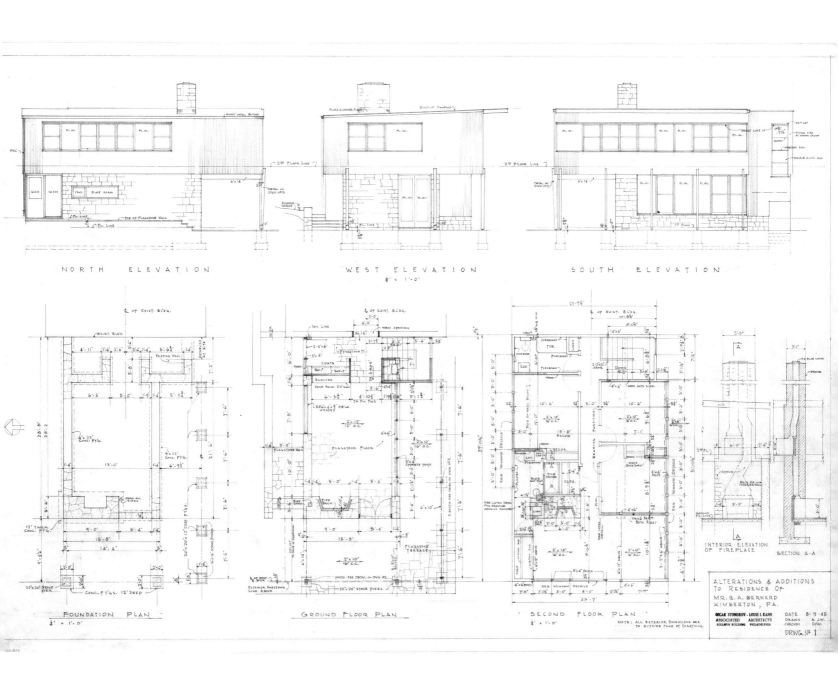

Fig. 40 Bernard and Reba Bernard House. Elevations and plans. Albert J. Webb, dated August 9, 1945. Kahn Collection

In 1945, when Libbey-Owens-Ford, the glass manufacturer, began to implement innovative glass technologies, the company commissioned Stonorov & Kahn in Pennsylvania, along with architects in each of the other forty-seven states, to design a solar house as part of a large publicity campaign (fig. 41). The designs were illustrated in a book accompanied by statements from the architects.[43] Unlike the other architects, who commented on the science of solar technology, modern design, or functional precepts, Kahn, taking responsibility for this project, provided an extensive statement (which was considerably reduced for publication) that considered the design in light of the tradition of vernacular architecture and its validity for modern expression:

> Pennsylvania has a long tradition in domestic architecture. Fine 18th century farm stone houses, 19th century Colonial brick manors and the informally eclectic English suburban houses of the early years of this century attest to this fact. A contemporary approach to living is decidedly within this tradition and not outside of it. Pennsylvania in its rural buildings is full of original architectural forms—functional in their way. Tobacco shelters, corn cribs, spring houses, barns combine skillfully proper materials into functional use. If one replaces the wood sections of a stone barn with glass areas, one obtains a remarkable "modern structure."… The "modern structure" can be as much a part of the Pennsylvania landscape as the old houses. Wood, glass, stone or brick, white-washed or not, are natural elements. With the availability of glass in large sheets and the desirability to make use of it for vistas or for sun-heating, one arrives easily at a formula for a Pennsylvania solar house.[44]

If, on the one hand, the Solar House spoke to its Pennsylvania context, it demonstrated, on the other hand, an emerging engagement with the recent work of the European émigrés Walter Gropius and Marcel Breuer. By 1945–46, when the Solar House was being designed, Kahn had already become acquainted with Gropius (the two met in 1944), and several of his Harvard students had come to work in Philadelphia, among them Frank Weiss (later Weise), Elizabeth Ware Carlihan, and, most significantly, Anne Griswold Tyng (who arrived in September of 1945). It was through Gropius's students that Kahn had his first exposure to what has come to be known as the "Harvard box," an expression of the minimal house promoted by the university's Graduate School of Design.[45] Architects at Harvard sought efficiency in construction; they took advantage of the particularities of large-scale mass-produced materials and used modular systems to help design for them. Their houses touched lightly on the ground; in using a minimal amount of material they relied on innovative thin-wall construction, which reduced costs while also referring to the precisely machined surface that was a central expression of modernity.

The Solar House was the first job that Tyng worked on, and although she was still a young architect, her immediate impact can be seen in it, notably in the layout of the house (fig. 42). The trapezoidal plan (the corners cut in to increase the southern exposure on the east and west sides) shows the living area on the sunny east and south side with a strong core in the center, and the dining room with an outdoor, screened-in dining area on the west side, held aloft on slender Lally columns not unlike those in Gropius's own house in Lincoln, Massachusetts (fig. 43). Facing north, where the house on its imaginary site was said to be relatively close to the street, is a solid wall, positioned to dampen street noise and to provide a thermal mass for solar heating. The diagrams

Fig. 41 Stonorov & Kahn, architects. Pennsylvania Solar House for Libbey-Owens-Ford, 1945–47. Perspective. Archival photograph of lost original. Louis Kahn, 1946. Kahn Collection

published in the book show various methods of modulating light: fins and screens that could rotate and be adjusted to the changing pattern of the sun over the course of the year. For Tyng, the knowledge of the houses that Breuer and Gropius built in Lincoln impacted fully on the design of the Solar House. The trapezoidal form derives perhaps from Breuer's own house of 1937–38, and the tight, efficient core is also seen there (fig. 44). While Breuer and Gropius, like others on the American scene, were also looking to vernacular building, selecting local materials, and talking about the advantages of the American balloon frame, these were incorporated in their work without any literal correlation with the earlier tradition. The stone fireplace wall in Breuer's exhibition house in the garden of the Museum of Modern Art in 1949, for example,

Fig. 43 Walter Gropius and Marcel Breuer, architects. Walter and Ise Gropius House, Lincoln, Massachusetts, 1937–38. From southeast. Photograph 1988

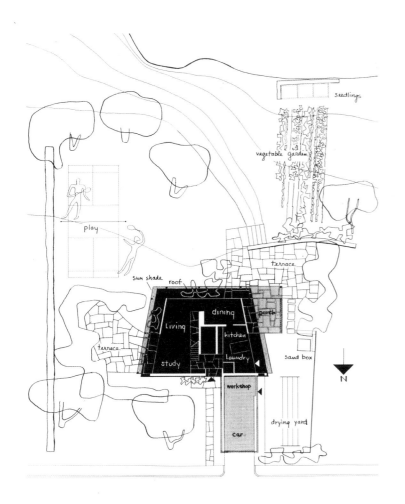

Fig. 42 Pennsylvania Solar House. Site Plan. Archival photograph of lost original. Kahn Collection

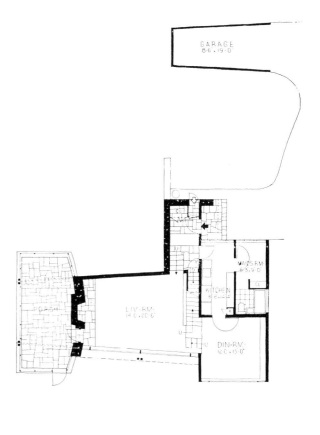

Fig. 44 Walter Gropius and Marcel Breuer, architects. Marcel Breuer House, Lincoln, Massachusetts, 1937–38. Plan. From *Modern Houses in America*, 1940

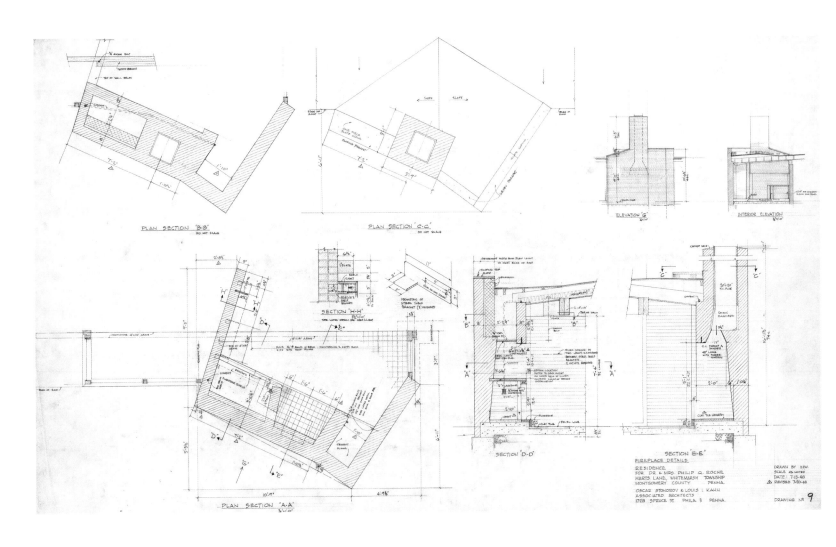

Fig. 45 Stonorov & Kahn, architects. Philip and Jocelyn Roche House, Whitemarsh Township, 1945–49. Fireplace details. David P. Wisdom, dated July 15, 1948. Kahn Collection

seems to deny its weight; it has a taut series of abstract planes and shapes, which presented a deliberate counterpoint to the earlier forms of building tradition (see fig. 110).[46]

The initial schemes of the Philip and Jocelyn Roche House, on which design resumed in 1947 (after the dissolution of Stonorov & Kahn), depict what seems to be a simple, efficient, minimal house with a characteristic chimney of stone at its core (see figs. 134, 135). Tyng, who was very much involved in this design, brought the discipline of a module into the house's planning, determining its overall dimensions. Then a remarkable change occurred: a massive inglenook, built of brick, not stone, appeared on the exterior wall (fig. 45, and see figs. 137, 138). Overscaled, and askew to everything else in the plan, this complex, multifaceted shape alluded in many ways to the forms of traditional inglenooks. It was "Lou's baby," Tyng later stated, and she must have felt extreme frustration at the imposition of this lopsided, sculptural element on the logic of the taut plan that they had designed for the house. It was "one of Lou's impulsive moments. He could be romantic at times, and the fireplace was one of those times," she added.[47] This rupture in an otherwise rational plan was not completely unprompted. Kahn was then being introduced to the historic precedents of the inglenook through his recently initiated friendship with Vincent Scully, who began to teach at Yale at the same time as he did, in the fall of 1947. Theirs was a close and warm friendship, which seems to have been formed on their first meeting. "I will always remember the first time he shook my hand, his openness and generosity," Scully recalled.[48] Scully had recently completed his dissertation on the late-nineteenth-century wooden domestic building form that he called the Shingle Style.[49] He remembered that Kahn "used to come often to my lectures," noting that he had been interested in history but "had been cut off from it because of the International Style; for him history was important since it was involved in everything. Besides, he had always learned from things, and that was the way he had always worked."[50] Scully's lectures would have reinforced for Kahn a sense of the psychological wellbeing of the household suggested by the warmth of the fireplace and the embracing inglenook, a central element in Shingle Style houses.

The Morton and Lenore Weiss House, built between 1947 and 1950, has the most disciplined of the plans that Kahn created during this period (fig. 46). Here in the countryside of Philadelphia he brought together many of the important

Fig. 46 Morton and Lenore Weiss House, East Norriton Township, 1947–50. From southeast. Photograph April 1958

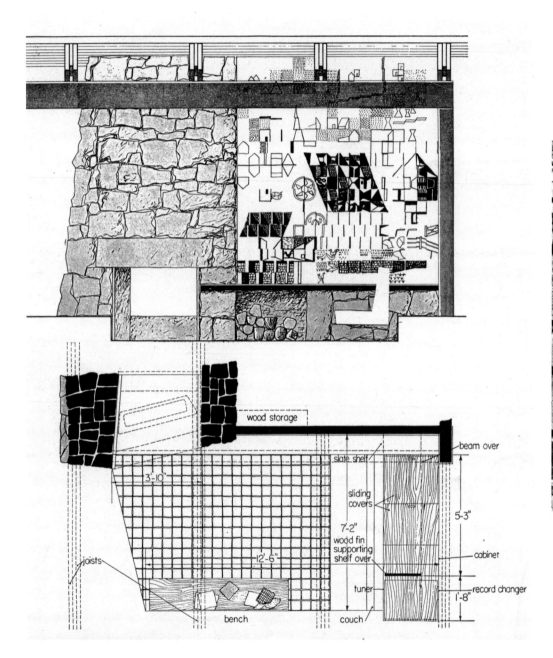

Fig. 47 Morton and Lenore Weiss House. Elevation and plan of inglenook, 1950. Archival photograph of lost original. Kahn Collection

Fig. 48 Morton and Lenore Weiss House. Stonework showing an area 7 by 5 feet. Photograph 1950. Kahn Collection

threads that he had investigated earlier. First was the distinction between living and sleeping areas, as seen in the bifurcated arrangement of the plan. Breuer had developed this planning principle in 1943–45, and Tyng brought it to this job, as Kahn acknowledged. "He often teased me about it being a Harvard bi-nuclear plan," she recounted.[51] The ease of movement throughout the house and the provisions for outdoor living were also indicative of this approach. More significant and distinctive, however, was the emphasis on structural expression. The wooden supports, organized on a 4-foot module, establish the logic of the plan. Set against them are a series of nonstructural stone walls, which reveal their screening role, especially on the west façade, where the top of the wall is held short of the structural beam (see fig. 139). The core of the house is the massive stone fireplace, with the living and dining rooms backing onto one another and setting up a relationship through their interconnection, the vertical edge tilted toward the conversation area in the living room. The roof is held up by a series of beams supported by the window wall and by the core elements, including the fireplace, which, along with the gentle changes in floor level and the roof pitch coming to a low point there, demonstrates Kahn's command of the design. This subtlety of expression is also found in the inglenook. In giving the fireplace a slight bulge to allow it to support the long-span beam above, Kahn acknowledged this as an exception to the otherwise nonstructural role of the walls and expressed this deviation with clarity (fig. 47).

When Kahn described the house, he associated it with the building traditions of the Pennsylvania German farmhouses. "The general compatibility of one material to another was well understood and well handled in Colonial days," he told a journalist in 1950. "We are still carrying out the same spirit if not in the same exact forms today."[52] The quality of the craftsmanship in stone and wood, and his feeling for the surface effects and the direct expression of structure and construction, recalled the buildings he had seen on his travels in the Gaspé region and Maine and his connections to George Howe. The wood siding, for example, would be allowed to silver through age and weathering. For the first time, his choice of stone and how he handled its detailing and construction can be documented. In choosing stone, Kahn looked to nearby quarries; in this he could connect to local building traditions and also provide a material familiar to the masons. For the Weiss house Kahn worked with Lemen quarry, which had been brought to his attention by a close friend, the craftsman Wharton Esherick, who had used its hard limestone for his own studio in 1926–27.[53] When Kahn suggested that the Weisses visit Esherick's studio to see the kind of stonework he had in mind, he must have been delighted to learn that they already knew it well, having frequently passed by it during their walks in the woods around Valley Forge. Kahn chose stones from the "top of the quarry," making his selection from the "original outcroppings" where the effects of weathering would be pronounced.[54]

For Kahn, stone was a material that required special attention. It is random as it comes to the building site, and it requires careful selection and precise execution to avoid grotesque effects or unwanted patterns. Kahn wanted to lay the stone carefully to establish a random pattern echoing Esherick's example, and he relied on the expertise of his stonemasons to achieve the desired result, although he made many trips to the site to inspect the work himself. Moreover, he wanted the mortar between the stones to be deeply raked to produce the effect of drywall construction, something that Esherick also insisted on, which allowed the individuality of each stone and each color to assert itself (fig. 48). This separation, Tyng explained, was what "Lou called the 'shadow joint' detail. He became very famous for that. The shadow joint is the idea of separation between materials so that if one has a door jamb in wood against rough stone-work, rather than to try to scribe the wood to the stone shape, one actually lets it be separate, with its own straight edge away from the irregular edge of the stone. The shadow joint is an indentation between them which would have depth at least equal to the distance between wood and stone."[55]

The Samuel and Ruth Genel House, designed shortly after the Weiss house was begun, and completed in 1951, carried forward many of its qualities, in particular, the expression of structure, which is more clearly rendered, and the ease of

Fig. 49 Samuel and Ruth Genel House, Wynnewood, 1948–51. Entry hall looking toward dining room. Photograph May 2011

flow to the exterior, with ample terraces and wide pergolas to provide shade (see figs. 149–65). While the inglenook remained at the core of its asymmetrical binuclear plan, it became a crystalline element, built of precisely cut pieces of Carrara marble and black slate (fig. 49; see fig. 161). It was geometrical, although purposely off square, and surrounded with an explosion of different materials and planes and angles, agitated shapes that suggested a profound change to come.

This was a moment when Kahn, as Mark Jarzombek describes it, began to question the "very nature of the American house," challenging the prevailing consumer-oriented suburban building style that Jarzombek calls Good-Life Modernism. Kahn created a series of simple plans that pronounced a "radical rethinking of the domestic environment."[56] He was coming to the realization that "a room is a defined space—defined by the way it is made—by the way it gets a roof or ceiling and has its walls to separate it from the rest of the spaces."[57] Jarzombek asserts that in these so-called pavilion plans—houses that are composed of separate, identical structures—the "fluidity of space, legibility of function, the hearth topos, and the organicist distinction between public and private have all been rejected. The repetition of identical spatial elements alone articulates the functional dynamic. The house is no longer a modernist machine, with its various parts designed according to the inner functional dynamic of suburban family life, but a conglomerate of smaller houses. . . . [It] no longer postulates a condition of suburban enlightenment, but rather aims to bring about an anthropological understanding of communal living. It makes allusions not to the conventional notion of modernity, but to African tribal huts."[58] This was not unlike the settlement at Percé or the arrangement of houses Kahn presented in his Philadelphia Row House Study of 1951–53 (fig. 50).

This new approach to planning first appeared in April 1952 in Kahn's designs for the unbuilt Leonard and Barbara Fruchter House, which was intended for a site in the Wynnefield section of Philadelphia.[59] The plan comprises three identical squares joined to form a triangular element at its core, which Kahn saw as a flexible space "best not defined" by a specific use (fig. 51).[60] A cylindrical volume, reminiscent of the central service element in Philip Johnson's recently completed Glass House, in New Canaan, Connecticut, is offset within the triangular core of the plan and contains a mechanical room and a fireplace. Each 24-foot-square block houses discrete functions. The living-room block (a volume several feet taller than the others) and bedroom block are positioned so as to maximize the potential of garden spaces on the rela-

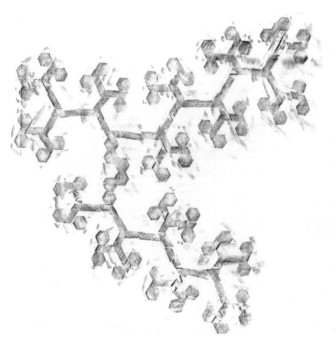

Fig. 50 Philadelphia Row House Study, 1951–53. Site plan. Kahn Collection

Fig. 51 Leonard and Barbara Fruchter House, Wynnefield, Philadelphia, 1951–52. Plan. Louis Kahn, c. May–June 1952. Kahn Collection

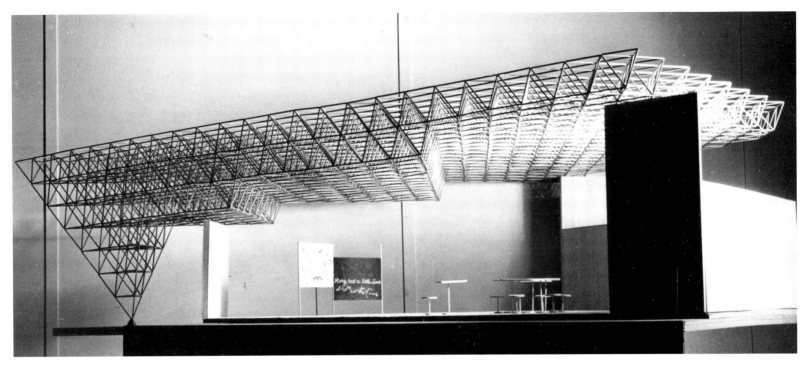

Fig. 52 Anne G. Tyng, architect. School for Bucks County, Pennsylvania, 1951–52. Model. Archival photograph of lost original. AAUP, by the gift of Anne G. Tyng

tively modest, flat site; these areas are enlivened by unusually shaped patios, a trellis for outdoor dining, a shallow pool at the entry, and walls built of terracotta chimney flues turned horizontally to create an engaging shadow effect. The service block, with kitchen, laundry, and storage and a guest room, has direct access from the entry court.[61]

Underlying the logic of the Fruchter house plan was a grid of equilateral triangles measuring 12 feet on each side, which was a mark of Tyng's increasing interest in geometry and her impact on Kahn's thinking at the time. Her project for an elementary school, a work developed independent of Kahn and completed by February 1952, had explored the potential of geometrical forming principles through the design of an individual classroom housed within a discrete structural unit, a variation on the octet truss with integrated vertical support (figs. 52, 53). Tyng's design preceded the Fruchter project and may have instigated the development of the pavilion-plan concept.[62] Tyng's hand can also be seen in a number of quick sketches made in the early weeks of October 1953 during the initial site visit to the property of Ralph Roberts, who was considering commissioning Kahn to design

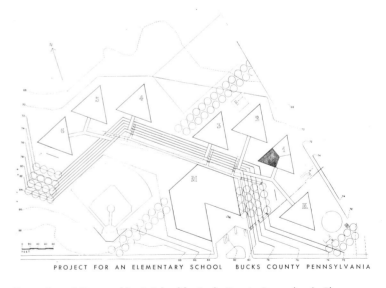

Fig. 53 Anne G. Tyng, architect. School for Bucks County, Pennsylvania. Plan. AAUP, by the gift of Anne G. Tyng

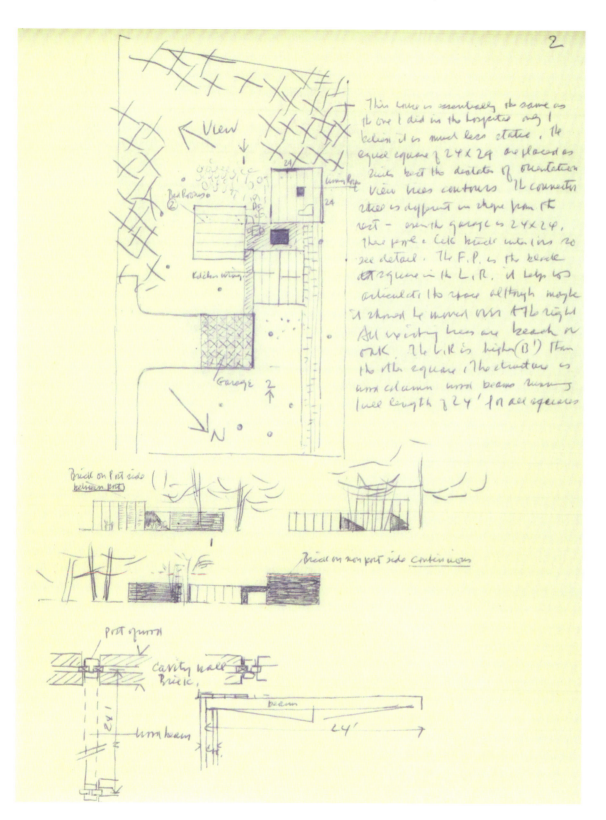

Fig. 54 Benjamin and Ida Jaffe House, Wynnewood, 1954. Site plan, elevations, and wall sections. Louis Kahn, dated March 16, 1954. Collection Alexandra Tyng

a house for his family in the Germantown section of Philadelphia.[63] While rudimentary, these sketches demonstrate a continuing interest in defining the relationship between the elemental blocks of a house through the use of geometry and, in this case, a hexagonal core. Clearly the question of how to separate these elements in a meaningful way was in the foreground of their discussions, but they went no further because at this moment Tyng discovered that she was pregnant with a child fathered by Kahn. To avoid a scandal, she decided to travel to Rome, departing in November 1953. While she and Kahn would be in regular correspondence over the next fifteen months, investigations of taut geometrical ordering systems slackened in Kahn's house designs in favor of more picturesque compositional strategies.[64]

In February 1954, several months after Tyng's departure, Kahn accepted the commission for the Benjamin and Ida Jaffe House, a work that demonstrates an important development in his linked-pavilion concept.[65] Here the radial symmetry of the Fruchter house gave way to a more loosely arranged grouping of pavilions. In a letter to Tyng, Kahn described the preliminary design that he had prepared for the couple, who were downsizing for retirement and had selected a site in Wynnewood surrounded by old beech and oak trees (fig. 54): "The house is essentially the same as [the Fruchter house] . . . only I believe it is much less static. The equal squares of 24 × 24 are placed as suits best the dictates of orientation view trees contours. The connector still is different in shape from the rest—even the garage is 24 × 24. . . . The F.P. [fireplace] is the black square in the L.R. [living room]. It helps to articulate the space although maybe it should be moved over to the right. . . . The L.R. is higher (13') than the other squares. The structure is wood columns wood beams running full length of 24' for all squares. . . . It is the general opinion that it is superior to [the Fruchter house,] which I also think is so. It is more adaptable and therefore more true to conditions of nature."[66]

If geometry had served as the ordering system for the Fruchter house, circumstantial considerations now came to the fore, as Kahn's sketches for the Jaffe house demonstrate. Kahn adapted the ideal form of the square to the realities of the site while simultaneously asserting a strong structural order. As they would have been viewed from the street (and as seen in the small elevation study at right below the site plan), the garage, kitchen, and living-room blocks—slightly offset to one another—maintain the same structural alignment and provide a distinct impression of wooden columns with brick infill. In contrast, the bedroom square (as seen in the elevation to the left) appears as a continuous surface of brick to distinguish its private function. This structural system advanced the one first put forward in the Genel house, now clearly aligned to the room unit. In devising this system of construction (as shown in the details at bottom), Kahn was reacting to what he saw as the "present-day . . . tendency to fair joints out of existence—in other words, to conceal how parts are put together." Developing further the example of Howe, he suggested that architects should "draw as we build, from the bottom up, stopping our pencils at the joints of pouring or erecting. . . . How it was done, how it works, should filter through the entire process of building, to architect, engineer, builder, and craftsman in the trades."[67]

The pavilion-plan concept crystallized in the Francis and Marty Adler and the Weber and Eleanor DeVore houses, which were commissioned at the same time, in June 1954, but were never built. Studies began immediately, although detailed investigations on the Adler house followed the development of the DeVore house.[68] They allowed Kahn to explore alternatives to an emerging set of principles. Kahn described his quest poetically in a 1955 statement called "Two Houses": "The Kitchen wants to be the Living Room. The Bed Room wants to be a little house by itself. The car is the room on wheels. In searching for the nature of the spaces of house might they not be separated a distance from each other theoretically before they are brought together. A predetermined total form might inhibit what the various spaces want to be. Architectural interpretations accepted without reflection could obscure the search for signs of a true nature and a higher order. The order of construction should suggest an even greater variety or design in the interpretations of what space aspires to become and more versatility in expression of the ever present problems of levels, services, the sun, the wind and the rain."[69]

For the DeVore house, which was to have been built in Wyndmoor, just across the city line from Chestnut Hill, Kahn chose brick, creating a series of four living pavilions loosely organized off a 4-foot-high stone retaining wall, which is delineated as a dark line on the plan (fig. 55). (The pavilion at the left is roofless, defining a small area of garden in its distinct precinct, and the one on the far right, a garage.) The six supporting members, creating a space 26 feet by 26 feet, form two bays or rooms measuring 13 by 26 feet. This system provided a subtle directionality and a logical location for room divisions where required. The articulation of the structure on the exterior recalls Howe's Square Shadows: for the columns, bricks were to be laid horizontally, as seen in the denser areas in the elevation drawing; for the infill, the bricks were to be laid on their edge, rendered in the elevation in a slightly less dense manner, as they also are in the areas directly above the column, which mark the transition where the roof structure begins (fig. 56). Visible in the bedroom block, projected forward from the retaining wall, is the ceiling and floor structure, consisting of a series of inclined 2-by-12-inch joists, paired into a triangulated form, which could house mechanical ductwork and other systems.

The Adler house was to have been built in a new subdivision in Chestnut Hill on a plot that faced the Wissahickon valley in Fairmount Park. For that wooded site, Kahn initially chose to use a structure comprising four stone columns, 3 feet, 6 inches square; wood for the roof; and brick for the large chimney. Like the DeVore house, it consists of a series of four living pavilions, 26 feet square, each freely arranged relative to the others (fig. 57). The kitchen and dining areas are in one volume, situated across from the garage area to form an entry court. The entry hall contains the service core, defined graphically in the plan by a tiled floor pattern, with bathrooms, closets, and utilities. Screened by that core, and given some distance from the rest of the house, are the two bedrooms; additional bedrooms, a music room, and mechanical spaces are downstairs. Living and dining spaces, on the south side of the house, are adjacent to outdoor living areas that are either paved or turf. An intriguing aspect of the Adler plan is the nondirectional quality of the supports. Acting as a single bay, the squares that make up the plan are the purest expression of Kahn's ideal form. As such, he specified a system of crisscrossed joists with metal connectors following suggestions made by Tyng, providing a nondirectional structure for the nondirectional space.[70]

Kahn's exploration of idealized form, embodied in the square pavilions, implied a search for a meaningful pattern to express the nature of a house and the human interactions and relationships that occur within it. This meant that one had to choose how to arrange the pavilions, considering not only the expression of functional relationships but also the conditions of the site, topography, orientation, and natural and built features. In the DeVore house, a sharp slope crossed the site in an east-west orientation, allowing the house to be arranged in a linear fashion, with the principal rooms afforded a southern exposure (fig. 58). Similarly, the Adler house site was sloped but the buildable area was tighter, requiring a clustered configuration, one that was centralized around a defined core. The south elevation shows the stone structural piers and the brick chimney—a strong vertical element—in two parts, the smaller for the furnace, the larger one for the

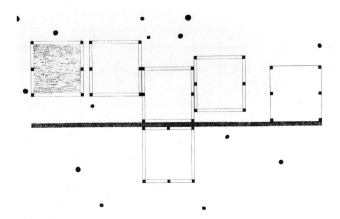

Fig. 55 Weber and Eleanor DeVore House, Wyndmoor, 1954–55. Diagrammatic plan. Kahn Collection

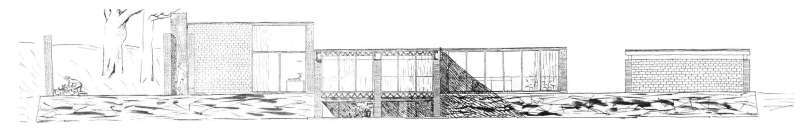

Fig. 56 Weber and Eleanor DeVore House. North elevation. Archival photograph of lost original. Louis Kahn, c. July 1954. Kahn Collection

fireplace (fig. 59). This is the side of house opposite the entrance, and part of Kahn's desire to make the chimney a full story higher than the house was to allow it to be seen and understood from the other side. The arrangement was carried forward into a series of revised schemes driven by economic considerations (column dimensions were reduced along with ceiling heights) and apparently by conflicts with the developers, who seem to have retained a say in what was to be built on the site.[71] A revised drawing of the south elevation, most likely made in the early winter of 1955, shows notable changes, in particular the introduction of individual, shallow hip roofs, an important development that clarified the expression of the individual room units (fig. 60).

The internal subdivision of a pavilion plan was a problem that challenged Kahn. If the Adler house was a "stronger" expression of an ideal form or order in Kahn's estimation, the set 26-foot dimensions and nondirectional character of the supports did not lend themselves to the "division which was necessary" to accommodate the partitioning of the space.[72] He solved this problem in the Bernard and Norma Shapiro House, designed and constructed with shallow hip roofs between 1958 and 1962, by establishing a hierarchy among the parts of the plan (see fig. 173). The key to this realization was the articulation of what he came to call "servant" and "served" spaces. In addition, he adjusted the space centered under each hip roof from the 26-foot-square dimension of the Adler house to 16 feet square, obviating the need for subdivision. Clustered around this served space were the servant spaces (such as closets, bathrooms, and vestibules), housed within "hollow columns" positioned at the pavilion corners. In

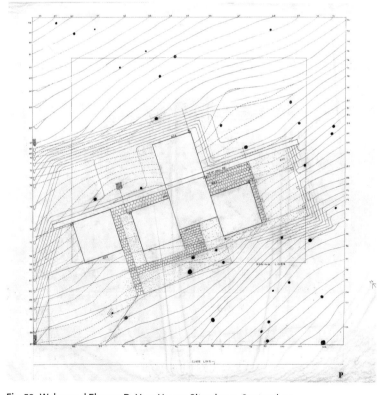

Fig. 57 Francis and Marty Adler House, Chestnut Hill, Philadelphia, 1954–55. Plan, c. September 1954. Kahn Collection

Fig. 58 Weber and Eleanor DeVore House. Site plan, c. September 1954. Kahn Collection

HOUSES   49

Fig. 59 Francis and Marty Adler House. South elevation. Archival photograph of lost original. Louis Kahn, c. September 1954. Kahn Collection

Fig. 60 Francis and Marty Adler House. South elevation, showing shallow hip roofs and reduced dimension of columns, Louis Kahn, c. January–March 1955. Kahn Collection

Fig. 61 Bernard and Norma Shapiro House, Narberth, 1958–62. From east. Photograph November 2011

essence, Kahn delineated a 4-foot zone wrapped around a 16-foot room, creating a pavilion 24 feet square as the basis of the Shapiro plan.

Overall, the Shapiro house consists of two pavilions, axially aligned to the contours of the steeply sloping site (fig. 61). Living areas were positioned at entry level with sleeping areas below. Dimensions of the servant areas were subtly varied according to circulation and functional requirements; where the flanking elements, containing closets, measured 4 feet, 6 inches by 8 feet, 6 inches, the central elements were 6 feet wide, extending the full 24-foot depth of the plan. These central elements were separated by a 3 foot, 6 inch gap—visible in the notched roofline—to accommodate vertical circulation and allow for more generous kitchen and entry areas. This core, and related service areas, established a hierarchical relationship to the primary spaces of the house, including the living room and dining room, emphasized by their robustly structured ceilings. Kahn's deft handling of the expression of functional relationships, an idea at the heart of the pavilion-plan concept, can be seen from the entrance court, where the shallow hip roofs float above the retaining wall, articulating the location of the principal rooms (fig. 62). These relationships are further refined by the finely proportioned, freestanding chimney offset to the left, which finds a counterpoint in the alcove, inset to the right, denoting the location of the dining room. If the outward thrust of the chimney volume suggests the presence of an inglenook on the interior (the living room has an added space that the dining room does not), the manner in which the two pavilions are separated or joined reveals developments in the relationship of the work to the landscape. This gap provides both a visual and physical connection between the front and back of the house as well as the upper and lower spaces. Here, the picturesque forms of his earlier pavilion plans yield to a more nuanced understanding of landscape, drawing the landscape through the house in a manner reminiscent of George Howe's High Hollow.

The reassertion of axial discipline can be traced to Kahn's bathhouse near Trenton, in Ewing Township, New Jersey, of 1955. The remarkable plan, with its striking composition of

Fig. 62 Bernard and Norma Shapiro House. Entry court from west. Photograph November 2011

four symmetrically arranged squares with hip roofs supported on 8-foot-square hollow columns, was a dramatic development of Kahn's nascent distinction of servant and served spaces, a conception that established, or reintroduced, hierarchy as a tool in ordering space (fig. 63). Again, Tyng's influence was at work. Tyng had just returned from Rome at the time the bathhouse plan was being considered, and it was through her studies of the problem that the solution emerged.[73] Even as the bathhouse served as the formal basis for the Shapiro house as built, and as a confirmation of Tyng's continuing influence on Kahn in general, her sustained interest in taut geometrical ordering systems as expressed in the use of hexagonal elements also marked the early development of the Shapiro project, as seen in a preliminary plan completed in June 1959 (fig. 64). Kahn also experimented with hexagonal geometry in a number of works during the period, including the Wharton Esherick workshop (1955–56), the only variant of this system to be built.

The question of hierarchy continued to be an important one for Kahn. One of the limitations of the pavilion-plan concept was the set dimension of each of the units. Kahn first explored the softening of this regularity through the introduction of spaces that varied in size in his design of the Fred and Elaine Clever house, initiated during the summer of 1957. Modest in proportion, the plan arranged a number of small rooms tightly clustered around a two-story living room lit on four sides by clerestory windows (see figs. 166–70).[74] Kahn also explored looser relationships in his designs for two houses of more generous proportions. For the house of Lawrence and Ruth Morris, hierarchy is clearly expressed in the preliminary design, with a series of centralized volumes under distinct hip roofs of various sizes, or in other iterations, occasionally flat roofs (fig. 65). Related to those spaces are small-scale secondary elements that extend out from the central spaces to provide functional flexibility (fig. 66). This design seems to have explored a little bit of everything, from distinctive corner windows to elaborate connections; its difficulty was in coming to terms with what holds these perhaps too arbitrary elements together.

Kahn explored a solution to this problem in his design of the Herbert and Roseline Gussman House. Documented by a single presentation sketch dated August 20, 1957, the house was commissioned for a site in Tulsa, Oklahoma, by a "pioneer of the modern oil industry" and art collector with strong ties

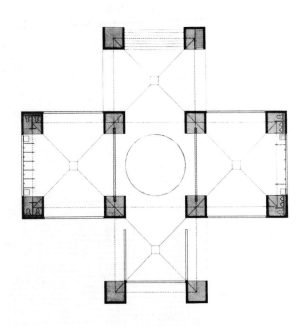

Fig. 63 Bathhouse, Jewish Community Center, Ewing Township, New Jersey, 1955. Plan. Archival photograph of lost original. Kahn Collection

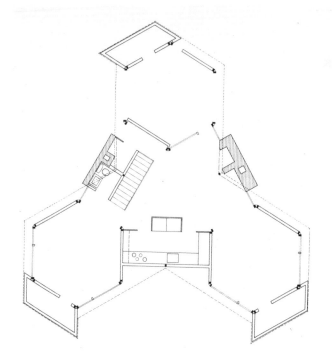

Fig. 64 Bernard and Norma Shapiro House. Entry level plan, hexagonal scheme. Dated 1959. Kahn Collection

to Cornell University (fig. 67).[75] During the previous April, Cornell's art museum had mounted the first one-man exhibition of Kahn's work, and it was perhaps this tie that brought the architect to Gussman's attention.[76] For this design, Kahn proposed a series of large square or rectilinear rooms unified by long galleries for circulation, elements he labeled "arcades." The linear arrangement of rooms, oriented along a north-to-south axis, provided ample space for dining, an inglenook-breakfast area, and a 32-foot-square living room.[77] A music room and library are situated within a cloistered garden and surrounded by an arcade off which four bedrooms are located. The master bedroom, with a private covered patio, and guest room are to the south, with the children's bedrooms to the west and a large open area in the landscape with a pool area beyond. Structural piers, both square and elongated, as well as a screen wall connected to the children's rooms, suggest a consideration of the sun's impact upon a structure, which would increasingly be of concern to Kahn.

Kahn returned to the Morris house design in the fall of 1958, following almost a year's hiatus during which he almost exclusively focused on the design of the Richards Medical Laboratories at the University of Pennsylvania. With the clients "restless to make progress," Kahn revised his previous scheme, compacting the loose-knit plan into a tight arrangement of volumes defined by a system of closely spaced masonry piers (fig. 68), recalling Frank Lloyd Wright's Richard Lloyd Jones house of 1929, in Tulsa (which Kahn could have visited if, in fact, he had traveled to that city to inspect the proposed site of the Gussman house).[78] Kahn was emphatic in expressing the logic of the individual rooms, which his use of these piers demonstrates. Each is based on a 1-foot module, but these could be doubled up or even presented as broad 4-foot slabs where individual room units joined. Entering into the double-height hall, lit by clerestories, one would have turned right into a pair of living rooms, oriented south and east, respectively, with a set of double columns and a change in ceiling height further distinguishing each. Beyond a fireplace inglenook, as Kahn referred to it, was the dining room, with kitchen and laundry spaces to the left and the master bedroom suite, including a small study, at the northern end of the plan. A monumental staircase in the hall would have provided access to additional bedrooms, two on a split level

Fig. 65 Lawrence and Ruth Morris House, Armonk, New York, 1955–58. East elevation. Louis Kahn, c. September 1957. Kahn Collection

Fig. 66 Lawrence and Ruth Morris House. Plan. Louis Kahn, c. August 1957. Kahn Collection

HOUSES   53

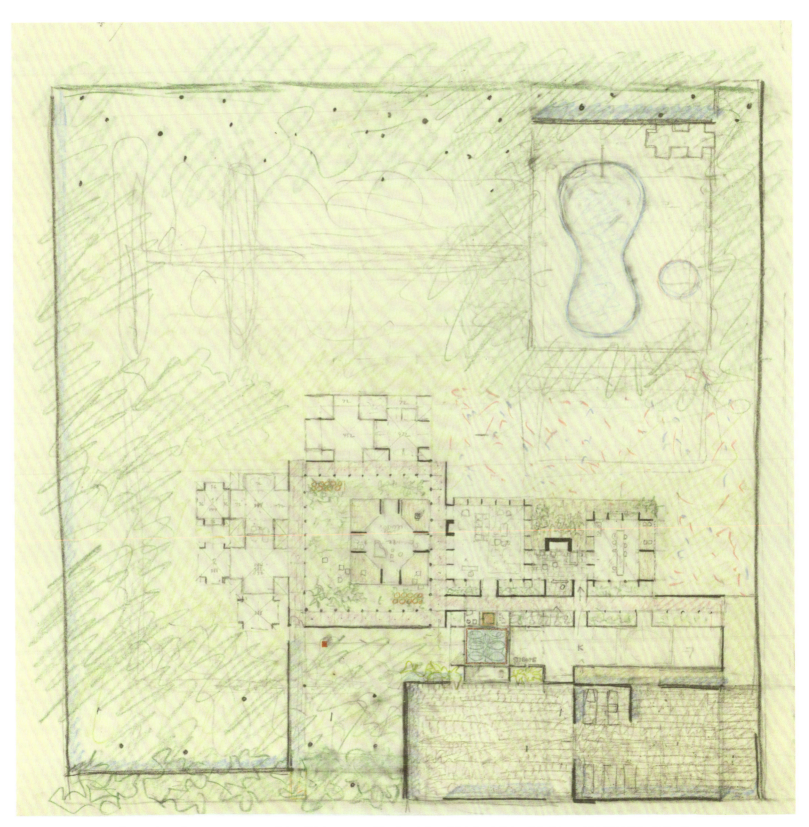

Fig. 67 Herbert and Roseline Gussman House, Tulsa, Oklahoma, 1957. Plan (north is at right). Louis Kahn, dated August 20, 1957. Kahn Collection

Fig. 68 Lawrence and Ruth Morris House. First-floor plan, c. September 1958. Kahn Collection

above the garage and a third located above the kitchen. A roof garden, framed by the broad wall elements, was proposed for the top level. The distinctive fenestration, rendered in alternating bands of glass and masonry block, reveals the structural system and gives the elevation a strong sense of mass (fig. 69).[79] But these designs left the clients "with a lot of questions," and by early October 1958, the project was dead.[80]

While Kahn, in his overarching pursuit of spatial and structural integration, had a difficult time realizing his house designs during the 1950s, he had succeeded in challenging the orthodoxy of fluid spatial sequences found in much of the work of the previous decades. His determination to uncover "what a space wants to be" had led him to the exploration of ideal forms, embodied in the individual units defined by his pavilion plans, finding poetry and inspiration in their joined separateness.[81] Kahn saw it as a virtue to "react . . . fluidly to environment," to account for the pressures, difficulties, and demands not only of location but also of modern mechanical systems. He was critical of "self centered" architects who "commend design immediately into steel glass boxes," where an imposed structural order denied the sensitivities he embraced.[82] Robert Venturi, whose interactions with Kahn

Fig. 69 Lawrence and Ruth Morris House. South elevation. Louis Kahn, c. September 1958. Kahn Collection

HOUSES   55

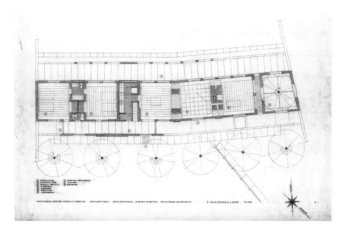

Fig. 70 Robert Venturi, architect. Forrest G. Pearson, Jr., House, Chestnut Hill, Philadelphia, 1957–58. First-floor plan. Robert Venturi. AAUP, by the Gift of Robert Venturi and Denise Scott Brown

during this period were complex and mutually enriching, certainly shared these views.[83] Venturi cited Kahn as a central influence in his design for the Forrest G. Pearson House in Chestnut Hill, commissioned shortly after he began his independent practice (fig. 70). Like the Adler house, next to which it would have stood had it been built, the Pearson house explored contained, nondirectional space articulated as a series of five "major rooms for living . . . interspersed in an orderly way, structurally and spatially, with . . . servant spaces."[84] These rooms were aligned between two long exterior screen walls, with a corridor on one side and an open terrace on the other. Whereas Kahn maintained the purity of the square form, Venturi distorted it, squeezing the individual rooms and bending the plan "slightly to give some feeling of direction and enclosure."[85] This solution provided an example for Kahn that maintained the clarity of the self-contained parts, or rooms, while also giving the whole an overall unity, a unity that was responsive to environment. Perhaps the most significant element of Venturi's design was the articulation of windows as holes in the wall and not the absence of wall (an aspect of modernism), a return to the traditional definition of a wall as a protective element.

For Kahn, the unbuilt Robert and Janet Fleisher House design, the development of which spanned only a few weeks during the spring of 1959, was a disciplined attempt to resolve his search for the logical definition of spaces within a neat spatial configuration.[86] The symmetrical plan is a tight cluster of square room units of varying size and use (fig. 71). The core consists of a hall laid out in a Greek-cross configuration, with a major axis leading to the living room, and a narrower transverse axis leading to the children's rooms and staircase. The core is bound by a series of four 12-foot squares, which comprise service areas, including bathrooms and a kitchen pantry on the ground level, and a master bedroom suite on the floor above (fig. 72). The rooms surrounding the core, including the living and dining rooms, kitchen and guest room, as well as the children's rooms, are contained in 18-foot-tall, 16-foot squares. The site was wooded but very tight, with the house to be situated close to an older house. The view up, toward the canopy of trees, would have been more desirable than the view across, and must have been a consideration in the design of the distinctive half-round windows. Elsewhere Kahn had noted the advantages this type of window held against glare, although the distinction that their canopylike form lent to each room unit was probably the determining factor here. The squares include a number of semi-enclosed, unroofed, private outdoor garden

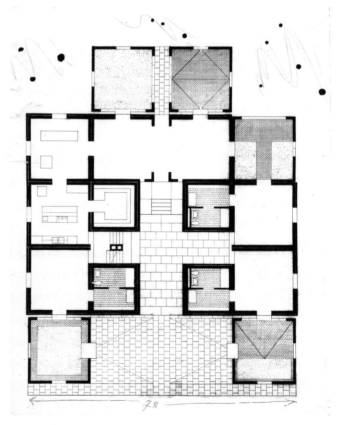

Fig. 71 Robert and Janet Fleisher House, Elkins Park, 1959. First-floor plan, c. May 1959. Kahn Collection

Fig. 72 Robert and Janet Fleisher House. Model. Archival photograph of lost original, c. May 1959. Kahn Collection

spaces, indicated on the plan by the thin profile, and again reasserting the bias toward containment that was so emblematic of Kahn's pavilion plans (and of the thinking of the 1950s). Just as the square entrance reconfirmed the architect's allegiance to that basic form, the vertical slit window above might be seen as a sign of changes to come. While the slit window denotes the verticality of the entry hall, it also reveals the overall weakness of the design, with Kahn's walls being at their thinnest, most insubstantial and the stiff arrangement of rooms requiring many adjustments and sacrifices to maintain the order of the—albeit preliminary—plan.

"This is not the Villa Rotunda!" Kahn was heard to exclaim in the drafting room one day in 1959 as work was under way on the Goldenberg house (fig. 73).[87] His observation that "a house is a building which is extremely sensitive to internal need" is a reflection of this, but if a house could not be "disciplined within a geometric shape," Kahn was left with the question of how to provide it with a strong sense of order.[88] For some years Kahn had shifted between two poles, on the one hand exploring picturesque compositional strategies, as in his DeVore and Adler houses, and on the other applying axial discipline and rules of symmetry, as in his Fleisher house. If the latter approach reflected a widespread interest among Kahn and contemporary architects—Philip

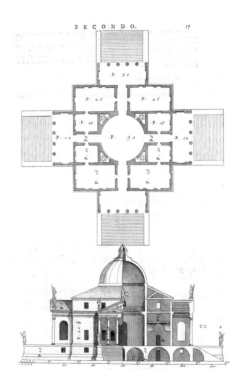

Fig. 73 Andrea Palladio, architect. Villa Capra, "La Rotunda," Vicenza, Italy, 1566. From *Quattro libri dell'architettura* [1767]. Fisher Fine Arts Library, University of Pennsylvania, by the Gift of G. Holmes Perkins

HOUSES   57

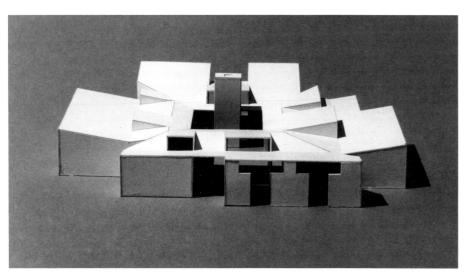

Fig. 74 Morton and Mitzi Goldenberg House, Rydal, 1959. Model, c. March 1959. AAUP, by the gift of Anne P. Meyers and Pamela Meyers Schaefer

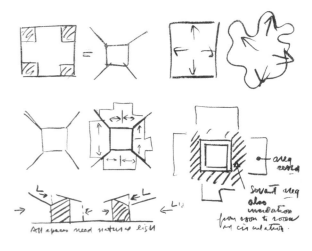

Fig. 75 Morton and Mitzi Goldenberg House. "Form" diagrams. Archival photograph of lost original drawn by Louis Kahn for publication, c. 1960. Kahn Collection

Johnson, in particular—regarding the implications of the Palladian plan in reshaping modernism, each saw the advantages differently. "If neo-Palladianism meant *piano nobile* and balanced façades to Philip Johnson and his admirers," William Huff explained, "it meant something else to Lou. To him [Palladio's] Villa Rotunda was a grand central space with clusters of small spaces serving the larger one, fitted into the ring between its inner circle and outer square of walls. . . . And so, he saw that the Palladian villa was served by persons from the cubicles, surrounding the master's space, and that the modern servants were no longer persons but mechanical equipment systems."[89]

In the Goldenberg house, which was canceled just as construction was about to begin, Kahn shifted the focus of interest from the simple form of the square as a planning element (although a square was still at its core) to the periphery, with the imposed symmetry of the Fleisher house giving way to a more relaxed outline and an animated roofline (fig. 74). The plan had started with a Greek cross similar to that of the Trenton Bathhouse (fig. 75). Each quadrant contained a working component of the house, but this configuration did not give Kahn the flexibility of planning that he wanted until he hit upon the diagonal, a device that provided both a strong ordering system and the flexibility to respond to internal need.[90] Each component, derived from functional requirement, could be any size or shape that was needed and still remain subservient to the ordering of the diagonal. This was not unlike Venturi's imposition of a giant order in the resolution of the Pearson house and perhaps owed something to the architects' shared interest in Rome, particularly the Baroque planning of its great boulevards.[91]

The final plan, dated July 10, 1959, reflects the functional needs of the family in its three sectors: four bedrooms; kitchen and eating areas, and a maid's, or guest, room; and the living area. Each is anchored to one of the diagonal arms (fig. 76). The entry is on one side, giving way to the open court, which one could walk around; it is slightly offset, suggesting that one should go left, not right, where the private areas are located. The living areas are to the south, and the chimney is positioned just to the north within the court. Kahn opened up the roof, providing a dormer that looks directly at the chimney, above a sunken seating area that, with the flanking columns, is reminiscent of a traditional inglenook. The notion of servant and served spaces is very clear in the plan: flanking the open court is a series of denser spaces, such as closets, bathrooms, utility areas. This clarity is also expressed in section, where changes in roof pitch accommodate clerestory windows that provide natural light to each of these spaces, a strategy Kahn had first explored in the Genel house (see fig. 165).

The core of the house is the open court, an embodiment of site specificity. Here the presence of nature would have

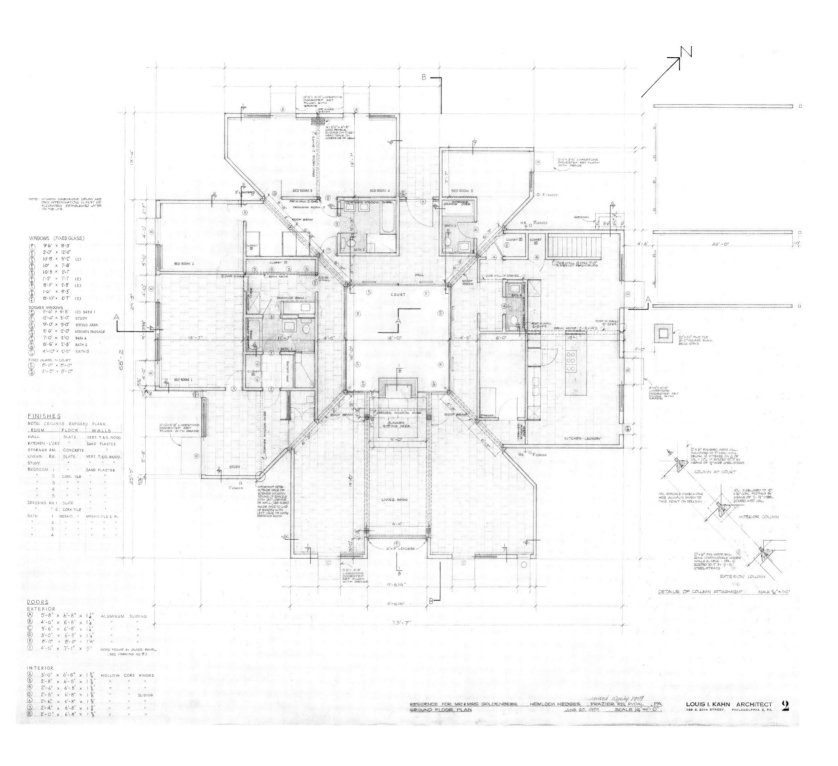

Fig. 76 Morton and Mitzi Goldenberg House. Plan. Thomas R. Vreeland, dated June 20, 1959, revised July 10, 1959. Kahn Collection

been felt in the way the changing seasons, and the changing qualities of light, were revealed. This is perhaps most beautifully accomplished in the living room, where the clerestory above the inglenook, partially screened by the mass of the chimney, would have presented a slice of light, transiting the floor over the course of the day. Up to this point Kahn had provided a connection to location through the use of local materials and building techniques, an extension of Howe's considerations. Natural light offered new avenues of expression. Like the diagonals in the Goldenberg house, which offered a means of unifying the plan literally, natural light offered a means of unifying spaces figuratively, brought into a meaningful arrangement as a society of rooms unified in light.

This new sensitivity to light was furthered dramatically in the design of the Margaret Esherick house, a work that Vincent Scully would come to characterize as a "brimming chalice of light."[92] Kahn's earlier houses had been intended for families, but here he was called upon to design a one-bedroom house for a single person. His first sketches for the house were most likely prepared during the summer of 1959, shortly after he received a survey of the site on July 24, when he must have enthusiastically put his first thoughts on paper, as he is known to have done in the immediacy of receiving commissions.[93] The four sketches, done in rapid succession (the torn edges of the sheets line up exactly), show an upright, two-story volume contained within a compact plan, a series of four squares organized around a stair hall (in subsequent versions its orientation would change from being on axis with to perpendicular to the fireplace; fig. 77).[94] Included in this plan were two semi-enclosed outdoor spaces, a forecourt and a covered terrace area, as well as suggestions for complex ceiling forms, possibly light monitors of the sort first proposed in the Morris house (see fig. 65). The tight clustering of squares and the clear articulation of the columnar structure demonstrate a connection to the earlier pavilion plans, as does the implied Greek cross of the circulation area, here with a column that notably interrupts the axis from stair to

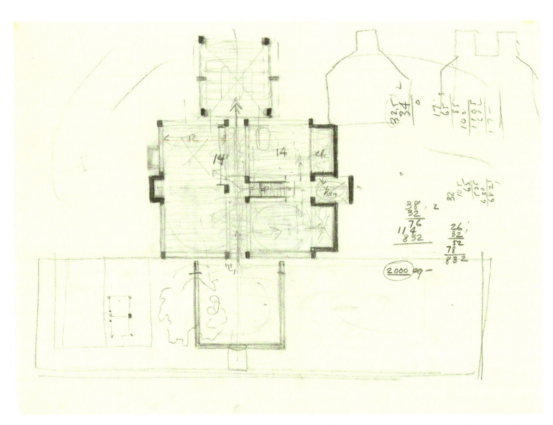

Fig. 77 Margaret Esherick House, Chestnut Hill, Philadelphia, 1959–62. First-floor plan. Louis Kahn, c. July–September 1959. Kahn Collection

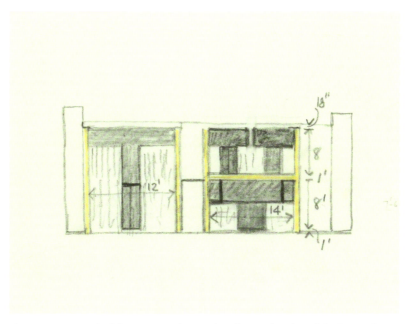

Fig. 78 Margaret Esherick House. Northwest elevation. Louis Kahn, c. July–September 1959. Kahn Collection

fireplace. The axial discipline is pronounced and more meaningfully and symbolically focused in the prominence given to both the fireplace and to the connection to the natural environment.

The elevation presents a clear articulation of the structure, here rendered in yellow, showing the columns and beam, with distinction given to the double-height living-room space to the left (fig. 78). This would be carried forward during the fall as the design developed (the plan would be flipped, with the living room switched from the eastern to the western side), and by winter it was resolved in a façade of concrete-block construction with a clear delineation of the structural piers (fig. 79). A study for the corresponding plan, from December 1959, shows a decided thickening of the window enclosures (the many details for which are also in evidence in the elevation), along with a more circuitous entry axis, now turned 90 degrees into an entry hall (fig. 80). Overall, the plan shows a dramatic shift from the pavilion form toward a simpler grouping of rooms familiar from examples of early American houses. Discussions with a builder who was furnishing cost estimates and references to signing a contract, perhaps to begin construction, suggest that work was taking a definitive form by this time. There are also provisions for such amenities as a desk by Margaret's uncle Wharton Esherick in the living room (placed next to a large built-in shelf system for her extensive library) and, upstairs, a luxuriant bath area, with a fireplace and a pull-out seat to cover the tub when it was not in use. The façade would take a step toward further simplification, becoming stucco clad in response to objections raised by the Woodwards, which emphasized a shift of interest from structure to surface and enclosure.

The most innovative development, however, was the fenestration. In his work of the early 1960s, Kahn would increasingly explore the modulation of light, and the expressive qualities of changing light, as aspects of a building's enclosing envelope, introducing a "perceivable, faceted thickness," as David G. De Long has suggested, that infused his buildings with "a quality of exaggerated mass that was new even to his work."[95] This quality first appeared in the Esherick house, and the source of this inspiration can now be traced. On September 3, 1959, Kahn departed on a two-week trip to Europe, where he had been invited to give the keynote address at the Congrès International d'Architecture Moderne (CIAM X) meeting in Otterlo, the Netherlands. Following the conference, at the suggestion of Le Corbusier's assistant André Wogenscky, Kahn rearranged his schedule to visit the architect's chapel at Ronchamp and his recently completed monastery of La Tourette.[96] He had not known of the monas-

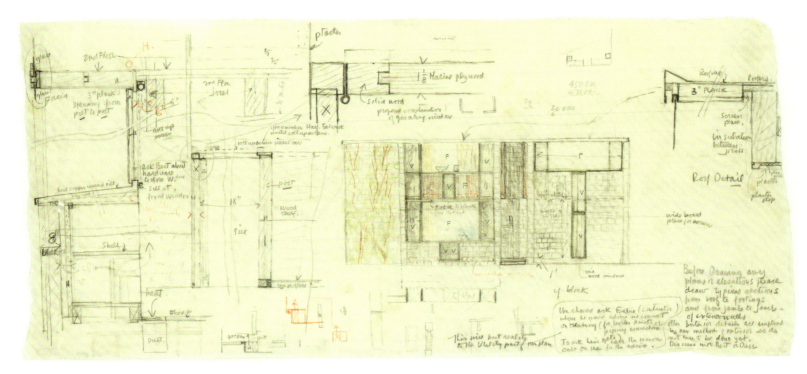

Fig. 79 Margaret Esherick House. Elevation and window details. Louis Kahn, c. December 1959–January 1960. Kahn Collection

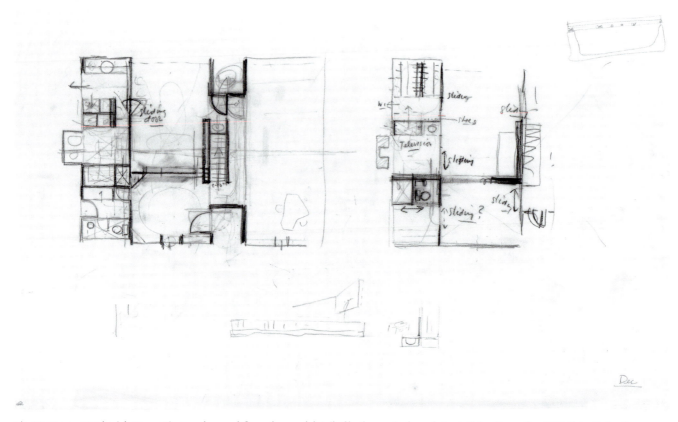

Fig. 80 Margaret Esherick House. First- and second-floor plans and detail of bathroom inglenook. Louis Kahn, December 1959. Kahn Collection

tery until he heard about it in Otterlo, and then "couldn't resist" visiting it, as he wrote in a letter to Harriet Pattison:

> The building is a coming together of spaces boldly and even violently meeting each with its own light quality. I felt all humility before this masterpiece of Corbusier's. I kept telling the monk who guided me thru of my reactions—the meaning profound in the nakedness of every form. The joyous courage that comes from realization in art and that only a religious man could act with such fearless invention for the sheer need rather than desire for the creation.
>
> All the time I talked to him I was thinking of course if my own realizations are testing against what I saw. I felt nothing but humility and strength and a powerful will to continue more than ever. This monk . . . readily saw my point that an artist never sets out to solve a problem for which there is a known solution and a known appearance (or feeling). He draws from the circumstances and need the essence of new clusters of affinities, which he models into a new image. The monks with the problem may well have envisioned a Gothic monastery. Now in the hands of the master it becomes a tough environment of spaces religious, all Corbusier's and all Everyone's.[97]

How exuberant Kahn must have been as he walked through the monastery, in which light is handled in a different way at every turn. At one point there is a rhythmic composition of verticals, geometric compositions elsewhere, and at the ends of hallways there are light scoops, with no view to the outside but which capture a beautiful, changing light. Finally, in the chapel, most dramatically, light illuminates the rituals of monastic worship. The handling of light throughout the building, so all-embracing of Le Corbusier's definition of architecture as the "masterly, correct and magnificent play of masses brought together in light," was a revelation to Kahn.[98] It instigated a focus on natural light as it affects the design of individual rooms, which was new to his thinking, especially in their forceful gathering that he would come to express as a "society of rooms brought together in natural light."

The visit would affect all of Kahn's subsequent work, especially the great rooms at Rochester, Dhaka, Exeter, and Fort Worth, although the lessons would be filtered through his sense of structure. But in the Esherick house the impact could be seen immediately. Keeping in mind that he was designing a house for a single woman, a bibliophile at that, Kahn would have been thinking of the singularity of the monks' cells, a place of private retreat and contemplation (fig. 81). At La Tourette the cells have a thick wall of brightly painted wood, with movable shutters for ventilation that are separate from the fixed glazed elements. This is precisely what Kahn brought into his work in the Esherick house, but he transformed it from the small-scale element set within Le Corbusier's deeply recessed balconies into a large-scale element, a gigantic order of deep recesses containing solid wood ventilating panels juxtaposed against large sheets of glass, pressed forward, almost to the very periphery of the house (fig. 82). Kahn also found in Le Corbusier's distinctive wooden latching a model for securing the shutters in his own design.

Fig. 81 Le Corbusier, architect. Sainte Marie de La Tourette, Eveux, Rhône-Alpes, France, 1953–58. Photograph 1959. Monk's cell, showing fixed glass and wooden ventilating shutters

Fig. 82 Margaret Esherick House. From southeast. Photograph fall 1962. Kahn Collection

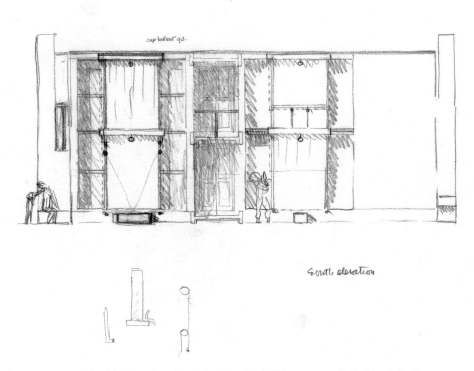

Fig. 83 Margaret Esherick House. Southeast elevation. Louis Kahn, summer 1960. Kahn Collection

When the ventilators are opened within these recesses the façade changes, bringing in not only the breeze on a warm day but also a different quality of light. The occupant and the house become active players in the experience of nature.

A second trip abroad also had a direct impact on the design. This came just as the final work was being done on the elevations of the house. In May 1960 Kahn traveled to Tokyo for the World Design Conference, where he lectured and interacted for ten to twelve days with leading architects. Afterward he visited Kyoto and the Katsura Imperial Villa, and Nara, where he saw how light was modulated in traditional Japanese architecture (as well as in modern interpretations of that tradition) through the use of sliding panels, or *shoji* screens, wooden shutters (*amado*), and reed blinds (*sudare*).[99] For the Esherick house he imported these blinds, and in the southeast elevation there are projecting enclosures to hold them on the exterior (along with the circular and triangular elements showing the lowering of a blind system; figs. 83, 84). The blinds were on the punch list waiting for completion but were never installed owing to Margaret Esherick's premature death.

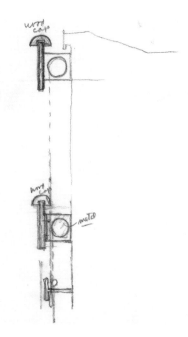

Fig. 84 Margaret Esherick House. Partial section of living-room window showing housing and mechanism of exterior blinds. Louis Kahn, summer 1960. Kahn Collection

Kahn was able to bring in a traditionally trained Japanese carpenter, Yukio Madokoro, who had just completed the interiors of Isamu Noguchi's house and studio in Long Island City, to finish important elements of the interior woodwork for the house, including the stair screen and balcony rail (see figs. 191, 196).[100] Initially this work was to have been executed by Wharton Esherick, but his highly individualistic design sense presented an unwelcome distraction in the logic of Kahn's interiors. The shift to a traditional craftsman, the "unknown craftsman" celebrated in Japan, was more in keeping with Kahn's sensibilities, to which the executed woodwork attests—in particular, the use of large planks with an emphasis on the grain (see fig. 191).[101]

The chimney that Kahn designed for the house was also articulated in an extraordinary way (see frontispiece). Here, in a house for a single woman, the symbolism of the chimney as a place of gathering for a family did not ring true, and he minimized its footprint. Instead, Kahn created a flush-mounted mantel of black Virginia soapstone, above which he cut out a vertical slice for a window (see fig. 190). There was a precedent for this in the work of earlier architects, among them Frank Furness in Philadelphia and Edwin Lutyens in Great Britain, where similar moves confounded expectations of the presence of a chimney and added tension to their buildings. Kahn's awareness of such precedents may be traced to his interaction with Robert Venturi, who at that time was actively designing his Mother's House and consulting with Kahn on it as it progressed.[102] Venturi was just beginning to work on his book *Complexity and Contradiction in Architecture* (published in 1966), in which illustrations of the work of both Furness and Lutyens would be included. If for Venturi a chimney could be an ironic element, for Kahn this was not a clever inversion, and certainly not an expression of irony. This was about light, like the light scoops at the end of the hallways at La Tourette. Kahn had originally detailed this element as a projecting bay and carried that through into the construction drawings, only to simplify the detail during construction. Kahn often made such decisions on the job site, and one can picture him walking into the unfinished room, seeing beautiful light entering the raw space, and deciding then and there to change his design. In the end it became a simple window with a chimney set in its view, made slightly smaller than the opening so that it could better shape natural light. In this configuration a memory of a traditional inglenook is maintained and expressed. Kahn carried this idea upstairs to the bath area, where he provided a fireplace and a pull-out seat above a bathtub next to a window, which was more directly reminiscent of an inglenook and yet transformed.

The transformation of the inglenook into a distinct, freestanding element freed from its traditional purpose or form appears in an early elevation study for the Norman and Doris Fisher House (see fig. 202). The house was commissioned in the fall of 1960 as construction was beginning on the Esherick house, and it took seven years to design and build. The elements of a separate inglenook had already emerged in the initial scheme, where the house has three components: a living area; a bedroom area, which in this scheme includes the kitchen; and a large volume, with thick stone walls, which incorporates the family's dining table along with a fireplace (see fig. 201). As the house developed, becoming more clearly articulated in terms of structure (4-by-4-inch posts, exposed to the interior, are seen throughout the plan) and location of service areas (quietly positioned between the major elements of the plan), it comprised a central entrance (note the column positioned in the middle of the face of the closet), with the sleeping areas to the right, and kitchen, storage (lit by a clerestory), utility, and living areas to the left (fig. 85). The stone inglenook, with thick walls and a complexity of deep windows and openings, is attached to the outside of the house, becoming a separate room unit—a juxtaposition that recalls Shingle Style examples (fig. 86).[103] The prominence of the inglenook as a massive and distinct architectural feature indicates that for Kahn the dining area was the most important part of the house, as he imagined the family seated around the table, and the day-to-day exchanges that would take place there and make the family a family. This is a notion that he later spoke of when he said, "I don't know of any greater seminar than the dining room."[104]

Because the cost of building these large volumes in stone was beyond the means of the client, the inglenook was distilled to a simple chimney as the design finally developed, a freestanding element set between the living and dining areas. As built, the house became a dynamic juxtaposition of parts, two self-contained cubes attached at an aggressive 45-degree angle, a duality unflinching in its expression of the often contradictory manner in which people lead their public

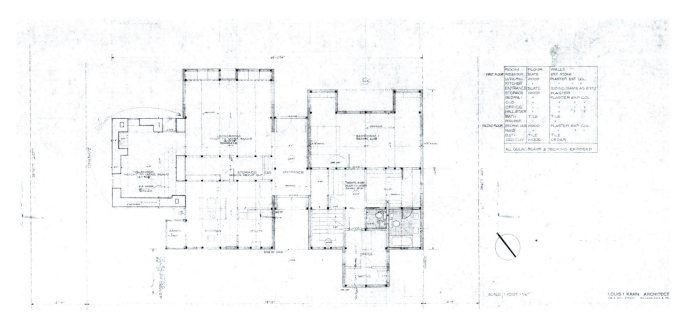

Fig. 85 Norman and Doris Fisher House, Hatboro, 1960–67. First-floor plan. Dated August 3, 1961. Collection of Doris and Norman Fisher Family

Fig. 86 Norman and Doris Fisher House. Northeast elevation. Louis Kahn, c. August 8, 1961. Kahn Collection

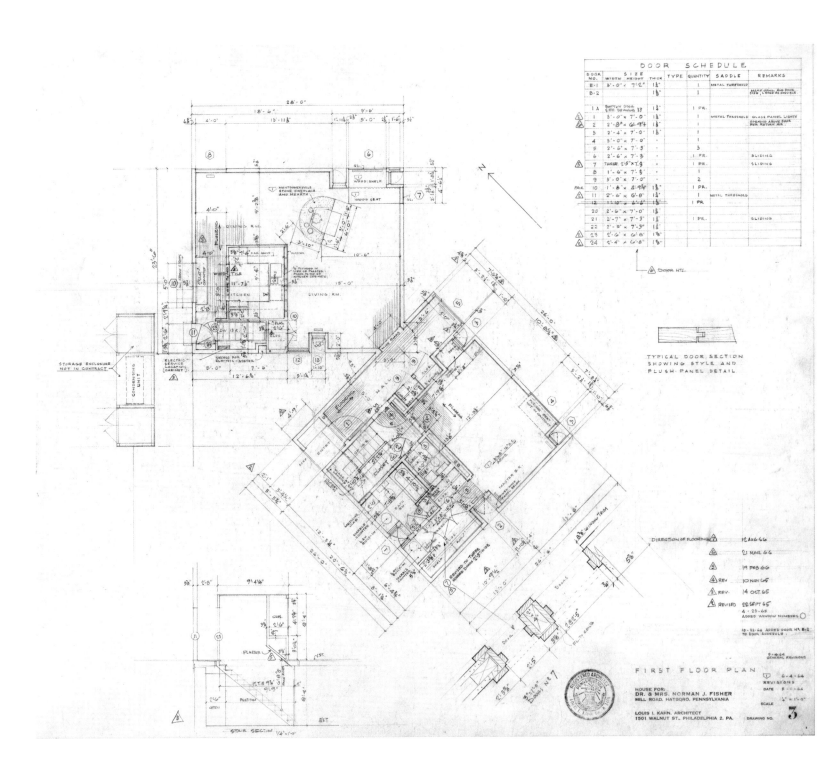

Fig. 87 Norman and Doris Fisher House. First-floor plan. Albert J. Webb, dated May 11, 1964. Kahn Collection

and private lives (fig. 87). The austere exterior, with its narrow, deeply inset windows; taut cypress siding; and string courses aligned to the logic of the openings but seemingly also gesturing to the hillside sloping downward to the right (see fig. 219), defies any conventional expression of a house.[105] The entrance is in the private, bedroom, section but in a distinct hallway that terminates in a broad window, which connects one immediately to the landscape beyond. An angled connection, where one corner of the living unit is cut away, opens up into the living areas. This is the part closest to the river, where the windows are the largest and where the seating area is placed at the heart of the house. It is here that one comes closest to Kahn's own understanding of nature and place (see fig. 224). Beyond the curve of the massive stone chimney is the dining area (which originally had only a small window at the corner). Here, the idea of a family focusing inward around a dining table was retained and celebrated.

Kahn described the Fisher house as "essentially a wood house on a stone plinth."[106] For the stone he selected a locally available limestone with a warm reddish-brown coloration, laid with deeply raked joints as he had first done at the Weiss house. In wood, his preferences leaned more to medieval traditions than the modern age. To Kahn, the timber framing of the Pennsylvania bank barn, with its clearly expressed bay system and direct expression of materials, revealed more. "His detailing was fundamental," recalled William Huff. His "detailing of doors and wood wall panels were strictly out of the Elizabethan Age; but he had his own profiles."[107] Underlying Kahn's detailing were Arts and Crafts impulses, shaped as much by his connection to Cret and Howe as by his admiration of the work of the Shakers.[108] Whenever he was required to become more frugal in his detailing, he noted: "I look to the Shakers to help me out."[109]

In Kahn's own search for sources he had looked to Colonial houses, their simple, upright volumes, and the sense of "agreement," expressed in the early settlements. While he was unsentimental in his use of these examples, he respected their inherent qualities. "The Colonial house is a marvelous house," he explained. "It has an eternal plan in my opinion. No matter how much variation you put into it, it's still an eternal plan. . . . The room separations make responsive places. One can become the place where you go away while somebody else is doing something else. If you blend spaces in the Colonial way, you have a society of rooms in which each one has its character, allowing delicate differences to express themselves. In a way, people meeting in them are different people from those who live in divisionless spaces."[110]

In the last years of his career Kahn was able to explore more elaborate conceptions of a "society of rooms" in the design of three houses, for Philip and Helen Stern, Harold and Lynne Honickman, and Steven and Toby Korman. These clients were affluent, worldly, and relatively young (Steven Korman and Lynne Honickman, brother and sister, were in their thirties), coming to him because of his prominence, which notably increased after his major exhibition at the Museum of Modern Art in 1966. Their programmatic requirements allowed him to explore the "delicate differences" inherent in complex plans. In the Stern house, designed for a site in Washington, D.C., but never built, there are prominent fireplaces and chimneys, especially the flanking chimneys that one would have seen on entering its central feature, which for a while was a garden, or atrium, space (fig. 88; see fig. 11). He explored complex room shapes, including circles, ovals, and hexagons, set within a framework of timber columns and heavy, thick floor beams, recalling examples found in early American interiors (fig. 89). As he had done in his design of the central court of the Goldenberg house, Kahn brought a strong sense of nature and natural lighting to the heart of the house, organizing the building around it. His inset shutter system and fine wood detailing also figured in the design, as did a consideration of integrated garden spaces, including walled, formal gardens, terraces, and grottos. For philosophical reasons the atrium space was rejected by the clients, and the final design took on a much more compact form, although in doing so it perhaps lost some of its elegance for hard-nosed realism. Here, Kahn was forced to redefine the living room as a place with "no privacy," as he described it, and charged to create a structure for living where "everyone is welcome."[111]

Kahn's mature attitude toward natural light, the use of local materials, and the expression of structure is explicit in plans for a pair of houses commissioned in the spring of 1971: the Korman house, which was completed in late 1973, and the Honickman house, which was never built. They were designed almost simultaneously, with the clients often meeting together with the architect to review the projects as they evolved. The generous and unobstructed adjacent sites were located on flat, beautiful former pastureland. Kahn had great freedom in

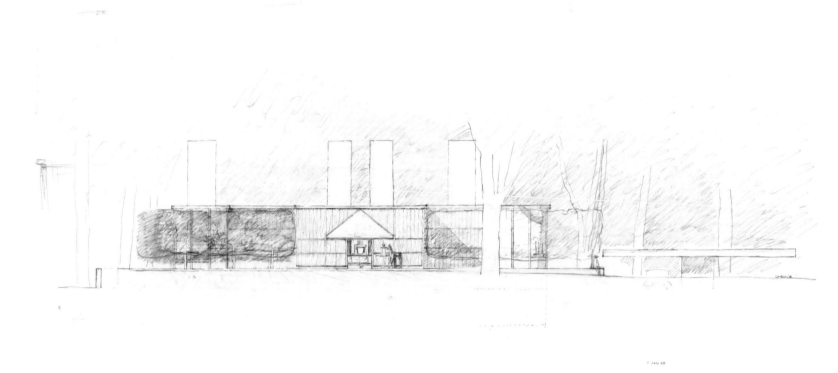

Fig. 88   Philip and Helen Stern House, Washington, D.C., 1966–70. Elevation. Louis Kahn, dated January 7, 1969. Kahn Collection.

Fig. 89   Philip and Helen Stern House. Section. Louis Kahn, dated June 1970. Kahn Collection

resolving the internal needs of the houses with the landscape beyond and was able to work closely with landscape architect Harriet Pattison to develop refined settings that included walled gardens, outdoor pavilions, and integrated plantings.[112]

In designing these houses Kahn continued to explore the potential of the inglenook as a focus. For the Honickmans' house Kahn situated a breakfast room within a towerlike inglenook enclosure (fig. 90, at right). This structure, to be built of 4-inch-thick slabs of cut limestone, was matched on the house's opposite side by a fireplace inglenook of equally monumental scale, with still others located in the bedroom wing. At the Korman house these features were initially consolidated into a single, semicircular inglenook terminating the living room's northern end (see fig. 228). But these elements were extravagant, fanciful expressions and, as the realities of cost set in, were reconsidered in both projects. In the end, three fireplaces were built in the Korman house using a brick selected by Kahn for its subtly variegated surface coloring (a by-product of the firing process). These fireplaces were animated by their distinct designs, details that helped to reveal the delicate differences between functional areas of the house.

These differences between spaces were further articulated through Kahn's ability to shape natural light and to integrate a structure into the landscape. The house sits low to the ground, just above the gently sloping lawns and groves that surround it, anchored, it seems, by the mass of the three chimneys. Kahn's finely proportioned, double-height living room was designed to accommodate natural light, making room—through careful placement of windows—for the sun to reveal its many moods on the taut, vertical surfaces within (see fig. 236). This sensitivity informs the finely orchestrated northeast-facing windows, detailed to the thinnest of dimensions. A simple cross axis establishes the logic of the plan and the movement from the entry hall to light-filled living room, with the landscape framed at each turn.

In an extraordinary position, visible and exposed to the entry court, and similar in concept to Kahn's early designs for the stone inglenook at the Fisher house, is the family dining room, set into the landscape and facing west, toward the late-day sun (fig. 91). This is a most compelling and unconventional expression of the face that a house puts forth—a beckoning gesture of the hospitality within. Housed in a distinct volume, which included the kitchen, and opened up with an elegant structure of floor-to-ceiling windows, this private space was placed front and center for all to see, bringing to mind that idealized vision of home that Kahn had spoken so wistfully about to his daughter many years before, where "if an outsider were looking in . . . he could see a woman cooking over a stove, a happy family with the light glowing."[113]

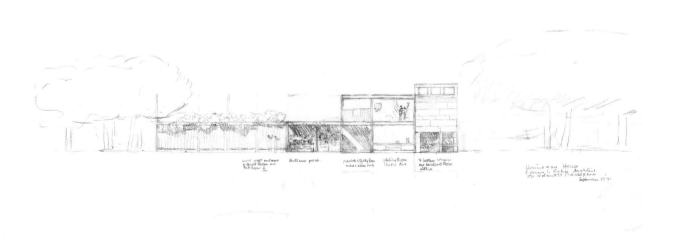

Fig. 90 Harold and Lynne Honickman House, Whitemarsh Township, 1971–73. Elevation. Louis Kahn, dated September 27, 1971. Kahn Collection

Fig. 91 Steven and Toby Korman House, Whitemarsh Township, 1971–73. From west. Photograph November 2011

FURNISHINGS

In his drawings of interiors Louis Kahn envisioned a structure for the life to be lived within them. He fitted out his rooms with modern furniture, decorations, knickknacks, and works of art that would make them seem inhabited and give them a sense of home (fig. 92). When Kahn first began to build houses, during the 1940s and early 1950s, he similarly approached them as complete works, taking great pains to control their furnishings and fittings, adding built-ins to his spaces, designing freestanding furniture, and choosing pieces from shops and showrooms to finish off the interiors. Kahn worked through the creation of his houses methodically, and he did not customarily give final form to their interior fittings until after the projects were designed, and redesigned, and often not even until construction had begun, or in some cases, was completed. His furnishings must have been especially important to him, for even when he was busy with other jobs and had several assistants to help him in his office, he detailed many of these elements himself (often on Sundays, when he could be alone in a quiet office), and his hand and his signature can be seen on a number of drawings for them (see fig. 114).

When he began to consider the interior design of the Oser house in 1940, he was still a neophyte. He had no experience in accommodating spaces and designing furnishings for a particular family. But finally, after almost a decade of working on public housing, he had in the Osers clients "whom you could talk to," as he later distinguished the process of designing a private house from that of mass housing.[1] He spent a great deal of time with the family trying to understand and meet their requirements. This included, as their daughter Julie recalled, "a whole day in the kitchen with mom, following all her steps as she worked."[2] Kahn tried to work with the tight spaces of the house by creating built-ins: a 12½-foot-long buffet/divider in the dining area, a cabinet in the inglenook, and a desk and bookshelves at the foot of the stairs (fig. 93; see fig. 132). Preliminary versions of these pieces are seen in his early perspectives of the interior and appear on the construction drawings, although their configurations changed as the house was being built (fig. 94; see fig. 128). He adapted these elements to what he had learned of the family's particular requirements by including such features as a compartment for the storage of a bridge table in the side of the buffet and housing for a radio, record player, and speaker in the cabinet beside the fireplace.[3]

For the modern form he gave to the buffet, with its semblance of four different cabinets set next to each other (as seen in the early construction drawings; fig. 95), Kahn relied on the concept of unit furniture, which had been introduced in the United States in the early 1930s by the American designer Gilbert Rohde and then imitated by many others. In 1927, Rohde had traveled to Germany, where he became acquainted firsthand with the strategy of the modular furniture that had been manufactured there since the early twentieth century and had been widely published.[4] Rohde's

Fig. 92 Stonorov & Kahn, architects. Kitchen interior. Perspective. Louis Kahn, c. 1945. Kahn Collection

Fig. 93 Jesse and Ruth Oser House, Elkins Park, 1940–42. Living and dining rooms. Photograph May 1944

transatlantic transposition of unit furniture included two modular concepts, sectional sofas and standardized cabinets, which he designed for a number of different companies. As a consultant designer for the Herman Miller Furniture Company beginning in 1932, Rohde created elegant seasonal lines of modular bedroom, living-room, and dining-room furniture; these were sold to a large middle-class market in department stores and furniture shops across the country in what Herman Miller designated as "groups" (fig. 96). These modular units were all of the same depth and could be set on legs or solid bases and placed next to each other to form a group. Although Kahn's side-by-side cabinet, drawer, and display components were built in, the buffet is meant to look as if it were made of four freestanding pieces put together as a group, and it expresses the asymmetry and variability characteristic of Rohde's unit furniture.

Kahn also designed a suite of oak unit furniture for the Osers' master bedroom, which was first mentioned only in February 1942, about the time the family was moving into the house, in an estimate from the Decorators' Cabinet Shop

Fig. 94 Jesse and Ruth Oser House. Living room. Perspective. Louis Kahn. Kahn Collection

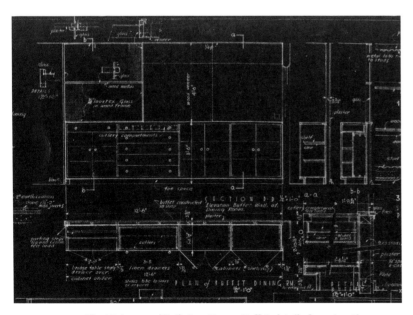

Fig. 95 Jesse and Ruth Oser House. Buffet, detail of construction drawing. Louis Kahn, dated November 11, 1940. AAUP, by the Gift of Mr. and Mrs. Paul Silver

Fig. 96. Gilbert Rohde. Mahogany Group. From 1939 Catalogue and Sales Guide, Herman Miller Furniture Company

FURNISHINGS   77

in Philadelphia. The suite, as listed in the invoice sent after the furniture was delivered in June, comprised a "Modern Bed" and "4 Sections, Drawers and Door combined, in straight white oak as per details and Instructions given by Mr. Kahn Architect." These four sections included two for the bedside that had open shelving on the ends next to the bed, a dresser, and an additional cabinet (fig. 97).[5] In October, the Decorators' Cabinet Shop billed Oser for a desk made of "one Walnut Veneered Door."[6] This is not extant, but a second desk, which is made of oak and shares most of the construction details and stylistic features with the bedroom furniture, remains with the family. Since there is no documentation for it among the other estimates and bills from the Decorators' Cabinet Shop, this desk may have been made for Jesse Oser's office in the city (and billed there) and then taken along with the household furniture when the family moved to Los Angeles in 1945. There is a refinement, however, that differentiates the desk from the bedroom furniture; it has mitered instead of butt joints where the top and sides meet. Mitered joints also distinguish two somewhat larger pieces that formed a group created for the architect's own sitting room in West Philadelphia, a chest of drawers and a cabinet lined in cedar for woolens storage, which has one full and two half-size doors with an unconventional offset arrangement of pulls (figs. 98–100).[7] The mitered joints suggest that Kahn revised the design after he saw the Oser household furniture and realized that the clarity of construction had not been resolved, and that the Decorators' Cabinet Shop did not make the Oser desk and Kahn's units until later.[8]

These pieces all feature distinctive walnut pulls, discs an inch and a half in diameter with ebony centers for the cabinet doors, and long and short bars for the drawers, which, unusu-

Fig. 97 Jesse and Ruth Oser House. Master bedroom. Photograph May 1944

Figs. 98–100 Unit furniture (chest of drawers and cabinet), c. 1942. Oak, walnut, and ebony. Made by Decorators' Cabinet Shop, Philadelphia, for Louis and Esther Kahn. Photographs 2012. Collection of Sue Ann Kahn

ally, are affixed at the base, not the center or the top, of the drawers. In designing these pulls Kahn was picking up on the ornamental hardware, often large in scale, that was prominent in the furniture of the 1930s, when many different types of metal, plastic, and wooden bars and discs appeared on the pieces created by Rohde and other contemporary designers. Rohde himself had used horizontal pulls at the base of the drawers, along with discs for the doors, on his Mahogany Group.

In tackling the bedroom set early in 1942, Kahn was moving into uncharted territory. He had never designed a suite of furniture before, and in his haste to do so he once again looked around for modern sources, which, as it happened, were close at hand. He must have drawn on the furniture (much of which was also influenced by Rohde's work) that had just been shown in the Organic Design in Home Furnishings exhibition at the Museum of Modern Art in New York from September to November 1941, and at the Pennsylvania (now Philadelphia) Museum of Art in January 1942, just when Kahn was designing these pieces.[9] The exhibition displayed the prize-winning furniture, fabrics, and lamps from a competition organized by the Museum of Modern Art, which had arranged with manufacturers and retailers to fabricate and merchandize these pieces. There can be little doubt that Kahn took careful note of this exhibition, for Noemi Raymond's printed-cotton textiles, used for curtains and upholstery throughout the Oser house, were introduced there (see figs. 93, 97).[10] Raymond's fabrics were probably bought from Gimbel Brothers department store in Philadelphia, where a selection of the Organic Design pieces was on sale in room settings concurrently with the museum exhibition.[11]

Included in the exhibition was a group of living-room unit furniture designed by Eero Saarinen and Charles Eames, mahogany-veneered drawer, cabinet, and shelf components with simple lines and clean expanses that were designed to be set on a base that doubled as a bench (fig. 101). A diagram in the *Organic Design* catalogue lays out the many advantages of Saarinen and Eames's designs, including the fact that by placing the chests and cabinets on benches high off the ground they would not interfere with base plugs, heating registers, and baseboards.[12] Kahn was probably alerted to this issue by the catalogue, for he made his own adjustments for this purpose: he added a lip at the rear of the top, which kept the mass of his cabinets away from the wall while allowing them to meet it at top and appear to be built in (see fig. 97).

The details of Kahn's cabinetry, freestanding and built in, indicate that an architect who was sensitive to Arts and Crafts precepts and who was thinking of structure and the expression of function created this furniture: the overhanging lip; the framing elements, which, drawing on the structural considerations of building, are considerably wider at top and bottom and thinner at the sides and center; the distinction between the pulls for drawers and pulls for doors; and the directional graining, horizontal for the drawers, which slide open, and vertical for the doors, which swing open. This last feature may have been Kahn's response to another group from the Organic Design exhibition, modular walnut bedroom furniture in which the directional graining is pronounced (fig. 102). These had been designed in 1940 by Oscar Stonorov, by now Kahn's partner, with Willo von Moltke, a German émigré who had spent time in the office of the Finnish architect and designer Alvar Aalto.[13]

When Kahn prepared to order freestanding furnishings for the Oser house he sought out work by Aalto, which he

Fig. 101 Eero Saarinen and Charles Eames. Living-room unit furniture, 1940. From *Organic Design in Home Furnishings,* 1941

would have first seen in 1938 at Aalto's introductory American exhibition at the Museum of Modern Art (and also the next year in his Finnish pavilion at the New York World's Fair). Aalto had rejected the cold metal and glass of International Style modernism for a warmer, more typically Scandinavian organic modernism, his pieces being made of natural materials, originally bent and laminated birch. Kahn responded positively to Aalto's work; there was little other inexpensive high-quality furniture available in the United States that could equal it for simplicity and its craftsmanlike truth to materials. Aalto's furniture was being fabricated of maple in Wisconsin and had just been introduced to the American market in this form. It could be bought from Artek-Pascoe, a collaborative branch of Aalto's Artek store in Helsinki, which fortuitously had opened on Madison Avenue in New York in 1940 (its predecessor, New Furniture Incorporated in Rockefeller Center, had sold limited quantities of Aalto's birch designs imported from Finland).[14] "The excellence of the Aalto furniture," *Time* reported when Artek-Pascoe opened, "may help to discourage manufacture of some furniture that now passes for modern. The Aalto purpose is to use U.S. mass production to get their designs into ordinary U.S. homes.'"[15]

Kahn drew liberally from the Artek-Pascoe catalogue to furnish the Oser house (except for the lighting, which came from the designer Kurt Versen). Period photographs of the Oser living and dining areas show the Aalto side chairs, child's chairs, dining table, and upholstered dining chairs that Kahn ordered (see figs. 93, 130). In addition to Aalto designs, the shop carried webbed bentwood chairs by the Swede Bruno Mathsson and pieces by several little-known American designers, whose works were commissioned to fill out the store's inventory. They also show a bentwood armchair with webbed upholstery evocative of Mathsson, which was listed as designed by Ewald Holtkamp (identified as production manager, New York City), and a webbed lounge and small webbed bench, also by Holtkamp (designed with Aalto's partner in the New York firm, Clifford Pascoe).[16] While Kahn attempted to create a unified up-to-date interior with these modern furnishings, some of the traditional furniture that the Osers brought with them was retained, including the maple coffee table, with its plank top and cleated ends, but Kahn had it rebuilt to fit in with his other pieces, probably lowering it and replacing the original legs with the splayed, rounded, and tapered ones.[17]

It is clear that Artek's catalogue colored Kahn's initial conception of the Oser interior given the unmistakable undulating screen that he drew at the left of a preliminary perspective drawing (along with the suggestion of an Aalto dining table and chair; see fig. 94). Artek offered flexible screens designed by Arthur Mack (identified as a New York stage designer; fig. 103), which were probably inspired by the flowing interior walls of Aalto's World's Fair pavilion. The Osers bought a screen made of gumwood (American mahogany), which matched the plywood paneling of the dining area, although it cannot be seen in any of the early photographs of the house. It was probably used, as shown in the drawing, to separate the living room from the dining room when people were invited for dinner. This was a continual problem for Kahn in the design of open living-dining areas, which he never got used to (early in his career he had poked fun at open planning in a cartoonish drawing with, for example, a man at a grand piano next to a kitchen sink, which he labeled "Dishwashing Concerto"; fig. 104). He later complained about open planning as an aside in a discussion of the Colonial house: "Today, we

Fig. 102 Oscar Stonorov and Willo von Moltke. Bedroom-unit furniture, 1940. From *Organic Design in Home Furnishings,* 1941

Fig. 103 Arthur Mack. Flexible screen, c. 1941. From Artek-Pascoe catalogue, 1941

Fig. 104 Stonorov & Kahn, architects. House planning diagram. Louis Kahn, c. 1943. Kahn Collection

put the dining room in the living room and when guests come they see the table. The hostess is constantly rushing in and out. She may go gracefully from place to place, be charming and all that, but the charisma of the house is disturbed."[18] He tried to deal with this in his next house, for the Roches, by adding a track for a curtain that could be pulled across to divide the rooms. Anne Tyng, who had recently arrived from Harvard to join Kahn's office, must have made him aware that Walter Gropius had used such a device in his own house in Lincoln (designed with Marcel Breuer in 1937–38), which she would have known from the students' annual forays there. Kahn was still wrestling with this drawback of open planning when he was designing the Genel house, and he asked his Yale students to work this out as part of its design problem; his own solution was to include removable wooden doors between the living and dining rooms.[19] Later, following a shift in outlook toward differentiated space, he either created separate dining rooms, as in the Clever, Shapiro, and Esherick houses, or used permanent architectural elements to separate the areas, as the stone chimney does in the Fisher house and the oak partition does in the Korman house.

Almost a decade after he completed the Oser house, Kahn undertook to design interiors for the Weiss and Genel houses, creating compositions that were substantially more assured and that relied heavily on his own built-in designs. In the Weiss house Kahn created a core of domestic livability around a massive fireplace, with plywood paneling and flush cabinetry of birch, except for that in the dining room, which was of walnut.[20] The cabinet designs for the living room, dining room, kitchen, and laundry room are documented in a sequence of working drawings dating from the fall of 1948 to the spring of 1949, and in a series of colored sketches that Kahn and Tyng, who was a close assistant on this project, seem to have worked on together. These sketches were probably made for discussions with the Weisses about their household needs, and Kahn and Tyng added notes from their conversations directly on the drawings, specifying the objects that the shelves, cabinets, and drawers were meant to hold. On the elevation of the kitchen cupboards they describe not only larger elements, such as vegetable bins and a copper rack for pots and pans, but also the location of a myriad of workaday items, such as chopping board, garbage, towels, soap, sugar, and flour (fig. 105). The elevation of the living room shows the fireplace wall with a preliminary sketch of a large mural, the sunken seating area with its armless orange settee, and the music center and bookcase behind it (fig. 106). The setting, at the heart of the house, is meant to look cozy and lived-in, with logs in the wood storage area, decorative objects on the shelves, and a still life of bottles in the liquor cabinet.

82 FURNISHINGS

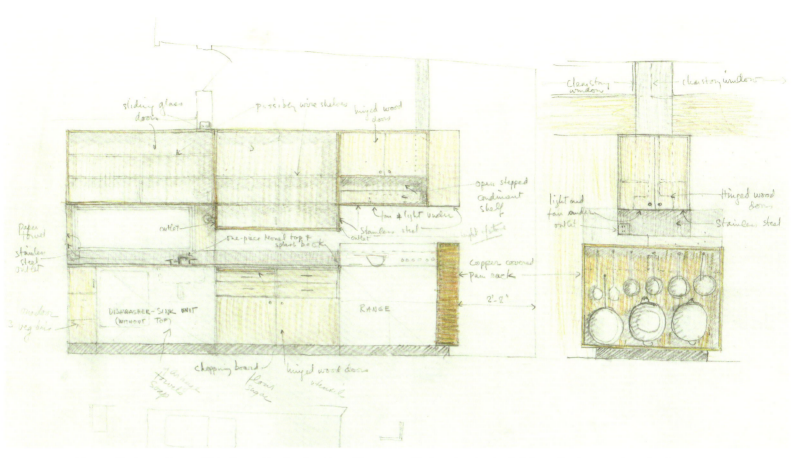

Fig. 105 Morton and Lenore Weiss House, East Norriton Township, 1947–50. Kitchen elevation. Louis Kahn, c. March 1949. Kahn Collection

Fig. 106 Morton and Lenore Weiss House. Living room. Elevation of inglenook. Louis Kahn, c. February 1949. Kahn Collection

Fig. 107 Morton and Lenore Weiss House. Study for mural. Charcoal on paper. Louis Kahn, c. 1950–51. Collection of Nathaniel Kahn

The design for the mural was only blocked out in the elevation, but it gave a sense of scale and of its architectonic structure, allowing Kahn to consider how his painting would look in its furnished setting. When the house was finished and the Weisses moved in, late in 1949, the mural had not yet been completed (see fig. 144), but Kahn worked up a diagram of its salient features for the first publication of the house, in *Architectural Forum* in 1950 (see fig. 47). The diagram must have been based on his only known full study for the mural (shown here as later revised; fig. 107 and see fig. 145).[21] This charcoal study, which the finished painting closely resembles, clearly shows Kahn's referencing of the Pennsylvania countryside and Pennsylvania-German folk motifs. Barns, farmhouses, steeples, shingled roofs, fields, forests—all are abstracted into a composition of black and white opposites, enlivened with images of a hex sign, flowers, a heart, and horses. The painting, according to Tyng, was based on Kahn's idea of a "giant pointillism," incorporating many small motifs within the grid that makes up the full composition,[22] and once again using "pieces and parts," as he had explained to Hochstim, and recombining them in another form.[23] The mural was not completed until after Kahn returned from the American Academy in Rome and his travels in the winter of 1950–51, when he and Tyng executed it. After it was finished the Weisses had second thoughts and asked that their beloved dog be added to the composition, so, as described by Tyng, "a black and white pattern to represent the . . . Dalmation was tucked into the lower right-hand corner."[24]

Kahn designed three walnut tables for the house, for which construction drawings in his own hand are extant: a built-in table in the kitchen, a table with tapered X-shaped legs and a large central drawer to serve as a desk in the living room (figs. 108, 109), and an extendable table for the dining room.[25] The dining table was never built, and, instead, a table

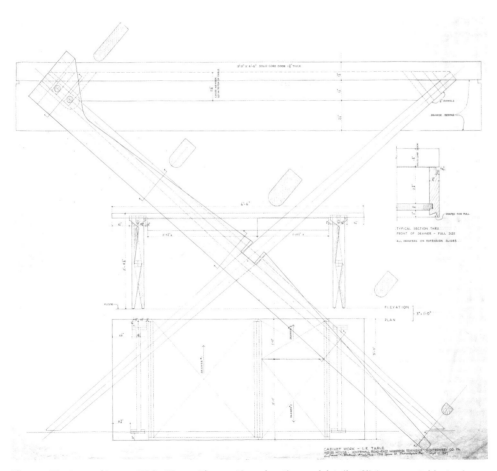

Fig. 108 Morton and Lenore Weiss House. Plan, section, elevation, and details of living-room table. Louis Kahn, dated September 11, 1949. Kahn Collection

Fig. 109 Morton and Lenore Weiss House. Living room. Photograph 1950. Kahn Collection

Fig. 110 Marcel Breuer. House in the Museum Garden, Museum of Modern Art, New York, 1949. Living room

Fig. 111   Anne Tyng and Louis Kahn reviewing samples of materials for the Weiss house, spring 1949. AAUP, by the gift of Anne G. Tyng

designed by Jens Risom was bought from the Knoll furniture company, where Tyng had worked for a short time before joining Kahn's office, and where she had gained the experience that helped her advise on the fittings of the house (see figs. 111, 143).[26] Two other Knoll pieces, Eero Saarinen's Grasshopper chair and a sofa designed by Florence Knoll, were also purchased. Examples of these two designs had recently been exhibited in Marcel Breuer's House in the Museum Garden, shown at the Museum of Modern Art in 1949 (along with a television stand with X-shaped legs that Breuer himself had designed; fig. 110).[27] Breuer's interior may have been the inspiration for the choice of Knoll seating, but other modern furniture was also bought for the house, including Charles and Ray Eames's molded-plywood side chair, George Nelson's modular cabinets and benches, and a headboard from Herman Miller—and, reminiscent of the Oser house, an Aalto stool from Artek (see figs. 142, 148). The House in the Museum Garden may also have been a source for the vivid colors (described in a newspaper account as dark green, red, beige, brown, and blue) that were used in the hallways and bedrooms of the Weiss house.[28] This would not have been Kahn's preference—it was probably done at Tyng's prompting—and this is the only known instance of painted wall colors in any of his residences. "I have no color applied on the walls of my home," he later explained. "I wouldn't want to disturb the wonder of natural light. The light really does make the room. The changing light according to the time of day and the seasons of the year gives color. Then there are reflections from the floors, the furniture, the materials, all contributing to make my space made by the light, mine. Light is mood. The color of light is very pronounced. We know that a red light will cast a green shadow and a green light will cast a red shadow. A blue light will cast a yellow shadow and a yellow light will cast a blue. Ever since I knew that to be true, I grew away from painting and depended on the light. The color you get that way is not applied, but simply a surprise."[29]

Kahn approached the furnishings for the Genel house in the same way as he did the Weiss house, placing a series of built-in pieces (which were removed by a subsequent owner) in wood-paneled rooms. The items designed for the living area included a cabinet for a television, record changer, and tuner, and one for record storage; suspended speaker and drawer units; a side table; and plywood shelves edged in birch, all of which are shown in a colored drawing of the outer wall of the living room (fig. 112). In scale with the large space, a long foam-rubber sofa made up of a 4- and an 8-foot section, seen in the drawing from the side, filled the end wall of the living room (see fig. 4). Like the settee in the Weiss house, it was upholstered in bright orange. A 10-foot-long sofa, the back covered in a patterned fabric, was built for the alcove (see fig. 161). To make these armless pieces more comfortable, Kahn designed three long, rectangular arm cushions for each. To separate the dining area from the entrance hall Kahn also designed a large built-in buffet, which was topped with translucent glass much like the divider in the Oser house (fig. 113; see fig. 159). With its long base combining a cabinet

FURNISHINGS   87

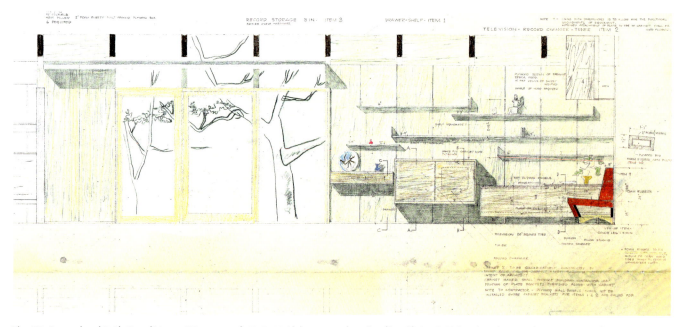

Fig. 112   Samuel and Ruth Genel House, Wynnewood, 1948–51. Living room elevation (detail). Louis Kahn, dated November 18, 1950. Kahn Collection

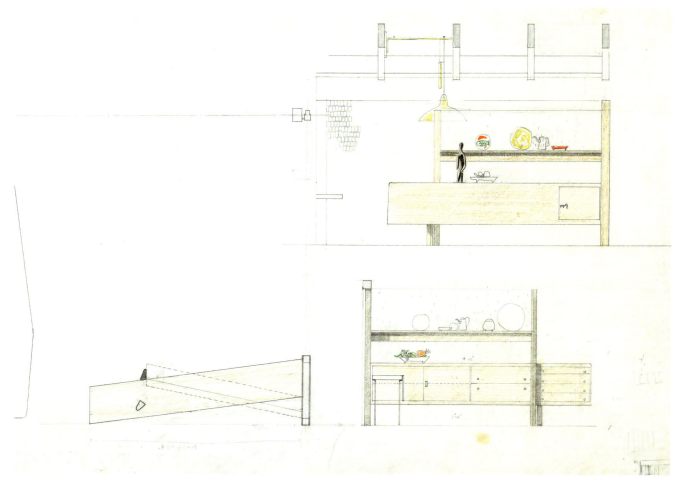

Fig. 113   Samuel and Ruth Genel House. Buffet. Louis Kahn, c. November 1950. Kahn Collection

and two drawer sections (cantilevered off one end) and the shelf above, which crisscrossed each other, this unusual construction played off the angles of the nearby fireplace and the trapezoidal counter in the pass-through between the dining room and the kitchen. Kahn also designed two tables of dark walnut for the dining room, each 6½-feet long, which could be put together for large parties (fig. 114). Modern seating, like that in the Weiss house, included Saarinen's Grasshopper chair and a webbed chair by Risom.

By the later 1950s, as Kahn was increasingly distancing himself from established modernism, he also modified his attitude toward his interiors and furnishings. He no longer thought that an ensemble of built-ins was necessary, telling the Shapiros that they "didn't give you flexibility."[30] What built-ins he continued to design were mostly architecturally determined, set into the structure like the bookcases between the windows of the Esherick house (see fig. 190) and not applied to the wall like the cabinets and seating in the Genel house. For the Kormans, however, who "love[d] built-ins and places to put things away," Kahn designed extensive cabinetry, with plain construction enhanced by directional graining (see fig. 246).[31] Domestic and monumental interiors began to meld, and Kahn conceived such elements as the encased window seat and desks in the Fisher house (see fig. 226) with the same sense of structural integrity and monumentality as the reading carrels he designed for the Phillips Exeter Academy library in New Hampshire.[32]

Kahn also abandoned midcentury-modern furniture and left behind the colored walls of the Weiss house (and the orange sofas used there and in the Genel house) for higher-end designs, a palette of earth tones, and a gray Kahn described as the "color of cigarette ash."[33] He offered to help his clients furnish their houses, planning shopping trips with them, but both the Shapiros and Fishers complained that it took too much time to arrange, and in any case, they had their own preferences and sources for their furnishings (and the Fishers had already acquired a number of objects of contemporary design).[34] The Kormans, eager to complete their house and move in quickly, placed its furnishing in the hands of an interior designer, where the conditions set for the work required that "natural materials and hues . . . be specified to harmonize with the construction materials" and that "in no way could the furnishings infringe upon the interiors' architectural purity" (fig. 115).[35]

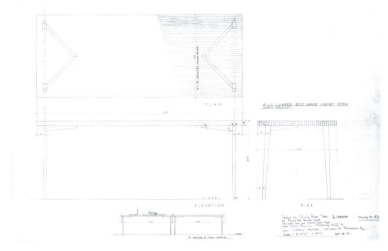

Fig. 114 Samuel and Ruth Genel House. Dining table construction drawing. Louis Kahn, dated April 28, 1951. Kahn Collection

Fig. 115 Steven and Toby Korman House, Whitemarsh Township, 1971–73. Living room. Cover of *Interior Design,* November 1974

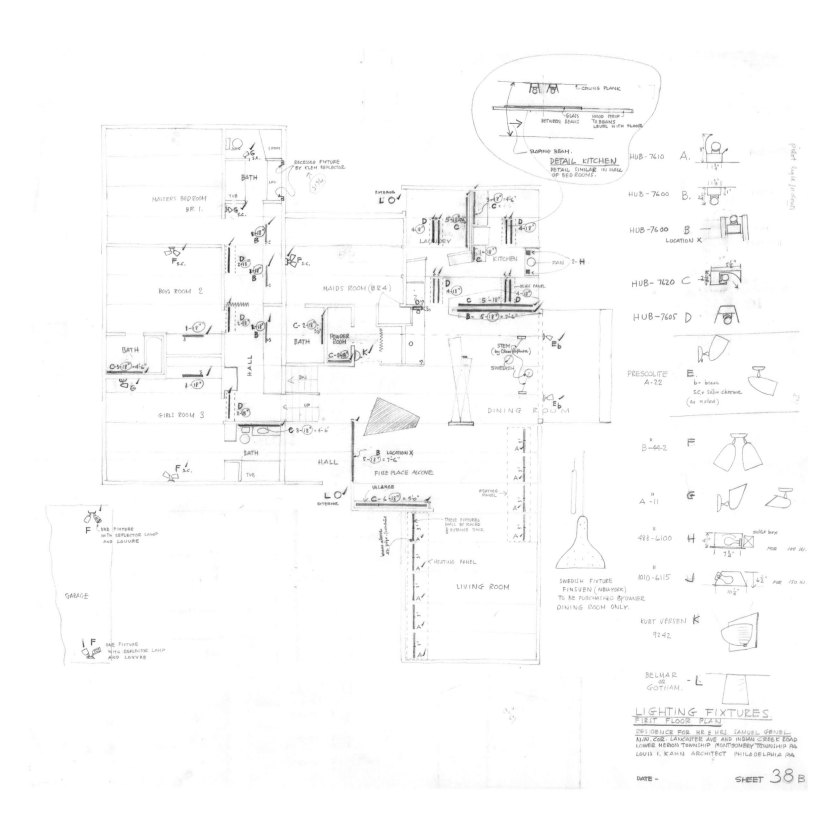

Fig. 116 Samuel and Ruth Genel House. Lighting plan. Louis Kahn. Kahn Collection

Kahn began to think more in terms of contemporary objects that would enhance his houses, not just furnish them. He offered (without success) to paint a mural above the Shapiros' ground-floor fireplace but was able to arrange for the Philadelphia weaver Yvonne Bobrowicz to design a hanging (long gone) for the large window next to the front door (later he engaged her to create weavings for the interior of the Kimbell Art Museum in Fort Worth[36]). He worked with Steven Korman and the artist Elaine Kurtz to develop the concept of the sizable red-hued painting *Warm Spectrum* for the Kormans' stair hall, its bands of colors in close values suggestive of the hangings that he had designed for the sanctuary of the First Unitarian Church in Rochester, New York (see fig. 243).[37] He also began to recommend furnishings that were themselves evocative objects, such as, for the Shapiros, the expressive woodwork of Wharton Esherick (who was then working with Kahn on the house for his niece Margaret Esherick); they could not afford it and so chose designs by another local craftsman, George Nakashima, whose work the Fishers bought as well.[38] Kahn also considered the possibility of using antiques, suggesting to the Kormans a "combination of heritages" and justifying this by explaining that a "fine refectory table, which would look very nice, is like a piece of sculpture.... I don't know where it would be," he added, "but it would be very excellent to have."[39]

While Kahn downplayed the furnishings of his later houses, he continued to design built-ins, furniture, and lighting for the reconfigured interiors of his renovations in Philadelphia.[40] As much as Kahn's rhetoric on the wonders of natural light makes it seem as if he had little interest in artificial lighting, he knew its characteristics well and had always been particularly attentive to the selection of his lighting fixtures. This is seen, for example, in the way he carefully considered and drew each of the lighting fixtures on his lighting plan for the Genel house (fig. 116). Between 1963 and 1967, Kahn made a number of alterations to his center-city row house before he and Esther could move into it, but he did not tackle the issue of lighting until after the couple was living there and he received a note from Esther in December 1968.[41] "Dear Lou," she wrote. "For the past 38 years I have never asked for a X Mas gift. Today I am asking, and it is within your favor to grant it easily. Since I know fixtures can't be ready at least you can act as a real Santa & present me with drawings of 3 outdoors fixtures; 2 kitchen & 1 2nd and 3rd floor hall hanging fixtures; 1 something for under kitchen cabinet; 4 fixtures for closets and ? number for rest of house. Please, E."[42] Although it took him another half a year, Kahn fulfilled his wife's request for new fixtures, reaching back to his 1930 "fascination with the early-modern Bauhaus work ... and [its] new lighting fixtures" to create simple, square, aluminum sconces with large, globular lightbulbs (fig. 117).[43]

In 1970–71, Kahn undertook the renovation of a grand nineteenth-century center-city townhouse for the president of the University of Pennsylvania, Martin Meyerson, and his wife, Margy.[44] The commission came at a period when Kahn's office was overflowing with work. At the same time as he was designing the Yale Center for British Art and the National Assembly complex in Dhaka, Bangladesh, he was personally measuring the Meyersons' rooms, drawing out electrical plans, and immersing himself in the minute details of designing new spaces, renovating others, and creating furnishings and fittings, all documented in twenty-seven drawings in

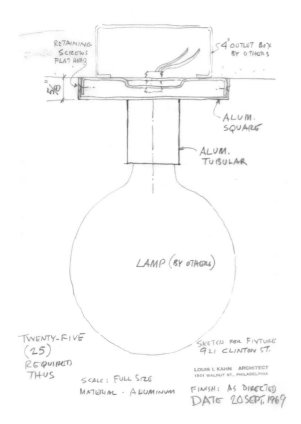

Fig. 117 Louis and Esther Kahn House, Philadelphia, 1963–67. Lighting fixture, dated September 20, 1969. Kahn Collection

his own hand.⁴⁵ Although he must have agreed to take the job out of friendship and obligation, he in fact found it hard to refuse commissions, for as he explained, he saw each as an "expressive possibility to be done."⁴⁶ Aside from satisfying such practical requirements as enlarging the kitchen and refurbishing bathrooms, this project was all about light. For daytime he constructed a charming sky-lit "garden room," which captured natural light and drew it into the Victorian interior (fig. 118). For night he imagined a shadowy sitting room lit by wall washers, a study with bookcases illuminated with fixtures of his own design, and the dining room brightened with only a large chandelier.

What Kahn had objected to in artificial lighting was having "electric lights where the sun comes in, because," as he said, it was "so ridiculous to try to imitate it." Instead, he had asked, "Why not make it entirely different? Have your chandeliers doing all sorts of gay things about being night."⁴⁷ Kahn followed his own advice with the designs for the chandelier, and his initial instinct was to evoke forms that would suggest the past life of the house. His color rendering of the Meyersons' dining room depicts two views of an evening reception, where guests mingle around a dining-room table set under a traditional chandelier and spill out through the garden room and onto the patio beyond (fig. 119). The inscriptions on this drawing and on studies for several other chandeliers give specifications for fabrication, bulbs, and dimmers, demonstrating that even what might look like preliminary, suggestive sketches were serious propositions for Kahn.⁴⁸ As he continued to work, however, he began to see the chandelier as a contemporary object, changing his vocabulary and adopting the modern glass globes and flat metal rods that he had introduced in his lighting for the dormitory at Bryn Mawr College.⁴⁹ He drew several configurations for a large fixture suspended 7 feet above the floor in the 16-foot-high room and measuring 5 or 6 feet across (fig. 120). Although his modern design may have left the traditional idiom behind, these fixtures were every bit as ornamental as his earlier schemes. The design was eventually resolved in a never realized chandelier of bare bulbs and rectilinear metal bars in which Kahn filtered his ideas of what the townhouse had been in the past in a design that was very much of the present.⁵⁰

Fig. 118 Martin and Margy Meyerson House, Philadelphia, 1970–71. Garden room. Photograph 2008

Fig. 119 Martin and Margy Meyerson House. Sections of dining room and garden room. Louis Kahn. Kahn Collection

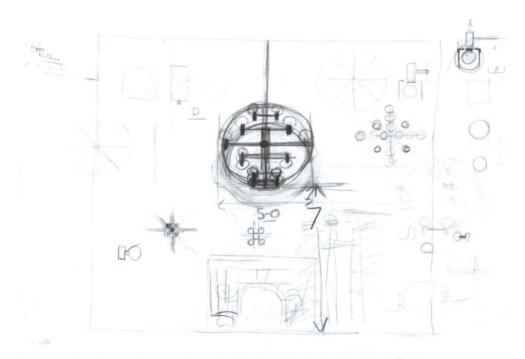

Fig. 120 Martin and Margy Meyerson House. Study for chandelier. Louis Kahn. Kahn Collection

FURNISHINGS

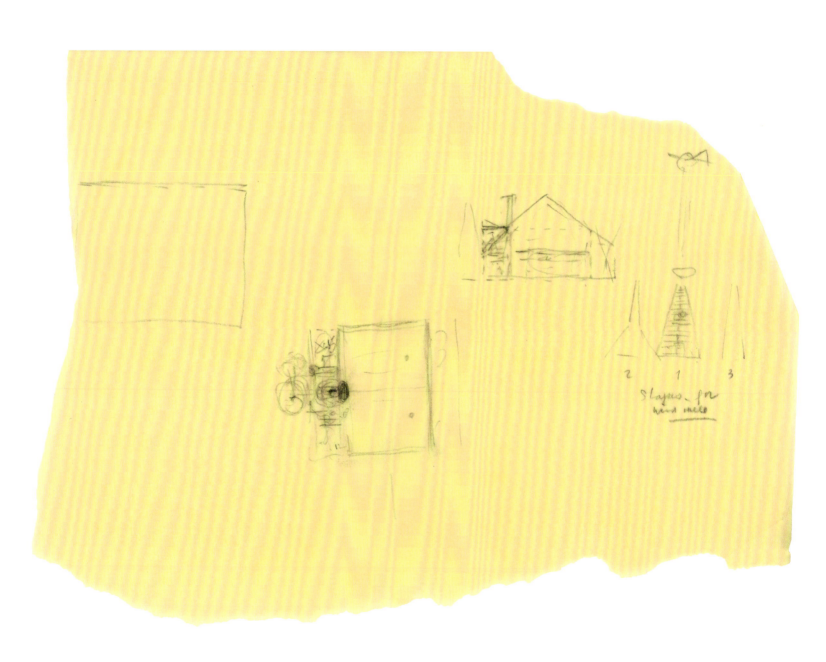

EPILOGUE

Louis Kahn never stopped designing houses, although the amount of work in his office during his later years prevented him from following through on many of the requests he received. Clients could become frustrated waiting for Kahn's attention and turn to other architects—but not Simone Swan, the last person for whom he would agree to design a house. Swan, who was executive vice president of the Menil Foundation and herself a patron of the arts, had met Kahn in connection with his commission for a museum in Houston for the art collection of John and Dominique de Menil.[1] In November 1973 she wrote him about her "dream house": "Several people offered to do it. . . . I kept them at bay having made the decision to have the patience to hear from you." When Kahn made it clear that, like the others, she was "free" to change her plans, she answered, "That's not the situation—quite the opposite. You don't know how I need and yearn for a home."[2]

William Marlin, who as editor-in-chief of *Architectural Forum* had a "deeply felt" friendship with Kahn, related the story of the commission: When Kahn learned that Swan had bought land on the North Fork of Long Island, "he immediately asked if she would mind if he designed her house. She protested, 'But Lou, it would be such a *modest* house.' . . . To which he replied, 'A modest house by, I hope, a modest man.'"[3] Kahn visited the site with Swan, and again with Swan's son Eric, who "was doing research in nutrition and agriculture, [and] had some thoughts about new energy sources, such as wind and solar power, for the house design." Marlin reported that a "deft, if tentative sketch came out of this encounter. And some notes to himself—dashed off as sonnets, which his notes invariably were, about how sunlight would be captured, the water kept."[4] This was the last design for a house that Kahn would sketch. It shows a floor plan, an elevation, and, at right, thoughts for "shapes for wind mill" (fig. 121).

During the intervening months Swan found out that a neighbor's barn was available, possibly for the taking. "Since all that old wood is there," she wrote to Kahn, "do you have any use for it?"[5] Swan eventually bought the barn "to be used as lumber,"[6] and in another letter to the office in February she announced: "I'm committed, now," and added, "Everyone connected with this house has strangely wonderful vibrations."[7] Despite all this hopefulness, the house would go no further, for Louis Kahn died a few weeks later, on March 17, 1974, just twelve days before a scheduled meeting in Philadelphia at which preliminary plans for the house would have been presented.[8]

Architectural Forum immediately planned a memorial issue for Kahn, and when Marlin contacted Kahn's office on March 22, the editors were holding up the April issue to do so. The idea, he explained, was to "include some thoughts about Lou—and to show, very simply in format, some of the last work. My friend, Simone Swan, has told me about his recent design for her house and of the beautiful relationship which emerged between Lou and her 23-year-old son. Simone and I agree that just this one design, if no other, would be the ideal metaphor to embrace Lou's love for learning, and his love for learning youth—his sense of constant growth."[9]

Fig. 121 Simone Swan House, Southold, New York, 1973–74. Elevation and details. Louis Kahn, c. January 1974. Kahn Collection

JESSE AND RUTH
OSER HOUSE

ELKINS PARK, 1940–42

Louis Kahn's earliest known private residential commission—for a modest house on a wooded site in Elkins Park—came from an old friend, Jesse Oser. They had been at Central High School together and may have met earlier, but even Kahn's wife, Esther, never knew how far back the friendship went. She recalled meeting Oser and his wife, Ruth, in 1930, when the Kahns were on their honeymoon and ran into them in Atlantic City; the acquaintance was renewed, and the two couples later became close friends and spent vacations together.[1] The Osers, who were leftist social activists, lived with their two children in an apartment in West Philadelphia, not far from the Kahns. Jesse worked in his family's printing business, and Ruth was a public-school mathematics teacher.[2]

In 1940, when the Osers decided to move to Elkins Park and build a house in the new Juniper Park development, a subdivision of the former estate of the prominent hat manufacturer J. B. Stetson, they asked Kahn to design it. Although formal transfer of the property did not take place until February 1941, the house already was designed—the final set of working drawings is dated November 11, 1940—and construction was under way shortly after the property was conveyed.[3] Work on the house was substantially completed during the winter of 1942, when the family moved in.

The house, with its simple cubic massing, juxtaposes large expanses of Wissahickon schist, a gray micaceous building stone strongly associated with Philadelphia's northwest

Fig. 123   From southeast. Photograph 1943

Fig. 122   Jesse and Ruth Oser House, Elkins Park, 1940–42. From northeast. Photograph 1990

suburbs, with clapboard siding of oiled cedar (fig. 122; see fig. 28). The site included a number of preexisting landscape features, among them a diminutive stone bridge crossing a creek lined with dry-laid masonry walls and topped with slender slate capstones, carryovers from the Stetson estate. These occupied the flat ground, and Kahn had little choice but to situate the house above, on a north-facing slope. Kahn used the site to his advantage; he elevated the living areas above a two-car garage, utility space, and workroom, enabling a south-facing orientation (fig. 123). This allowed ample room for a bank of large windows in the rear visually connected to an adjoining terrace with a pergola-covered dining area and exterior fireplace (fig. 124) and directly accessible to the kitchen and the dining room. Sleeping quarters on the second floor were also afforded a southern exposure, and the master bedroom opened onto a terrace (fig. 125).

Described in an early article in the *Philadelphia Inquirer* as "a marvel of compactness," the house has an open floor plan clearly shown in the cutaway drawing published in *Architectural Forum* in 1945 (figs. 126, 127).[4] A fireplace inglenook with a floor of 4½-inch-square red tiles forms the core of the social life of the house, a place for "Conversation," as he labeled it on the drawing, separated from the "Music" and "Dining" areas, which had tongue-and-groove oak flooring (fig. 128). The fireplace wall was clad with 2-inch-square tan and gray ceramic tiles (which were "placed back-side-out to

Fig. 124 Terrace, outdoor fireplace, and pergola (later removed), from south. Photograph May 4, 1944

OSER HOUSE

Fig. 125 From southwest. Photograph 1990

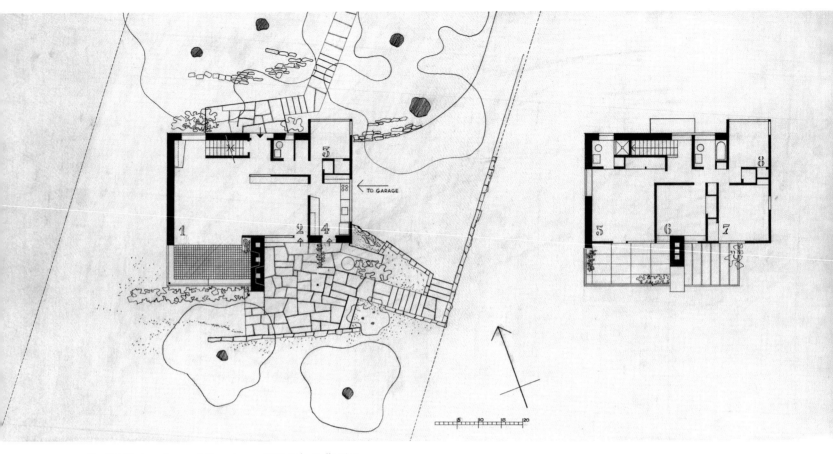

Fig. 126 First- and second-floor plans, c. 1943. Kahn Collection

expose an unusual matte texture"), an early example of Kahn's preference for mottled surfaces that would reveal the subtlety of light and color (figs. 129, 130; see fig. 29).[5] Kahn warmed and personalized the interior with plywood paneling and his own freestanding and built-in furniture, and the house was furnished additionally with the designs of Alvar Aalto (fig. 132; see fig. 93).

The Oser house received timely attention in the press: commenting that it was "new and different" for a functional house to have a "delightfully intimate, friendly quality," *House and Garden* introduced Kahn's work to its wide readership in 1944 while *Architectural Forum* presented it to a professional audience the next year.[6] The fireplace inglenook, in particular, was called on as a vivid example of new design, appearing in articles and advertising into the early 1950s.[7]

The Osers moved to Los Angeles in 1945, seeking "fresh air" to relieve Jesse's asthma and better opportunities in the printing industry. Ruth cherished Kahn's furniture and took it with them. The house was sold in 1947 to Nelson and Bobette Leidner, who gave it the name Stonebridge. In 1950 Kahn designed a 5-foot extension to the east side after a large tree fell on the house, as well as a small playroom addition (later removed).[8]

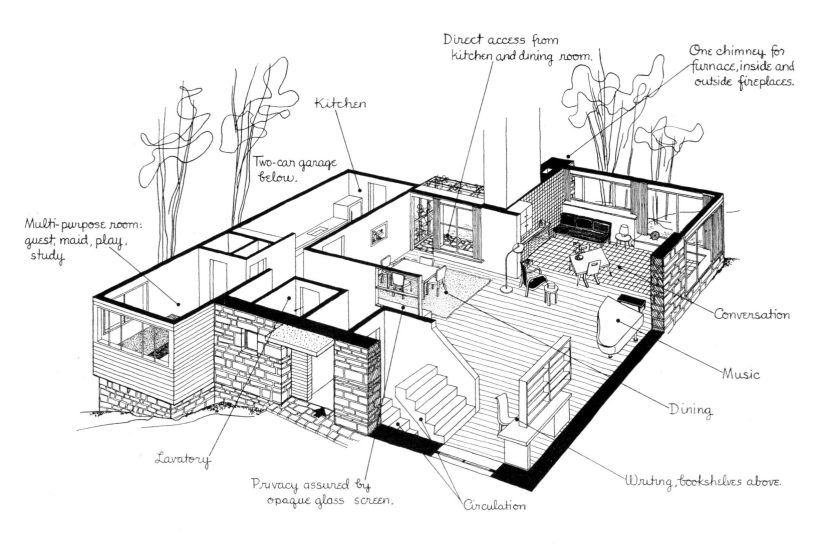

Fig. 127 Cutaway perspective. From *Architectural Forum*, August 1945

Fig. 128 Inglenook and dining room, 1940. Perspective. Kahn Collection

Fig. 129 Fireplace, with Mercer tile surround. Photograph June 2011

Fig. 130 Inglenook. Photograph May 4, 1944

Fig. 131 Dining room. Photograph June 2011

Fig. 132 Living room with built-in desk. Photograph May 4, 1944

PHILIP AND JOCELYN
ROCHE HOUSE

WHITEMARSH TOWNSHIP
MONTGOMERY COUNTY
1945–49, STONOROV & KAHN

The single-story Roche house is situated on a secluded, almost 4-acre site in Whitemarsh Township, ten miles from downtown Philadelphia and just beyond the city's northwest boundary (fig. 133). This sparsely populated area along the Schuylkill River was largely controlled by the estate of Henry H. Houston, whose descendants, the Woodwards, developed much of this and the neighboring Andorra and Chestnut Hill neighborhoods. Philip Q. Roche, a prominent psychiatrist, purchased the site from the Houston estate on December 31, 1943, and in March 1948 (coinciding with the date of completion of construction documents for the house), transferred the property into joint ownership with his wife, Jocelyn, a celebrated Washington, D.C., debutante whose father's family was from Pennsylvania. When the Roches were married early in 1944, both having been recently divorced, Curtis Bok, president judge of the Philadelphia court of common pleas and patron of both George Howe and Wharton Esherick, performed the ceremony.[1]

Much of Roche's professional experience had come as head psychiatrist at Eastern State Penitentiary in Philadelphia from 1934 to 1945. The notorious bank robber Willie Sutton had served as his secretary there during the Second World War, and the two had developed a close relationship, which was described in Sutton's autobiography *Where the Money Was*.[2] Roche later became widely known for his seminal study of criminal law and psychiatry, *The Criminal Mind*, published in 1958.[3]

No contract for the house survives. It is unclear how or why Roche chose Kahn as his architect, although his acquaintance with Curtis Bok may have been the connection. In any case, he would surely have been aware of Kahn through the architect's ongoing work for the Philadelphia Psychiatric Hospital. The preliminary version of the catalogue of Kahn's complete work, compiled with Kahn's collaboration and published in 1969, dates the start of the project to 1945,[4] but the earliest known drawings are considerably later, signed and dated "Louis I. Kahn 47."[5] The construction drawings bear the name of Stonorov & Kahn but are dated March 17, 1948, twelve months after the firm was dissolved, which suggests that the job may well have entered the office before the architects split up and likewise points to an earlier date for the beginning of the job. The explanation for the gap between the 1945 start date given in the early catalogue of Kahn's projects and the presentation drawings of 1947 must lie in a much larger event, the heated contest over the location of the United Nations Headquarters, for the site intended for the Roche house was right in the middle of the land that Philadelphia had offered to donate to the United Nations in order to bring the headquarters to the city.

Beginning in the fall of 1945, Philadelphia was among a few American cities under consideration by the United Nations Permanent Headquarters committee. Philadelphia had offered two possible sites, locations on the Belmont Plateau in the city's Fairmount Park and in the "Roxborough-Chestnut Hill section," where the Roche house was to be built.[6] Kahn followed the process closely and in the spring of 1946 took an active role by composing a "Preliminary Draft of Recommendations for the Planning and Development of UNO Site" on behalf of the American Society of Planners and Architects.[7] Later that year he contributed to the site materials

Fig. 133 Stonorov & Kahn, architects. Philip and Jocelyn Roche House, Whitemarsh Township, 1945–49. Chimney and terrace from south. Photograph June 2011

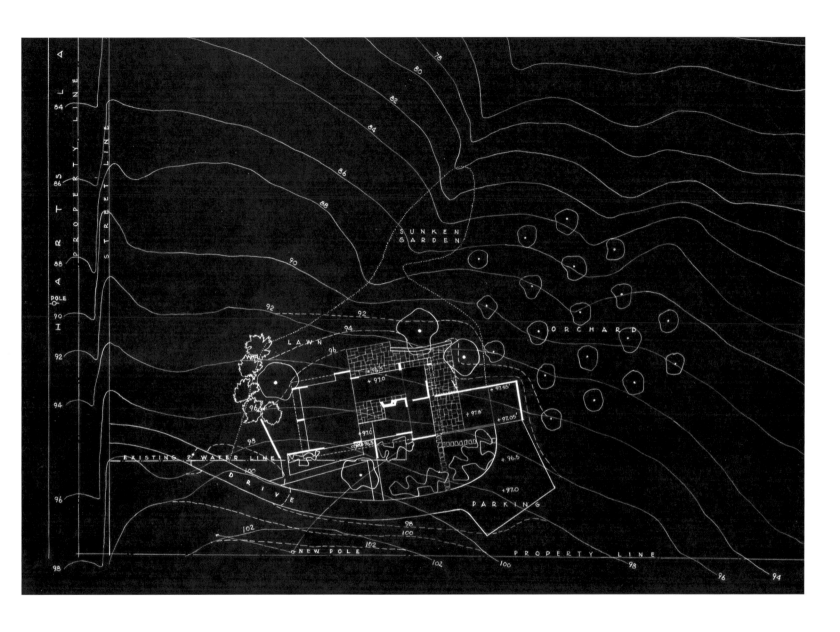

Fig. 134 Site plan. Archival photograph of lost original, 1947. Kahn Collection

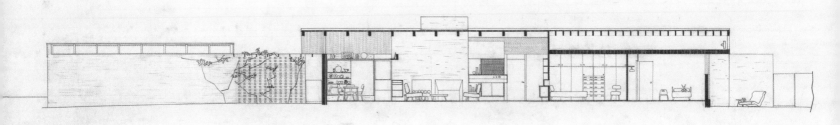

Fig. 135 Longitudinal section, 1947. Kahn Collection

provided in Philadelphia's bid.[8] When the United Nations delegation visited Philadelphia in November they stopped at the house of Kenneth Day, a landmark of early modernism in the Delaware Valley. At the house, which stands across the street from the Roche property and "in the center of the ten-square-mile site,"[9] delegates were directed to "observe view of site in all directions from flat roof."[10] While Philadelphia made a very strong case, and was one of two sites recommended on December 2, 1946, New York proved victorious with the donation of the present East River site in an eleventh-hour bid brokered by John D. Rockefeller, Jr., which effectively stopped the selection process by the end of the month.[11] Kahn and his client would certainly have put the project on a back burner throughout the selection process, and all evidence points to a restart date for design by mid-1947.

A preliminary set of drawings for the house remains, including a site plan and a longitudinal section, which show the house with the same dimensions as it was built but with a somewhat different interior configuration (figs. 134, 135). Kahn presented the house in the section as he imagined it with built-in and freestanding furniture and decorations.

It is clear from these drawings that Kahn had originally meant for the house to have an interior stone fireplace at the center of the plan, not set obliquely on the exterior wall as in the final plans. As built, the house is simple and compact, with four bedrooms on one end and an open-plan living area on the other. The regular outline of the building is broken by the large, obliquely set chimney, which animates the exterior with its whitewashed brick projection and provides an intimate fireplace alcove on the interior (figs. 136, 138; see fig. 45). A band of red-clay tiles forms a hearth, parallel to the walls of the house, and it is taken up on the other side of the angled inglenook wall, where it continues along the dining-room window, providing a sunny spot for potted plants. A curtain track running from the end of the angled wall to the wall next to the kitchen door allowed for the separation of the living room from the dining room. The only built-in known to have been executed (but which is no longer extant) was a 7½-foot-long birch wall unit in the dining room.[12]

The Roches sold the house in 1965 and moved to Chestnut Hill.[13]

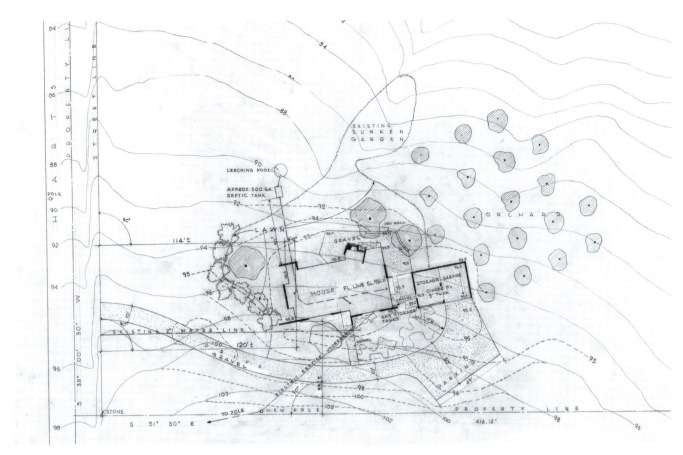

Fig. 136 Site plan. Anne G. Tyng and William Sayre, dated March 17, 1948. Kahn Collection

Fig. 137 From south. Photograph c. 1949

ROCHE HOUSE

Fig. 138 Living room and inglenook. Photograph June 2011

MORTON AND LENORE
WEISS HOUSE
EAST NORRITON TOWNSHIP
1947–50

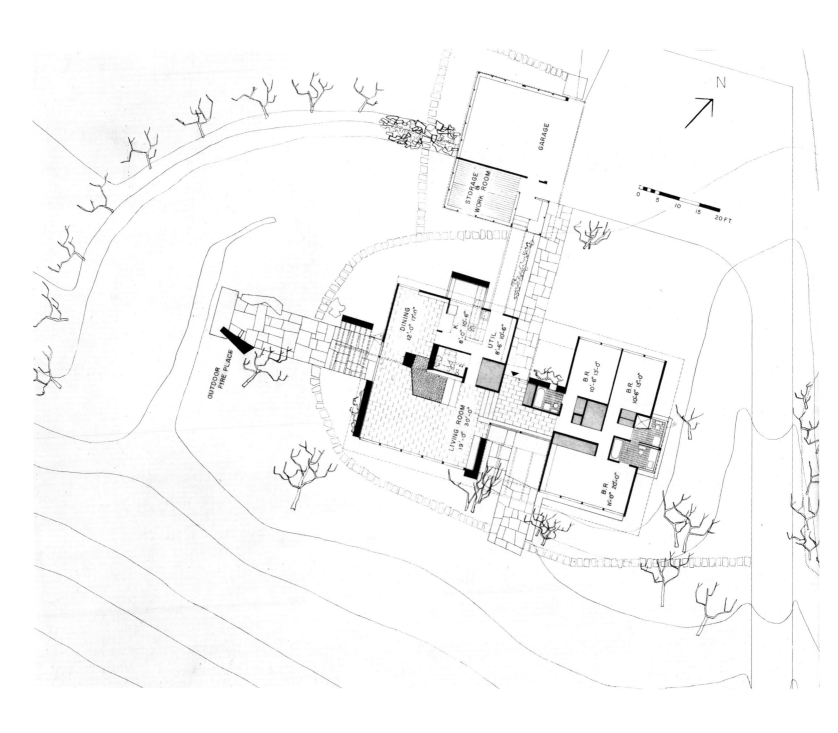

Fig. 140 Site plan. Archival photograph of lost original, 1950. Kahn Collection

Fig. 139 Morton and Lenore Weiss House, East Norriton Township, 1947–50. From south. Photograph 1950. Kahn Collection

The warm wood and stone house that Louis Kahn created for Morton and Lenore Weiss on a tree-covered hilltop in southern Montgomery County was meant to respect its surroundings and the building traditions of its area (fig. 139; see fig. 46). "A HOUSE that is contemporary, but does not break away from tradition," is the way Kahn described it.[1] This was in keeping with the Weisses' preferences, as reflected in the architect's account of them: "Desire for informal country living. A lively interest in contemporary art. Love for countryside of historic Norristown and its barns."[2]

Morton Weiss, affectionately known as Bubby, was born in the Norristown area to parents of Hungarian descent. His father, Harry, was a merchant who for many years ran a menswear shop, Gilberts Clothes, on Main Street in Norristown, and Morton continued operating the business into the 1980s. His wife, Lenore, five years younger than he, also lived in the area, and a love of the outdoors and the rural countryside must have drawn them together. The Weisses were strong boosters of their community, supporting, among other causes, open-space preservation and Norristown's Elmwood Park Zoo.[3] They continued to live in their house until their deaths in 2004.

The Weisses probably connected with Kahn through their synagogue. In 1945, Kahn wrote to a prospective client in Harrisburg: "I was the Architect of the Ahavath Israel, Philadelphia, erected in 1936; and we [Stonorov & Kahn] are to be the architects of the synagogue and community building for the Tiferes Israel Community Center of Norristown."[4] Although the buildings never went any further, the Weisses must have learned enough about Kahn from discussions there to engage him as their architect, signing a contract on October 24, 1947.[5] Kahn began preliminary studies in early November following the completion of his teaching duties at Yale.[6] Construction was under way by the fall of 1948, and the Weisses were in residence by the end of 1949. Additional finishing work continued into the spring of 1950, with the first publication of the house occurring that April. The total cost for construction was $50,000, including extensive cabinetry and furniture that Kahn himself designed.[7]

Early relations with the Weisses were not always smooth (Kahn had to write a stern, formal letter in 1950 complaining about their withholding payment for the extra work done on the house[8]) yet Anne Tyng, who worked closely with Kahn on the design and construction of the house, called them "wonderful clients,"[9] notable for their "pluckish enthusiasm" and the impromptu picnics organized at the job site during Kahn and Tyng's frequent visits.[10] Their disagreements must have been smoothed over with little difficulty, however, since Lenore later wrote warmly inviting Lou Kahn to visit,[11] while Esther Kahn recalled that afterward they became "close friends."[12]

The Weisses selected a site four miles from Norristown with distant views of farmland in all directions.[13] Their choice was an ideal one, providing good orientation, privacy, and a gentle, sun-filled slope for the architect to work with. He sited the house in the northern corner of the 5-acre property—over 450 feet from the road—near the crest of the hill. The rectangular plan of the house is bifurcated at the entry to provide a separation between living and sleeping quarters (fig. 140). Kahn used subtle variations of floor level to heighten these distinctions, and, through the centralization of utility and circulation elements at the core of the rectangle, he expressed for the first time in built form what he would later characterize as "servant" space.

The discipline and clarity of the plan was reinforced by the simplicity of Kahn's design of the roof structure (fig. 141). Timber-framed, the "butterfly" roof was laid out on a 5-foot, 4-inch module with variations in ceiling height ranging from 7 feet at the entrance to over 12 feet at the south side of the living room. The resulting sense of spatial uplift provided by the roof structure served to intensify the connection to the outdoors. That connection could be manipulated through Kahn's innovative design of an overscaled, reversible, double-hung sash window system that provided for alternating arrangements of opaque and transparent panels that allowed for the modulation of natural light throughout the course of the day (fig. 142).

Just as Kahn carefully thought through the way he could manipulate natural lighting with these movable panels, he showed an overriding concern for the choice of materials and their detailing. "Richness," Kahn said of his work at the Weiss house, would come from the "materials themselves" and through the "exposure of construction."[14] The warm-toned stone was to be laid in a random rubble configuration in a manner drawn from "the best examples in old Pennsylvania barns" (fig. 143).[15] Structural elements of wood and exterior sheathing were detailed in cypress, chosen for its durability and with the knowledge that the surfaces would remain unpainted. In connecting the rough-edged stone to the finely milled wood, Kahn created a "shadow joint"—a 1-inch inset reveal that cast the joint in shadow. During construction Kahn used this concept to further clarify the structure, lowering the height of the stone wall on the west elevation to reveal the structural timber—which, as detailed in the construction drawing, would have hidden the beam and denied, in Kahn's view, the nonstructural nature of the wall (see figs. 139, 141). Elsewhere—the central fireplace, in particular—stone would serve a structural role. Kahn subtly articulated this through the angling-in of the face of the fireplace toward the settee, affording a location to receive an unusually long timber that supported the low valley of the roof and creating a more intimate setting (fig. 144).

During the spring of 1949—six months into construction—Kahn turned his attention to the fittings of the house, personally preparing numerous sketches and final construction drawings for lighting, built-ins, and freestanding furniture (figs. 145–47; see figs. 105, 106). He also designed a mural for the living room, its motif the surrounding rural countryside and traditional buildings, that would not be completed until after his return from his stay abroad in the winter of 1950–51 (see figs. 144, 145). Stonework similar to that of the fireplace was used for the exterior "room" and barbecue that Kahn created in response to the Weisses' request for outdoor country living. *Architectural Forum* described it as a "deliberately brutal stone fireplace, a landmark, almost, from a moonscape" (fig. 148).[16]

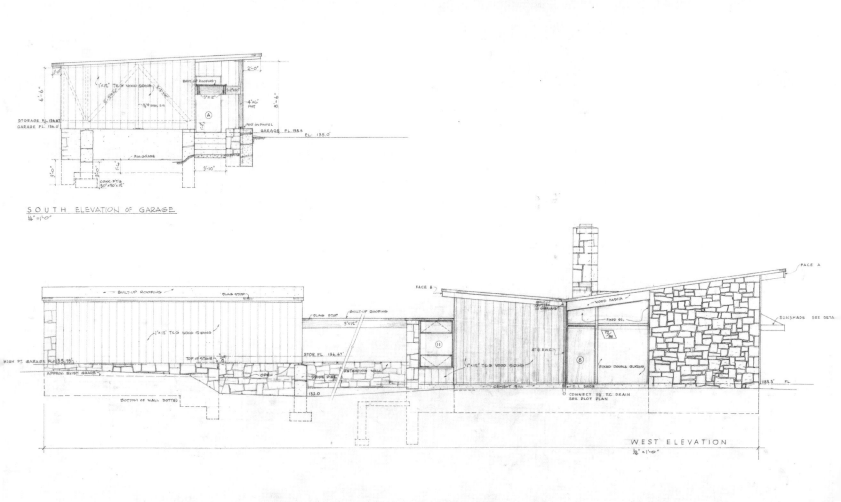

Fig. 141 West elevation of house and south elevation of garage. Louis Kahn, dated June 23, 1948. Anne G. Tyng and David P. Wisdom. Kahn Collection

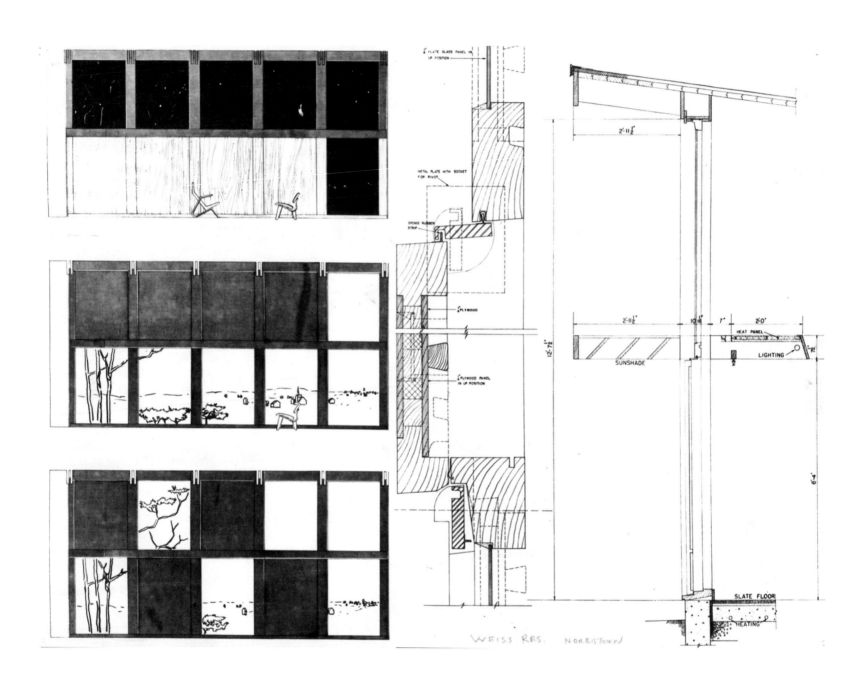

Fig. 142 Diagrams of living-room window. Archival photograph of lost original 1950. Kahn Collection

Fig. 143 Fireplace, with dining room beyond. Photograph 1950. Kahn Collection

Fig. 144 Living room prior to completion of mural. Photograph 1950. Kahn Collection

Fig. 145 Living room, with mural, built-in cabinet, and seating area. Photograph 1990

Fig. 146   Elevation of kitchen cabinet and breakfast area, c. March 1949. Kahn Collection

Fig. 147   Laundry with Dutch door to garage. Photograph 1950. Kahn Collection

Fig. 148 Outdoor seating area and barbecue from northwest. Photograph 1950. Kahn Collection

SAMUEL AND RUTH
GENEL HOUSE

WYNNEWOOD, LOWER MERION TOWNSHIP
1948–51

Fig. 150 Site plan. Louis Kahn, c. May–June 1948. Kahn Collection

Fig. 149 Samuel and Ruth Genel House, Wynnewood, 1948–51. From east. Photograph May 2011

In the spring of 1948, old family friends Samuel and Ruth Genel asked Kahn to design a five-bedroom, five-bath house for them in Wynnewood, a near western suburb of Philadelphia (fig. 149). They were then living in a row house in the nearby Wynnefield section of Philadelphia but wanted to move to Lower Merion to take advantage of its better schools. Samuel's sister Helen had belonged to the same sorority as Esther Kahn at the University of Pennsylvania, and Esther and Samuel, a student at Penn's Wharton School, had briefly dated. Samuel, who directed his family business, the Old English Printing and Labeling Company, was active in a number of local and national Jewish organizations. He also sat on the board of the Philadelphia Psychiatric Hospital, then a small but expanding institution supported by the Jewish community, where Kahn was working on two buildings at this time.[1]

Kahn chose the Genel house as the basis for a problem he assigned to his advanced design studio at Yale during the fall semester of 1948, much as he would do with a number of his other commissions throughout his teaching career. Calling it A Suburban Residence, Kahn clearly laid out in his problem statement the relevant information about the house, including all the details of his own Wynnewood project (even naming the intersecting streets as the location of the house). He gave his students a profile of his clients and described the site, the type and square footage of each of the rooms (the entire house was not to exceed 4,500 square feet), and the proposed cost of the house ($72,000, including 10 percent architect's fee, a luxurious sum at the time). The square footage he provided for each of the rooms was very specific—280 square feet for the dining room, for example, and 170 square feet for the guest room (including bath and 4 linear feet of closet). Most likely Kahn drew these figures from his own current plans for the house, which at the time of the studio assignment had progressed beyond preliminaries into the design development phase.[2]

"The Clients," Kahn told his students, were "a man, his wife and two children—girl 11, boy 6 and a resident maid. Man's occupation—head of an inherited printing establishment in Philadelphia. Woman's occupation—housewife, artistically inclined, enjoys painting and music in addition to keeping house and entertaining. Children are busy growing up. The grownups respect but do not live in the past. They try to understand our present mode of living, thinking, and methods of doing things. They are interested in getting a house which will serve their children when they grow up as well as answer their needs for space to make a home today. They are not afraid of new forms of architectural expression provided they are developed thoughtfully and are easy to build."[3]

Breaking down the principal rooms, he added: "Living room is the area of the house where the family intends to entertain their friends and neighbors for their fun, cultural and community interests. The Dining Room is made large to accommodate a large party and should be separated from the Living Room for table preparation and clearing. The mode of separation is optional with the planner. The client visualizes the so called study more as the family get together place rather than for seclusion and study."

The Wynnewood site was the last lot to be developed within the initial subdivision of the former estate of W. Percy Simpson, heir to wealthy mill owners and industrialists. His 16-acre property, noted for its "pretty open woods" and "low rustic wall" in a turn-of-the-century description of the suburbs of Philadelphia, had been broken up in the early 1920s, and the fashionable residences built before the Depression remain as neighbors to Kahn's completed design.[4] In discussing the site in his problem statement, Kahn singled out its proximity to Lancaster Pike, a busy stretch of the Lincoln Highway—America's first coast-to-coast road—which at the time was the primary westerly truck route in and out of Philadelphia. He suggested that existing trees "should be preserved as far as possible and be used to best advantage to give privacy and to protect from the noise of the main highway" and that the "stone wall of the ruin" located on the southwest side of the property could be employed to shield the "lot from the house beyond."

It appears that the house was built without a contract between the two friends. The Genels purchased the property from the neighboring McGlinn family on April 9, 1948, and three months later, on July 1, Kahn sent out his first invoice for design work.[5] Construction began in October 1949, and the family moved in some sixteen months later. Of Kahn's preliminary design studies, six original undated drawings survive, with a seventh, an east elevation, preserved in photographic form only.[6] As the only surviving preliminary plan shows, Kahn sited the house to take advantage of the existing trees and topographic features, in particular an area of level ground marking the site of an abandoned tennis court (fig. 150). He positioned the living areas, along with the entry, kitchen, study, and maid's quarters, a step above the former courts on the northern half of the plan. Working with the change in slope beyond the court, he arranged the family's sleeping quarters in a split-level configuration over a playroom, utility area, and two-car garage. While the plan clearly bifurcates these two zones, the elevations suggest a more subtle approach, with the stone walls oriented north to south in the area of the sleeping quarters and east to west in the area of the living quarters (fig. 151). The smooth limestone facing of the massive living-room fireplace strongly contrasts with the random rubble pattern of the exterior masonry (fig. 152).

In his final design for the house Kahn asserted its structure more forcefully, using a 3-foot, 8½-inch module to unify the plan (fig. 153). Whereas the initial design presented continuous surfaces of stone or wood siding, here Kahn broke the surfaces and revealed the structure with strong vertical elements—4-by-6-inch posts—that support long-span timber beams (fig. 154). The structural logic is further reinforced by the orientation of the clear-heart California redwood siding, which is set in 8-inch-high planks laid horizontally in the north and south façades, where the structural columns are located (the panels were replaced with vertical ones on Kahn's

Fig. 151 East elevation. Archival photograph of lost original. Louis Kahn, c. May–June 1948. Kahn Collection

instructions, apparently because they were not weathering well; fig. 155). The nonstructural east and west elevations were made of a continual surface of vertically oriented 4-inch-wide tongue-and-groove redwood.

Kahn relocated the garage to a semidetached structure in the final plan, affording a generous pergola-covered outdoor entry court complete with terraced planting beds and a seating area (fig. 156), but the pergola was later removed (fig. 157). The south-facing playroom and den opened onto a loggia, which provided protection from the sun just as the roof overhang protected the bedrooms above (fig. 158).

Refinements made during the summer of 1949 freed the terrace from an awkward pylon support, allowing a more generous area, which was realigned, through a skewed geometry, to reference the triangular fireplace within. Off the dining room Kahn created an entertainment terrace, with two 10-foot-long cypress-and-steel benches along the sides and, a few steps below, a large outdoor grill with a soapstone hood (see fig. 149, at right).

Kahn designed an imposing fireplace of white Carrara marble and black slate, once again locating it apart, an obliquely set, freestanding triangular form in an alcove that

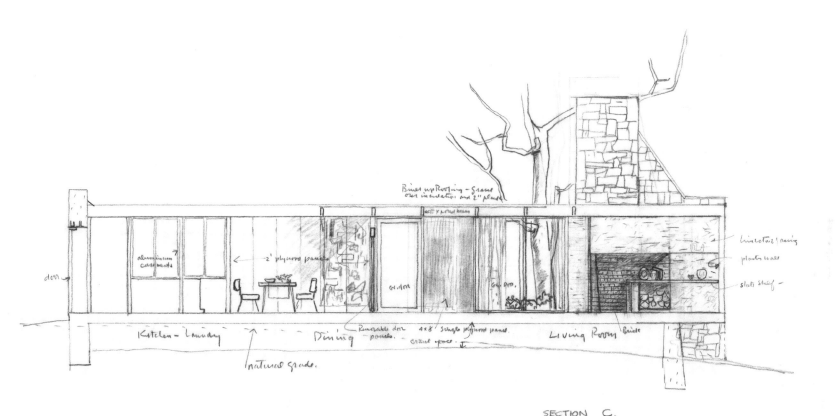

Fig. 152 Section through living block. Louis Kahn, c. May–June 1948. Kahn Collection

serves as a transitional space (fig. 159; see fig. 49). One walked from the entrance hall around the back of the fireplace and between the built-in buffet, which served to divide the hall and the dining room, and along the side of the alcove to enter the living room (figs. 159–62). These areas—hall, alcove, and a narrow runner leading to a side door off the living room—are unified with a continuous red-tile floor, which demarcates the core of the house as well as a pattern of circulation (fig. 163). The dining room, housed partially within its own alcove, extended out, providing access to exterior spaces (fig. 164). The wood paneling and wooden ceilings of the living areas continue into the sleeping quarters and the connecting hallway, which comprises a row of closets with sliding doors (fig. 165).

Well after construction of the house had begun Kahn developed designs for a number of built-in furnishings for the principal rooms (for which Genel later agreed that Kahn could charge a 20 percent fee; see figs. 112, 113).[7] He also designed two walnut dining tables, which could be placed end to end to reach 13 feet, suitable for the large parties described in the design problem. The buffet and some of the other pieces can be seen in early photographs of the house, but none of the furniture is known to exist (fig. 159; see fig. 4).

In a letter of February 1954 to Anne Tyng, who was then in Rome, Kahn described reactions that a Mrs. Jaffe had to the house: She "happened to drive on the Pike—spotted something brown in the trees—looked—liked—called Genel—Genel invited her to come look around—and she came home entranced (as she put it) with the 'Fugue' of the house." Another set of visitors had liked the house "very much and thought it was far superior to the Weiss house," to which Kahn added, "I do agree in many ways that they showed good judgment."[8]

The Genels occupied the house only a short time. Ruth died of cancer in October 1955 and Samuel later remarried, but his new wife had three children, so they sold the house in 1956 and moved into a larger one.[9]

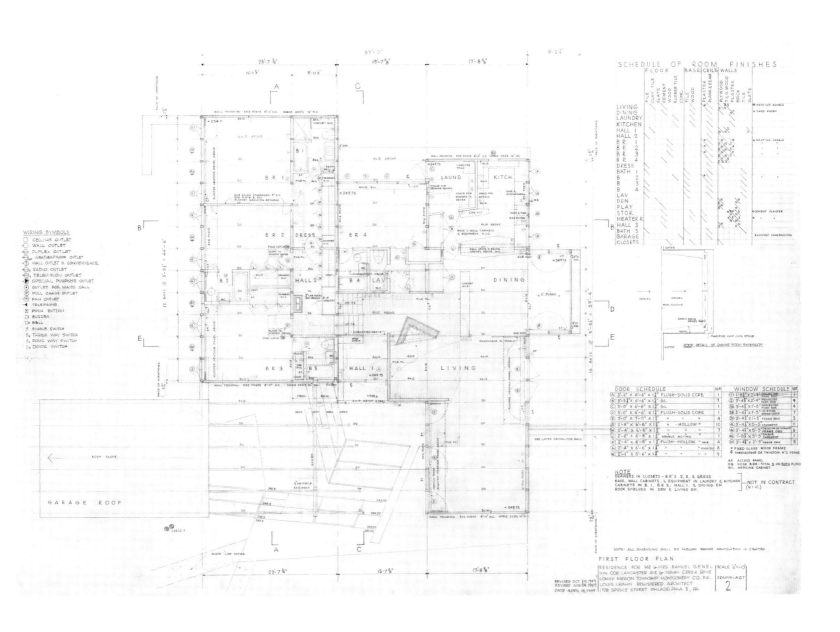

Fig. 153　First-floor plan. Anne G. Tyng, dated April 18, 1949. Kahn Collection

Fig. 154 Two-story bedroom block and garage from southeast. Photograph October 1952. Kahn Collection

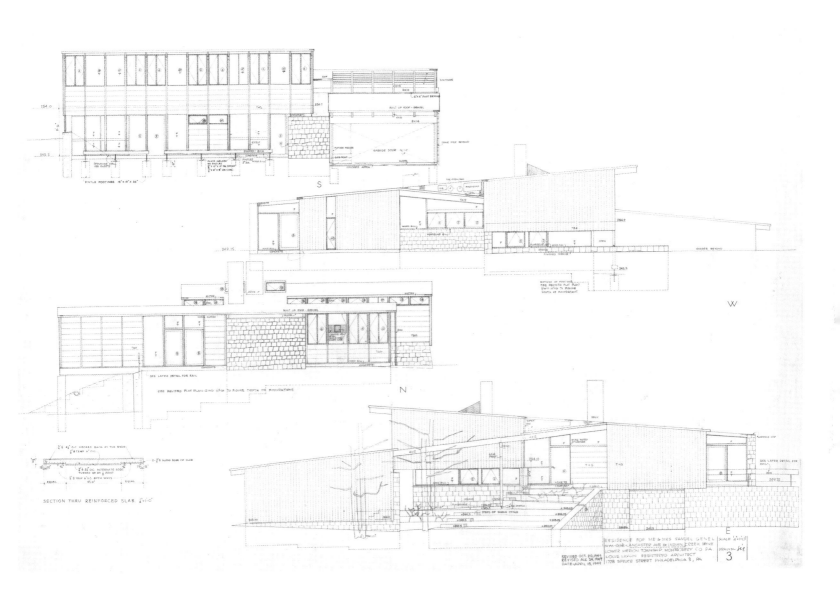

Fig. 155 Elevations. Louis Kahn, dated April 18, 1949. Kahn Collection

GENEL HOUSE

Fig. 156 Entry court and pergola (later removed). Photograph October 1952. Kahn Collection

Fig. 157 Entry court from southeast. Photograph May 2011

Fig. 158 Loggia from east. Photograph May 2011

Fig. 159 Entry hall, from bedroom hall. Photograph October 1952. Kahn Collection

Fig. 160 Entry hall, with chimney back and niche. Photograph May 2011

Fig. 161 Inglenook. Photograph October 1952. Kahn Collection

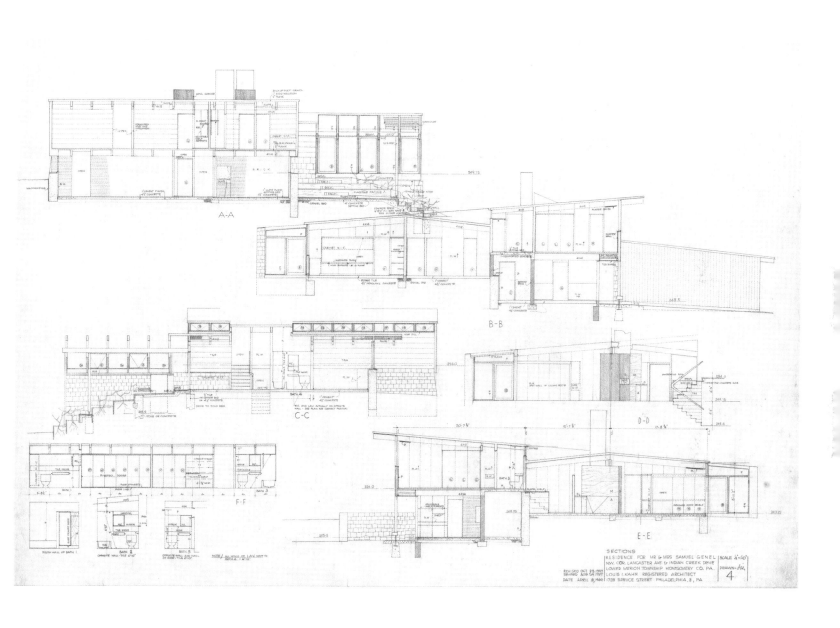

Fig. 162   Sections. Louis Kahn, dated April 18, 1949. Kahn Collection

Fig. 163 Dining room and living room with inglenook. Photograph May 2011

Fig. 164 Dining room. Photograph May 2011

Fig. 165 Bedroom with clerestory. Photograph May 2011

FRED AND ELAINE
CLEVER HOUSE

CHERRY HILL, NEW JERSEY
1957–62

In the fall of 1957, Fred and Elaine Cox Clever signed a contract with Louis Kahn to design a house for them and their teenage son Eric in Cherry Hill, New Jersey, a suburb of Philadelphia, ten miles from center city and six miles from their home in Collingswood, New Jersey (fig. 166). The house was built in the new Holly Glen development on a flat, wooded, 200-by-150-foot parcel of land, using a pavilion format related to that of Kahn's Trenton Bathhouse, which Kahn must have taken them to see.[1] Kahn had just begun to design the Richards Medical Laboratories at the University of Pennsylvania when the contract was signed, and with such a large undertaking in the office, he seems to have turned over much of the creative activity on the house to his associate Anne Tyng. Beginning as early as July 8, 1957—a full eleven weeks before the contract was signed—office time sheets document the long hours Tyng devoted to the project and confirm that significant elements of the design's development can be attributed to her.[2] Her centrality to the project is supported by the fact that when the Clevers contemplated building an addition in 1972 they went directly to Tyng, who then got the go-ahead from Kahn to design it herself; it was never built.[3]

Fred Clever had known Kahn at least since 1952, when he was executive director of Philadelphia's Citizens' Council on City Planning and Kahn was invited to join its Regional Committee, formed that year.[4] Both Kahn and Tyng became active members of the Council, supporting its goal of keeping an eye on the integrity of Philadelphia's planning activities. Clever, who worked in public relations at the Insurance Company of North America, was, like his wife, a Quaker; he was a civil rights activist, a member of a number of socially progressive organizations, and instrumental in founding the New Jersey chapter of the American Civil Liberties Union.[5] The Clevers had met during the war years when they were students at Penn State and worked together on the college newspaper.[6] Fred studied journalism, and Elaine became a librarian, eventually serving as head of Access Services at the Temple University library.[7]

Relations between the architects and clients were good, with Kahn and Tyng given a fairly free rein over the design. Problems arose, however, almost immediately after they received a bid from the builder Walter Cope for $27,680 in mid-March 1959, when they sought financing to cover construction costs.[8] After nearly a year of delay, a frustrated Fred Clever made an appeal directly to the president of the Philadelphia Savings Fund Society, whose organization had rejected the Clevers' most recent application.

> Two weeks ago I spent a pleasant hour in your mortgage department discussing with Charles Myrtetus the house I plan to build and the possibility of doing it with a PSFS mortgage....
>
> Last week Mr. Myrtetus called to tell me that your mortgage committee had met and reviewed the plans and had decided that PSFS "isn't interested in investing."
>
> At first I misunderstood Mr. Myrtetus. I thought that he meant that PSFS wasn't interested in writing as large a mortgage as I had requested.
>
> Perhaps you can imagine my surprise when he pointed out that such was not the case—that the committee had decided that it wasn't interested because they felt that the house "isn't marketable."
>
> My surprise might have turned to indignation at such a cavalier opinion of what I believe will be a

Fig. 166 Fred and Elaine Clever House, Cherry Hill, New Jersey, 1957–62. From north. Photograph February 1983

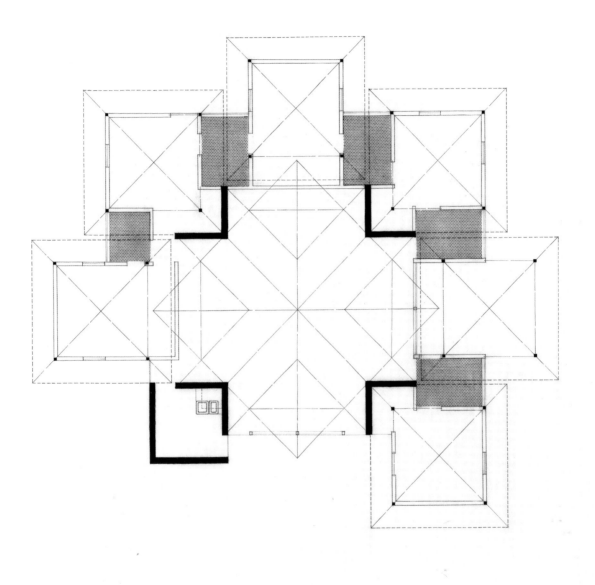

Fig. 167   Plan. 1959. Kahn Collection

unusually beautiful house by a truly great architect had not another thought kept intruding itself. I could not put from my mind a mental picture of a group of men poring over drawings of the PSFS building and muttering, "Yes, but who would ever buy it."

As it is, I am somewhat confused. All the evidence indicated to me that PSFS would be the financial institution most likely to venture outside the split-level-colonial-development category: the PSFS building, still a classic contemporary design; your own personal involvement in the Citizens Council on City Planning and other groups interested in good design; the several modern homes I know to be mortgaged by PSFS; and, not least, the reputation PSFS has had among architects.[9]

The letter did not achieve its goal and the design languished yet another year before financing was arranged elsewhere and construction began, but building the house went fairly quickly and the Clevers moved in by the spring of 1962.

The single-story, 1,700-square-foot house centers on a spacious 17-foot-high living room defined by two steeply sloped roofs that intersect to form a Greek cross in plan (figs. 167, 168). Ridge beams of Douglas fir projecting beyond the triangular clerestory windows provide shelter for hinged wooden ventilation panels and add depth and complexity to the natural lighting (figs. 169, 170). The central space—which was ideal for the many meetings and events the Clevers held there—is surrounded by a cluster of six gently sloped pyramidal roofs, which are supported by columns that establish 11-foot-square units. The interstitial areas, where two overhangs meet, are utilized for bathrooms, closets, and other service spaces. The dining room occupies a square initially intended to be a covered terrace. A two-story masonry square attached to the corner of the Greek cross contains the fireplace and mechanical equipment and has direct access from the exterior.

The Clevers lived in the house until their deaths, Elaine's in 2000 and Fred's the following year, and the house remains with the family.

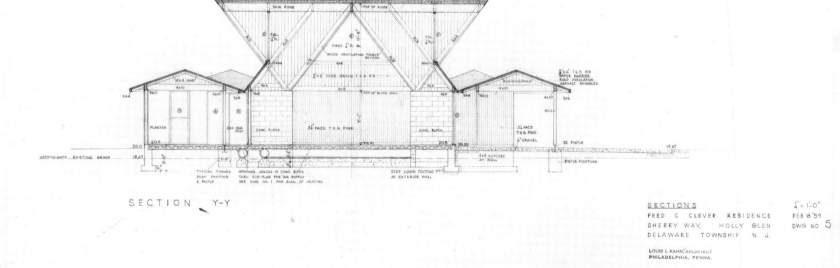

Fig. 168 Sections. Anne G. Tyng, dated February 18, 1959. Kahn Collection

Fig. 169 Living room. Photograph February 1983

Fig. 170 Ceiling detail. Photograph February 1983

BERNARD AND NORMA SHAPIRO HOUSE

NARBERTH, LOWER MERION TOWNSHIP, 1958–62 ADDITION BY KAHN AND ANNE G. TYNG, ASSOCIATED ARCHITECTS, BUILT 1972–75

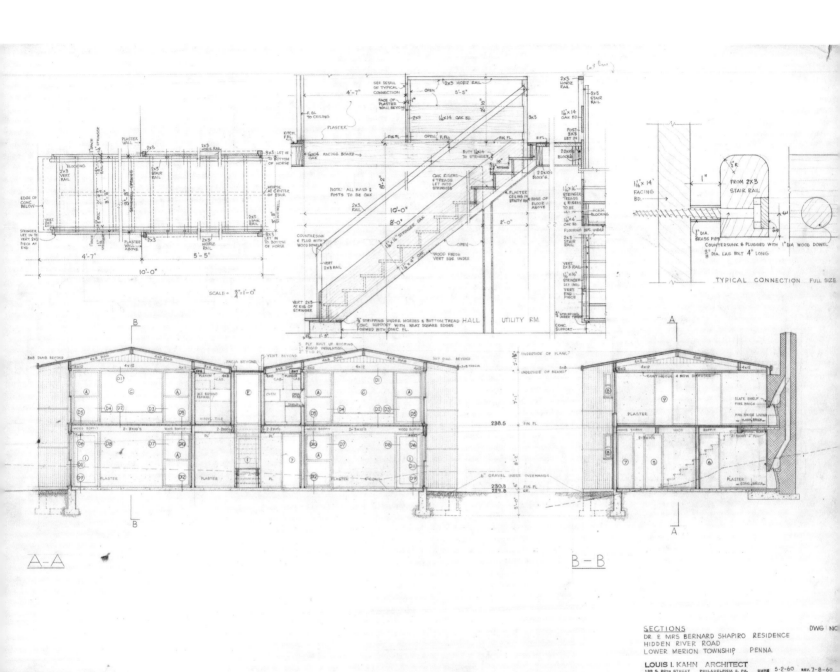

Fig. 172 Sections and stair details. Anne G. Tyng, dated May 2, 1960. Kahn Collection

Fig. 171 Bernard and Norma Shapiro House, Narberth, 1958–62. Entry court from west. Photograph December 2011

The house that Louis Kahn designed for Bernard and Norma Shapiro is set on a narrow, heavily wooded slope overlooking the picturesque Schuylkill valley and the Flat Rock dam and falls. With its blank stucco walls facing the street and large windows open to the view, it perfectly satisfied one of the couple's key requirements: to "provide as much privacy as possible" (fig. 171). This request appears in a practical and comprehensive checklist that includes a rundown of the couple themselves, their needs, and their desires, which they presented to the architect around the time the contract was signed in 1958.[1] The family was small, described in the checklist as "Norma Shapiro—Housewife & lawyer, age 30; Bernard Shapiro—Physician (Research medicine at Southern Division AEMC [Albert Einstein Medical Center]), age 33, photography & electronics hobbies . . .; and Finley Shapiro—age 2 weeks, hobby: breast feeding." They specified a house with three bedrooms, study, and family room, along with the kitchen, living room, and dining room (or dining area). They were very much aware of the setting and wanted the "outside readily accessible from inside . . . [and] as much natural light as is compatible with preserving woods."

It was Norma who favored a contemporary house, and she especially wanted "something of architectural value." The Shapiros did not seek out Kahn immediately, even though Norma had lived for many years around the corner from the Osers, whose house she had liked and to whom she was related.[2] They first thought of contacting the West Coast architect Richard Neutra, who had built a modern house in nearby East Falls, but then talked to the Philadelphian Norman Rice, who was building in the same area. When they did meet Kahn, he took them to visit the Weiss house and drove them by the Roche house, so they could see what his work was like. Most of all they were impressed with Kahn's Trenton Bathhouse, and after seeing it they contracted with him to be their architect.

The house took more than three years to complete, with the first, spectacular version shaped from two hexagonal pavilions rejected because it greatly exceeded the funds they had allotted for construction (see fig. 64). But when they saw the revised drawings for a smaller house with two square pavilions, they were suitably pleased: "We think this is a lovely design for the house," Bernard wrote. "The arrangement of rooms is perfect for our needs. Norma is happy with the study. The exterior is very attractive. The plans seem ingenious to us."[3] By the time the Shapiros moved into the revised but still not completely finished house in November 1961, the family had grown to include two more sons. The Shapiros had expended great amounts of energy on the house and were reeling from the effort of overseeing its construction at the same time as they were expanding and raising their family. "It was tiring having a house built," Norma recalled. "We had to approve everything, even whether a light switch should have a matte or gloss finish."

Kahn's symmetrical design is divided into two pyramidal roofed pavilions (fig. 172). Responding to the steep slope of the site, the living areas are on an upper, entry level, and the sleeping areas, a den, and service spaces are on the lower level (figs. 173, 174), which, according to Norma, Kahn pictured like "a cave where you would be protected." A narrow space set between the two pavilions provides a location for the staircase and the kitchen, with large windows adding definition to it (figs. 175, 176). Expanding upon the principles set forth in his Trenton Bathhouse, Kahn modified the "hollow columns" introduced in the earlier work to incorporate corner closets, connecting hallways, and entryways. These columnar elements also serve to brace against the outward thrust of the low-pitch pyramidal roof.

The uphill entry façade comprises a stucco-faced concrete-block wall ("No brick," the couple had specified), which extends the poured-in-place concrete retaining wall below (see fig. 62). The downhill façades are wooden frame sheathed in "Japanese" mahogany (fig. 179; see fig. 61). Horizontal water tables divide the sheathing at regular intervals that were determined by the length of available stock. On the interior Kahn specified plaster for the walls, oak flooring for the upper level, and carpet for the floors of the lower level (fig. 177). The roof structure is exposed timber ridge beams with a distinctive boss element at the center (fig. 178).

In 1972, wanting a guest room, the Shapiros hired Kahn to design an addition to the house, which had been built with expansion in mind. Working with Anne Tyng, Kahn added a guest suite, family room, and recreation room to the house.

The house is still owned by the original family.

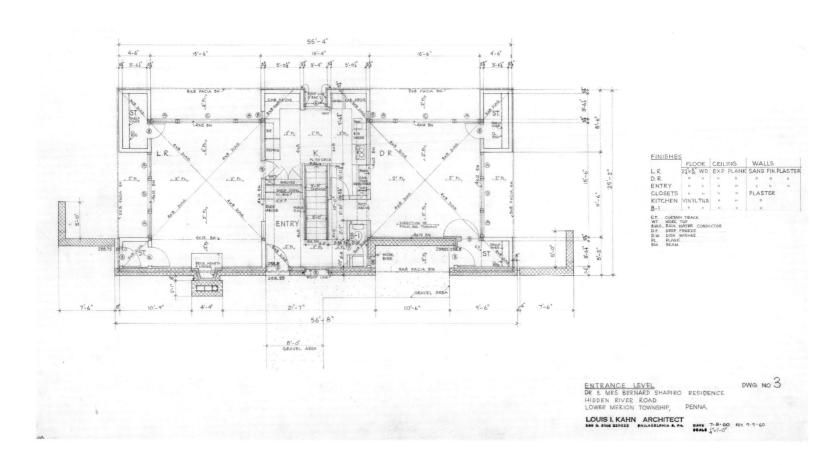

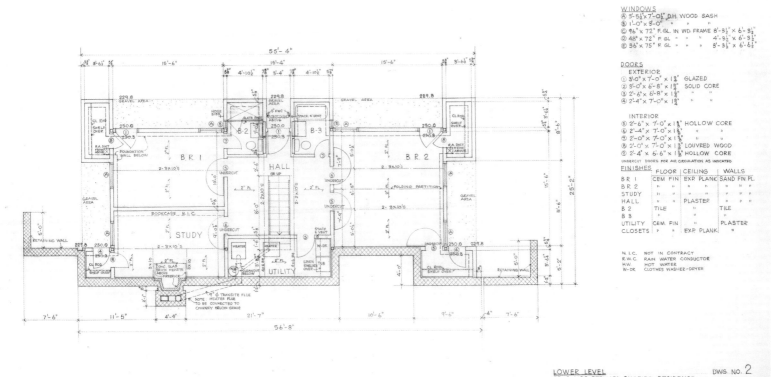

SHAPIRO HOUSE

Fig. 175   Living room block and entry from southwest. Photograph December 2011

Fig. 173   Entry-level plan. Anne G. Tyng, dated May 2, 1960. Kahn Collection

Fig. 174   Lower-level plan. Anne G. Tyng, dated May 2, 1960. Kahn Collection

Fig. 176 Entry hall. Photograph December 2011

Fig. 177 Fireplace inglenook. Photograph December 2011

Fig. 178 Living room. Photograph December 2011

Fig. 179 From northeast. Photograph December 2011

MARGARET
ESHERICK HOUSE
CHESTNUT HILL, PHILADELPHIA, 1959–62

Fig. 181 Perspective. Louis Kahn, c. March 1960. Kahn Collection

Fig. 180 Margaret Esherick House, Chestnut Hill, Philadelphia, 1959–62. From southwest. Photograph 2003

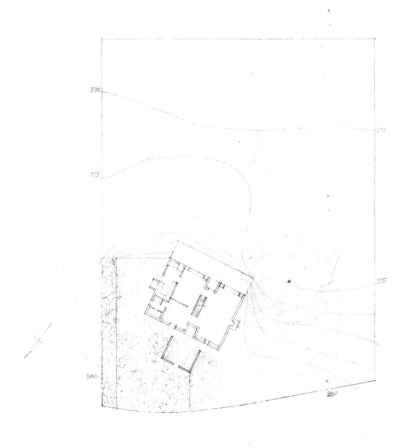

Fig. 182 Site plan. c. March 1960. Kahn Collection

Taking "beauty and logic" as his working principles and the "character of the community" as a consideration, Louis Kahn designed a superb masonry and wood house for the bookseller Margaret Esherick in Philadelphia's leafy Chestnut Hill neighborhood (fig. 180).[1] Esherick, who had been living nearby with her parents, commissioned the house after the death of her father in November 1958, presumably using money from her inheritance to pay for the land and the construction. Discussions with Kahn began during the summer of 1959, and the contract was signed the following October. Construction began in November 1960, and the house was well enough along for her to move in late in October 1961.[2] She lived in the house for only about six months, however, for she died unexpectedly in April 1962, leaving minor cabinetwork and landscaping unfinished.[3]

Margaret Esherick was born in Philadelphia in 1919, daughter of an engineer, and grew up in Mt. Airy, on the boundary of Chestnut Hill. She attended the University of Vermont, where she majored in elementary education. In about 1950, after an extended stay on the West Coast, and with experience working for the antiquarian bookseller David Magee in San Francisco,[4] she returned to Philadelphia and took over the Fireside Bookstore on Germantown Avenue, two blocks away from her parents' house.[5] Five years later she moved the store around the corner to a house on East Evergreen Avenue, which she renovated with the help of her brother, Joseph, then a young architect working in San Francisco.[6] "She bought an old building," he recalled. "In the front was an old residence. It was a neat old Chestnut Hill house.... That was a book store, and then in the back she converted the garages to a toy store. We cut holes in the upper floor so things could hang down, kites and toys hanging from the ceiling. It was a pretty exciting thing."[7]

When Margaret decided to build a house in 1959, she asked her brother to design it, but reeling from his experiences at the bookstore "trying to work with people at long distance, and having them not at all used to western detailing," he decided against it.[8] Joseph, a half generation younger than Kahn, had studied architecture at the University of Pennsylvania; in 1938 he had moved to San Francisco, where in 1946 he opened his own office and began what would become a celebrated career in the Bay Area.[9] He was familiar with Kahn's work, for Kahn had designed a workshop in

1955–56 for his uncle, the craftsman Wharton Esherick, and apparently recommended Kahn for the job. Most likely he introduced his sister to Kahn during the visit he made to Philadelphia in June 1959, during which, as he conveyed in a letter to Kahn, he intended to devote a weekend to seeing "something of you and your work."[10] As the project developed, he continued to advise his sister on elements of the design, even drawing out a "lighting fixture to go over the medicine cabinet," and the end fittings for a towel bar.[11]

The house was to be built on the wooded edge of Pastorius Park in the early twentieth-century model suburb Chestnut Hill, much of it exhibiting a uniformity of color and texture that the ubiquitous use of local stone created. It had been developed by the family of Dr. George Woodward, the reform-minded scion of the nineteenth-century multimillionaire Henry H. Houston, who had amassed over 3,000 acres in this western region of Philadelphia and in the adjacent counties. When they sold parcels from their holdings the Woodwards tried to assure that new construction, even if modern in style, would maintain the character of the area.

Woodward's youngest son, Charles, represented the family in the sale of the land to Margaret Esherick, and is the person to whom she sent a preliminary "sketch of the front elevation with trees and entourage" (as Kahn described it in mid-March 1960)[12] and a related site plan orienting the house to the cardinal directions and not the street front, both drawings mounted on identical boards for presentation (figs. 181, 182). Charles, a graduate of Yale and of the University of Pennsylvania law school, worked with his brother George in overseeing the family's real-estate interests. He had "turned out to be something of a thwarted architect," notes David Contosta, historian of Chestnut Hill, but he "discovered his real ambition much too late in life to make the family's preoccupation with fine housing into a lifetime career."[13] Thus his concerned reaction to the design of the proposed house was perhaps more personal than professional. "Since sending you the letter yesterday about the design of your house," he wrote Margaret on April 29,

> I have been giving some thought as to what might be done to make the appearance less controversial.
>
> If it were my own house I would have a sloping roof with the ceiling of the bedroom and upper part of the living room following the line of the roof; that is, the ceiling would not be flat.... But roofs are expensive and there are other ways of solving the appearance problem.
>
> Enclosed are some pictures of houses taken from Town and Country.... Three of these pictures show how other architects have solved the problem by a frieze, which is better than the parapet mentioned yesterday.
>
> Too many contemporary architects are disciples of the "bare naked" school. Nakedness (of a house) is not beautiful when maturity sets in. Or, some architects, like artists, want to create a sensational house; unfortunately only the canvas can be relegated to the closet.
>
> I like your plan; your fenestration is interesting, but the roof line is not good in my opinion. It needs some softening element. A mosaic frieze like the one in the enclosed picture is stupendous, but I guess we can't have a mosaic frieze on Sunrise Lane, although it could be a painted frieze. A simpler solution is merely a colored fascia board like the green one trimming the house shown by the pool.
>
> I am sending an extra copy of this letter which you may send to your architect. I suggest that thought be given by him to breaking the naked line of the top of the walls (naked because the eye has no where to go) by a fascia board, with or without design, but colored differently than the walls of the house to give a terminal effect to these bare walls.

Woodward's postscript to the letter, "I don't want to discourage you, I think you have something, but it could be softer," sounds a note of gentlemanly persuasion, to which Kahn responded in his revised scheme for the façade (fig. 183).[14] In his perspective sketch, which was probably made in early May 1960, Kahn's drawing and annotations seem to answer directly Woodward's concerns (although he did not add a fascia board): "House of Dark Stucco, stained natural wood

Fig. 183   Perspective. Archival photograph of lost original, c. May 1960. Kahn Collection

ESHERICK HOUSE   175

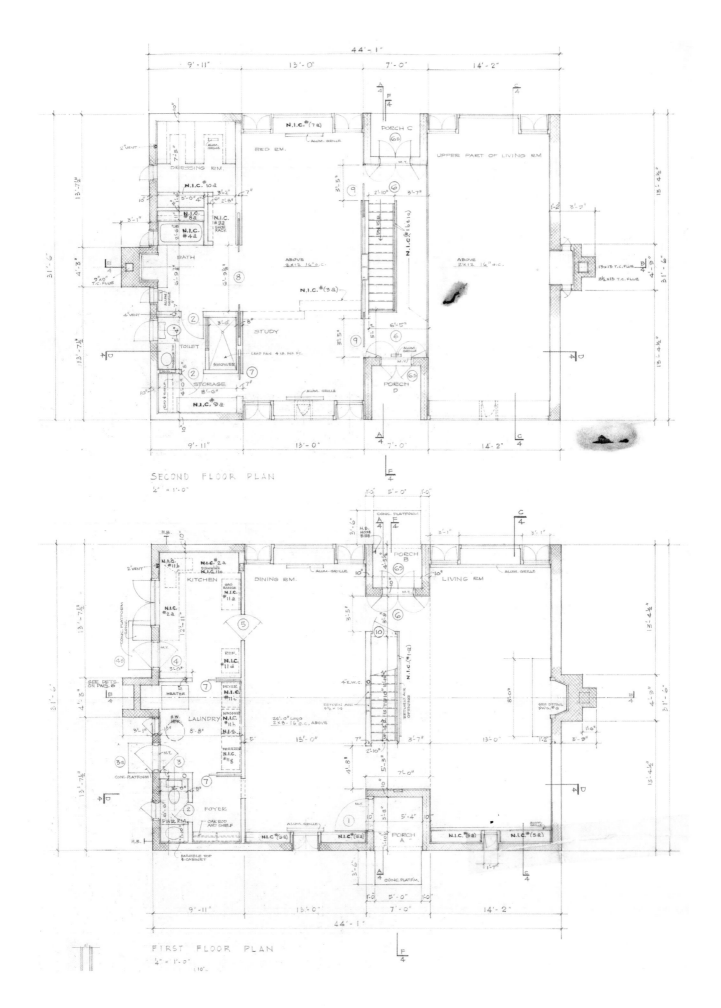

reveals for windows. The building will not look flat. The deep reveal of windows, entrance alcoves and 2nd floor flower porches will give it an alive look at all times. The 2 parts of the building divided by the alcoves should offer subtle silhouette."[15] Kahn, unrelenting in his preference for a flat roof, emphasized the animation of the façade through the changing quality of natural light as well as through the use of finely detailed, deeply inset windows built in naturally finished wood. The insertion of a balcony above the entry alcove, softened by the suggested boxed plantings, as well as the break in the roofline were augmented by both a heightening and thickening of the chimneys. In addition, Kahn now situated the house parallel to the street. These revisions seem to have settled matters with Woodward, and Kahn's office turned its attention toward the completion of construction drawings.

As built, the house features a compact plan, 44 feet by 31 feet, 6 inches in exterior dimension, organized into what Kahn referred to by then as servant and served spaces (fig. 184). Circulation was consolidated between a double-height living room (27 feet, 6 inches deep by 13 feet wide and 16 feet, 3 inches high) on the right side and the entry hall, dining room, and a single bedroom in the middle; baths, kitchen, storage, and utility spaces were combined in a distinct zone at the left side, with direct access to the driveway and outdoor service area (an earlier plan had these elements flipped, with the living areas on the left and the service areas on the right; see fig. 81). The sunken forecourt provides a distinctive note of formality to the entrance of the house (fig. 185). The logic of the plan is emphasized in the treatment of the façades, with each element maintaining the clarity of the servant and served areas of the interior. As such, the northwest, or street, façade presents on the right side a narrow alcove, one-and-a-half-stories tall, surmounted by a high window, which expresses both the double height of the living room inside and the client's desire for privacy (fig. 186). To the left are the narrow window of the entry hall and the large window of the bedroom above, seen here with the inset shutters open (the difference in the color of the hardwood apitong in the photograph is attributable to exposure to the weather). A cast-in-place concrete balcony with bronze railing provides shelter for the entry alcove, distinguishing this as the zone of circulation, a note emphasized by the break in the roof profile determined by the detailing of the balcony roof (fig. 187). Lead-coated copper was used for the roof soffits as well as for the drip pans that protect the base of the deeply inset windows. From the north corner of the house the service zone is revealed in the blank area of stucco on the street façade and through the irregular placement of windows on the northeast façade, each positioned to meet the functional requirements of the interior (fig. 188). The conventionally detailed windows of the service zone provide an important counterpoint to the deep reveals that characterize the windows of the served zones. The dramatic interplay of the glazing of the served zones, detailed so that the glass is set to within an inch of the exterior surface, and the deeply inset shutters, set 15 inches from the glass, can best be appreciated during summer from the southeast, especially at dusk, when the warmer weather allows for the shutters to be fully opened (fig. 189).

For Kahn, it was the interplay of natural light, the change of mood brought as the sun emerges from the obscurity of clouds, or the nature of light revealed as one season yields to another that gave the Esherick house an "alive look at all times." Nowhere is this better seen than in the living room: the high, horizontal window facing northwest catches the brilliant sunsets of late summer; the floor-to-ceiling glass to the

Fig. 184 First- and second-floor plans. Albert J. Webb, dated November 2, 1960. Kahn Collection

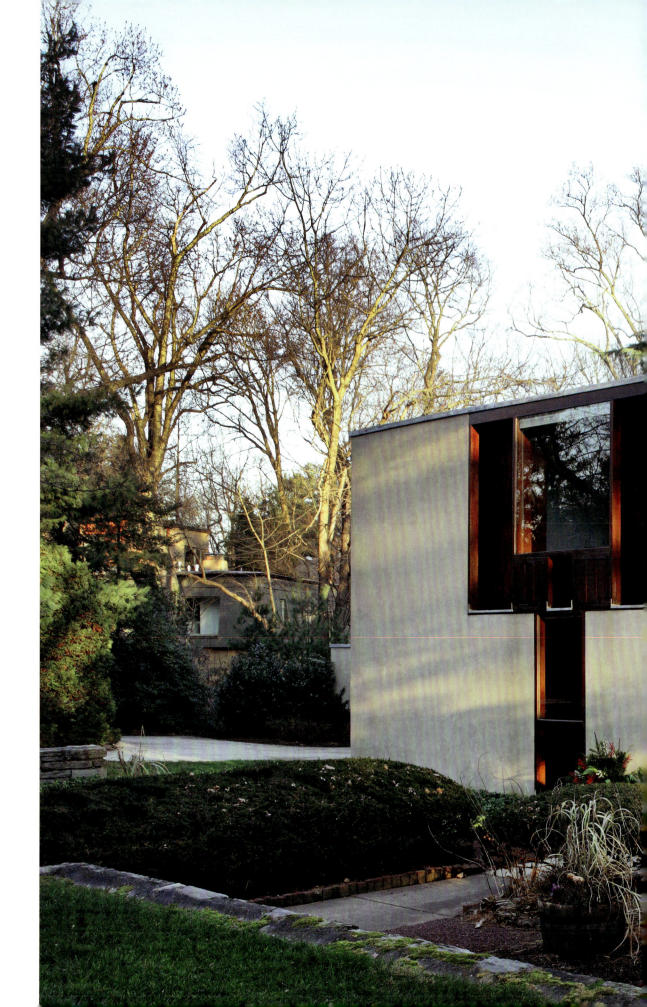

Fig. 185 From west. Photograph December 2011

Fig. 186　From northwest. Photograph 1990

Fig. 187　Railing. Photograph December 2011

Fig. 188 From north. Photograph December 2011

ESHERICK HOUSE 183

Fig. 189 From southeast. Photograph 2008

Fig. 190 Living room, with inset shutters open. Photograph December 2011

southeast captures the long rays of winter sun; and the strong vertical window above the Virginia soapstone fireplace, facing southwest (see frontispiece), permits a slice of light to traverse the long dimension of the room (figs. 190, 191).

When the construction drawings were given to the contractor in November 1960, most of the interior woodwork and fittings were excluded from the job. The list of not-in-contract items on the sheet of revised drawings begins with this note: "It is intended that Wharton Esherick—sculptor and cabinetmaker will make & install N.I.C. items #1 to #4 inclusive." These included the panel wall in front of the stairs in the living room and the gallery above, and the railings (the stairs themselves were in the contract); kitchen and laundry cabinets; sliding cabinets and shelves in the bedroom and study; and the sliding seat that would cover the bath tub next to the fireplace.[16] Not all of this was completed by Esherick, and his hand can be seen in only two of these elements, the stairway and the kitchen. Little information remains about the interaction between Kahn and Esherick on this job, and what occurred to limit the extent of the cabinetmaker's involvement. It is evident that Esherick had begun to work on the stairway, for it was he who had introduced the large, rough-sawn oak beam that supports the gallery above the living room.[17] There must have been some dispute, however, for a note of March 1961 told the contractor to "stop all work on stairway to 2nd floor until further notice."[18] Joseph Esherick commented later on a possible reason: "Lou's design didn't leave Wharton a lot of scope. The stair is just a stair, bloomp, like that, right straight up the stairs to the second floor—no room for Wharton's love for movement or the unexpected."[19]

Esherick never returned to the stairway and Kahn was left with the incongruous 6-by-12-inch oak beam, distinctly cambered and slightly warped, as Esherick's design preferences surely would have dictated. Kahn's plans for the stairway and railings, which were not completed until October 1961, after Margaret had moved in, returned to the general scheme that had been used as a placeholder in the revised construction drawings of November 1960 (fig. 192). As detailed, the stair screen and balcony rail were built of large-

Fig. 191 Living room and balcony. Photograph December 2011

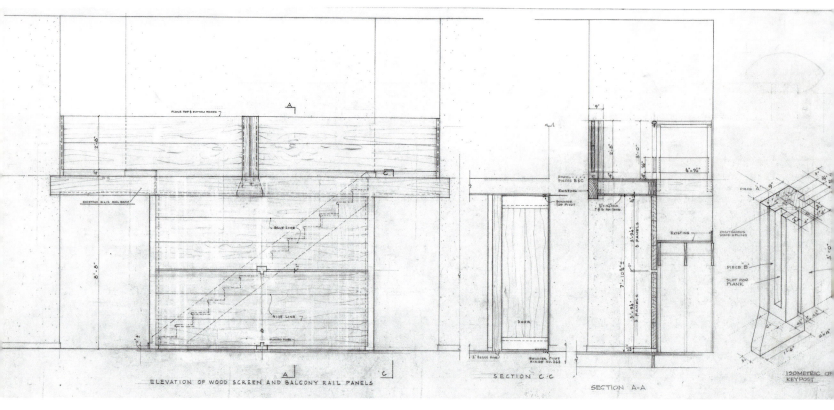

Fig. 192 Details for wood screen, balcony rail, and key post. Dated June 2, 1961. Kahn Collection

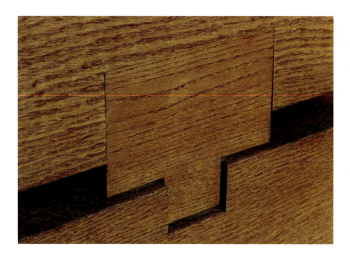

Fig. 193 Oak key. Photograph December 2011

dimension white-oak planks measuring 3 by 16 inches in section, beautifully planed to reveal the natural wood grain; their crisp corners and intricate joinery were more in keeping with Kahn's own design preferences. The overall composition is that of a T comprising two pairs of planks for the balcony rail, each 9 foot, 6 inches in length, connected at the middle by an intricate key post. Below, the stair screen comprises two sets of three planks, bisected horizontally by a two-inch void. The screen is subtly offset to afford a more gracious opening between the entry hall and living room. That shift is marked by a pair of intriguing elements, oak keys shaped, like the overall composition, in a T form (fig. 193). Construction of these parts (along with the pullout seat over the bath and the extensive shoe rack in the closet) continued into 1962.[20] Kahn's detailing of material here distinguished for the first time in his house designs those elements intended to be touched by the hand, such as a balustrade or a built-in desk, from those that used the mediation of metal hardware, such as windows and doors (fig. 194).

188 ESHERICK HOUSE

Fig. 194 Living room, with inset shutters open. Photograph December 2011

A second incongruity that would similarly disturb the concentrated formality of Kahn's interior was Esherick's kitchen, a tour de force of undulating counters, organic craftsmanship, and well-considered utility (fig. 195). This bold act of expressiveness could not have set well with Kahn, and the recollections of the subsequent owner of the house support this: "Louis Kahn visited us here many, many times. But he would always avoid the kitchen. Either ignore it completely, or walk through it muttering to himself."[21]

Upstairs, overlooking the living room, is a generous balcony, its solid rail in stark contrast to the delicacy and openness of the sculpted handrail of the staircase, with its bronze support (fig. 196). The bedroom looks out onto the garden and Pastorius Park beyond, providing, through a variety of operable shutters, a sense of changing qualities of light and nature (fig. 197). While Kahn acquiesced to Margaret's request for a bath adjacent to a fireplace, he made a provision for a pullout seat that would cover the bath when it was not in use (see fig. 80).

The Esherick house was published almost immediately. Ezra Stoller, the East Coast architectural photographer of choice, photographed the exterior in the summer of 1962, and his images appeared in *House and Garden* in October and *Architecture d'Aujourd'hui* in December.[22] Robert Lautman's photographs taken for *Architectural Record* later that year remained unpublished, however, owing to the "poor" condition of the house and especially the grounds (see fig. 82).[23] Following Margaret Esherick's death, the house remained

Fig. 195 Kitchen. Designed and made by Wharton Esherick. Photograph 2010

Fig. 196 Balcony and stair rails. Photograph December 2011

vacant for over two years, and Kahn had little or no input into the development of the landscape by the house's second owners, Burnap and Ann Post. When Vincent Scully reviewed Kahn's newest buildings in *Architectural Forum* in 1964, he illustrated the house and provided in his caption its first critical appreciation. He zeroed in on the distinctive windows, which, he rhapsodized, "can fill a volume up to the rim with light, so that the house is a cup, high-shouldered to contain air like a substance—a brimming chalice of light" (fig. 198).[24]

Fig. 197 Master bedroom, with inset shutters open. Photograph December 2011

Fig. 198 From southeast. Photograph 2008

NORMAN AND DORIS
FISHER HOUSE
HATBORO, 1960–67

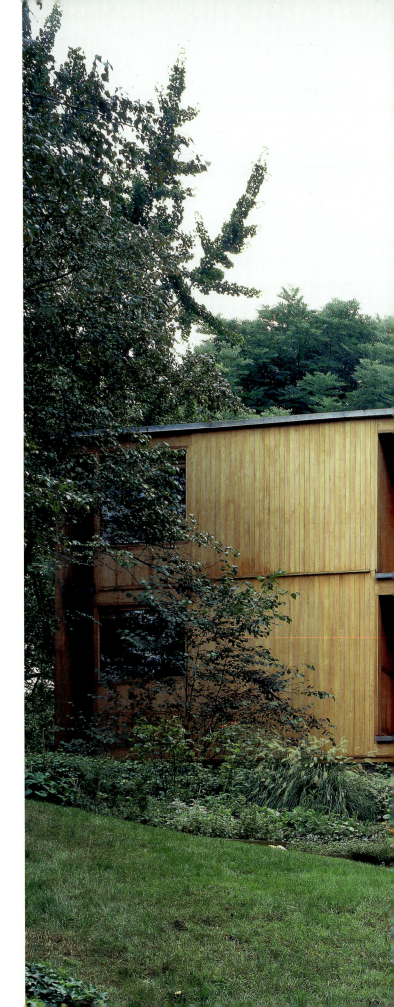

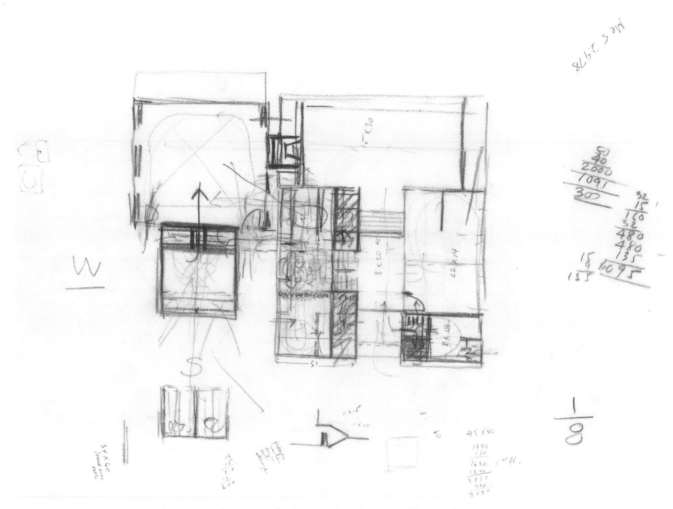

Fig. 200 First-floor plan. Louis Kahn, c. September 1960. Collection of Doris and Norman Fisher Family

In 1957, with the goal of building a new house for themselves and their two daughters, Norman and Doris Fisher purchased a 1½-acre lot bisected by the picturesque Pennypack Creek in Hatboro, a small municipality in southern Montgomery County.[1] This was just three blocks from the house they were living in, where Norman also had his medical office. The Fishers, who had met on a blind date, were married in 1953. Both had been born and raised in Philadelphia, Norman in the predominantly Jewish neighborhood of Oak Lane in North Philadelphia, and Doris, daughter of a sporting equipment manufacturer, in the Wynnefield section of the city, just across the city line from the affluent suburb of Lower Merion.[2]

Having earlier sought out contemporary furnishings, the Fishers would certainly have wanted to build a modern house, but they were not familiar with any architects and had to turn to the telephone directories to find them. They interviewed several before reaching Kahn, including the Philadelphia firm Geddes Brecher Qualls Cunningham. Intrigued by a reference to Kahn during an interview, they decided to pursue him although they knew nothing of his work. With the help of the Yellow Pages, they contacted him directly and hit it off immediately.[3] Assured by the architect's "intellect, energy, humor and warmth,"[4] and especially by his engaging discussions of their needs, they signed a contract on August 23, 1960.[5] Owing in part to Kahn's engagement with the Salk Institute, as well as his commissions in south Asia, the Fishers would persevere through long periods when the design process came to a "standstill." It would take nearly seven years

Fig. 199 Norman and Doris Fisher House, Hatboro, 1960–67. From east. Photograph 1990

Fig. 201 Section through inglenook. Louis Kahn, c. October 1960. Collection of Doris and Norman Fisher Family

before the family moved into the house on June 14, 1967, with four years having been spent on design and almost three years in construction (fig. 199).

Kahn produced four distinct schemes for the house. His earliest known study, probably done in September 1960,[6] set the private functions, including the bedrooms, kitchen, bathrooms, and an office for Dr. Fisher, in a unified, two-story volume; this was bisected by an entry hall that led, on axis, to a high-ceilinged, 15-by-30-foot living room (fig. 200). The principal walls of the living room were bound on the north by a broad window wall oriented toward a wooded landscape and on the west by a large stone fireplace. Beyond the fireplace was the initial form of an extraordinary, large dining area, the walls of which, suggested by the heavy double lines, were to be built of stone.

By October 20, Kahn had refined the scheme, setting the dining area within a tighter volume measuring 16 by 20 feet in plan and 16 feet high. The inglenook, as he would come to call this area, now contained a monumental fireplace (the only fireplace in the house), an adjacent seating area, as well as a dining table set in front of a large window (fig. 201). The house had a tripartite arrangement that was clearly defined on the exterior: the stone inglenook in the foreground, distinguished by a niche for wood or sculpture; the living room protruding to the left, matching the inglenook in height, but with a suggestion of strong vertical fenestration facing northward toward the woods; and a two-story volume to the right, accommodating the kitchen and the private functions (fig. 202). These last two volumes would have been built of wood, indicated by the vertical lines that suggest tongue-and-groove siding. The plan, however, was difficult to resolve to the site. Chief among the problems, from the point of view of the clients, was the fact that all the bedrooms faced the side yard with the adjacent house being visible through

FISHER HOUSE

the trees, the result of setting the long axis of the plan perpendicular to the grade (in his next scheme, Kahn would turn that axis). This preliminary scheme did, however, establish working principles for the design: living and dining functions were to be distinguished from private functions and stone was to be used as an expressive element to designate the center of the house.

Kahn's second scheme, begun during the winter of 1960–61, was first presented in a meeting with the Fishers on March 25, 1961, and then developed over the coming months, culminating in a set of drawings that were completed in August.[7] Kahn realigned the principal elements of the house into a linear arrangement parallel to the slope of the land, with private areas situated six steps above the living room, kitchen, and utility areas (fig. 203). The inglenook remained, and a substantial paved terrace now augmented it outside. Generous views from the bedrooms were afforded, and the plan was further articulated by the addition of alcoves that provided areas for relaxation or study in the master bedroom and living room. These alcoves were developed further as Kahn studied the elevations (fig. 204). Here, the architect's sense for the drama of changing light began to come into focus, with Kahn favoring "a lot of little exciting vistas," Norman recalled, not a large expanse of windows.[8]

The developed second scheme was presented in August in a set of five carefully detailed drawings by Kahn's staff, as well as three lively elevation studies by the architect himself. These drawings resolved issues related to topography and reasserted the significance of the inglenook. The complex entry sequence of the earlier plan for this scheme, necessitated by the split-level arrangement of the private and living areas, was simplified, bringing the entrance and living room onto an equal level (see fig. 85). More importantly, the roof levels were unified, shown in an elevation of August 1961 (see fig. 86). This established the clarity, and significance, of the inglenook as the dominant element of the house, enlivened by the narrowing of the upper walls and the deep-set openings. Further distinction was added to the interior by the

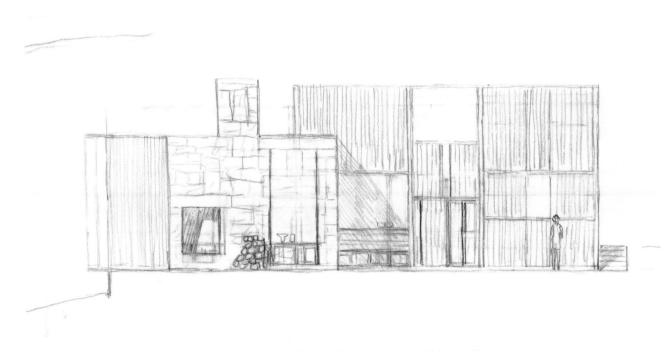

Fig. 202 Northwest elevation. Louis Kahn, c. October 1960. Collection of Doris and Norman Fisher Family

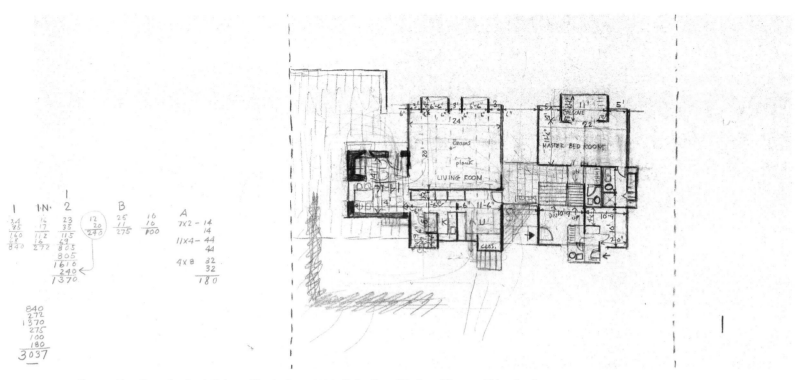

Fig. 203 First-floor plan. Louis Kahn, c. March–August 1961. Collection of Doris and Norman Fisher Family

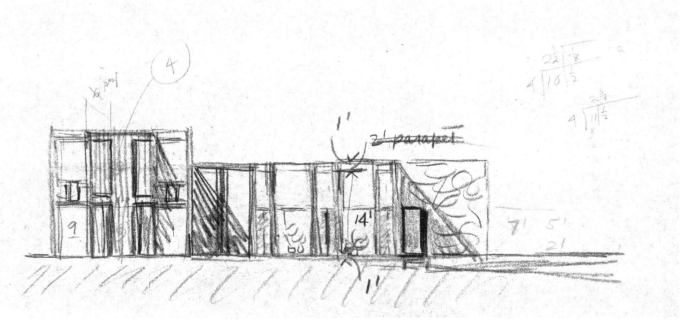

Fig. 204 Northeast elevation. Louis Kahn, c. March–August 1961. Collection of Doris and Norman Fisher Family

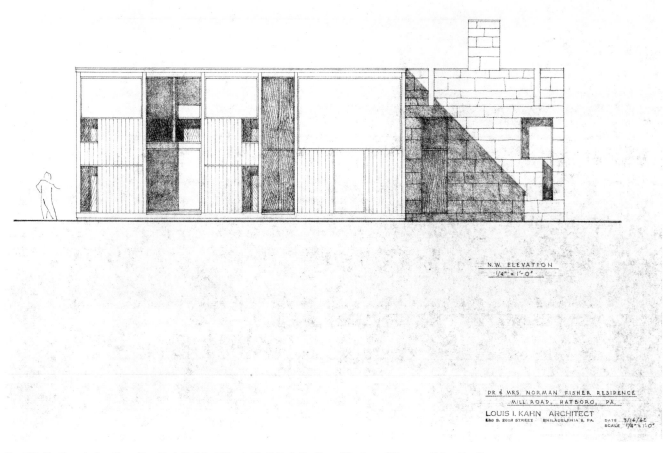

Fig. 205   Northeast elevation. Alan Hartell, dated March 16, 1962. Collection of Doris and Norman Fisher Family

explicitness of the structural system, with all columns, beams, and decking left exposed. As a sign of the times, a bomb shelter, to be housed in the lower level of the inglenook, was added to the plan.

During the winter of 1961–62, cost considerations seem to have come to the fore, necessitating a significant revision to the design.[9] In the third scheme the overall square footage of the August plan was reduced by 20 percent (from 3,000 square feet to 2,400 square feet), although the dimensions and mass of the inglenook increased by 25 percent. While certain progress had been made, much of the refinement of the previous design was lost, most noticeably in elevation, where the level change between the private and living areas, as well as the distinctive expression of the entry area, was eliminated (fig. 205). The entry lost the view to the delightful landscape, and the living room, reduced in size, its clarity of fenestration (fig. 206). Perhaps the only element strengthened in its design was the inglenook, now cylindrical within, its archaic, thick-walled, castlelike expression adding a romantic touch to the house.

More than a year would pass before Kahn had the opportunity to focus once again on the design, and perhaps in an effort to urge Kahn to carry on, Norman visited the office in December 1962.[10] Kahn, who was just back from his first trip to India, made a good-faith effort to demonstrate his commitment to the Fishers by assigning their site and the house program to his master class at the University of Pennsylvania in the spring 1963 semester. Notes kept by David De Long, a

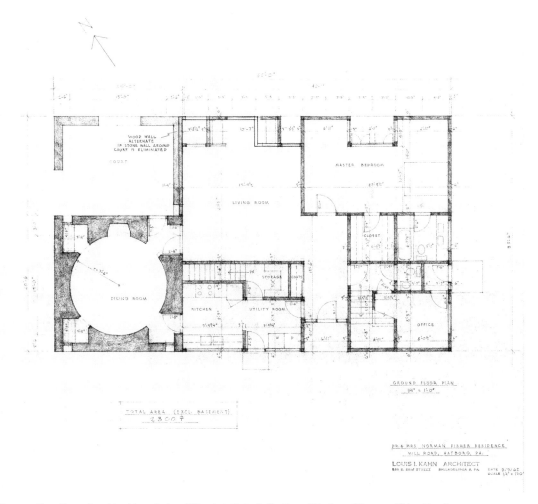

Fig. 206 First-floor plan. Alan Hartell, dated March 9, 1962. Collection of Doris and Norman Fisher Family

student in the class, state the problem as it was presented: "To discover from [the] sense of living today what these rooms really are" and to "eliminate artificial charm and pretentiousness." The couple "love stone—would like a fireplace," Kahn added. Although the Fishers never veered from their budget of $50,000, Kahn gave his students a figure of $75,000, probably realizing at this point that his own designs had already greatly exceeded the budgeted amounts.[11] None of the student work is known to have influenced Kahn's next design for the house, which would be a radical departure from his three previous schemes.

The fourth scheme, while in stark contrast to scheme two, recaptured its spirit, returning to the working principles by which Kahn sought both to elevate the living functions and to distinguish them from the private functions of the house. Meeting on June 2, 1963, Kahn presented the Fishers with a set of three drawings.[12] The elevation featured a three-story volume of stone, with a series of sharply tapered openings punctuating the massive walls (fig. 207). To the left, cast partly in shadow, is a second volume of wood construction, which is suggested by means of Kahn's own lively rendering technique. The remarkable plan with two obliquely set "cubes" reveals the inherent duality of the scheme, capturing both the singularity and interdependence of the constituent parts (fig. 208). The cubes are of identical dimensions, 32 by 27 feet. Situated in the cube to the north are the double-height living spaces, including the dining area and kitchen (with an open loft area above); in the cube to the south,

Fig. 207   Northeast elevation, c. June 1963. Diazo-type print of lost original. Collection of Doris and Norman Fisher Family

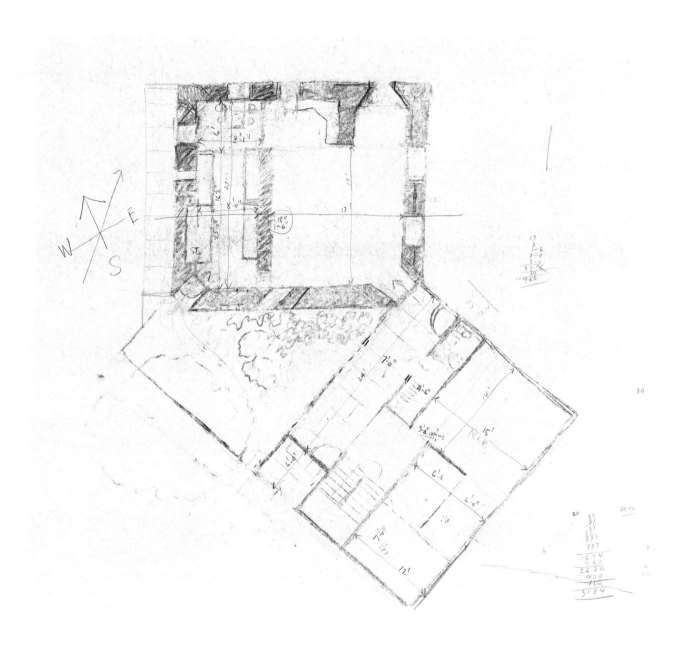

Fig. 208 First-floor plan. Louis Kahn, c. June 1963. Diazo-type print of lost original. Collection of Doris and Norman Fisher Family

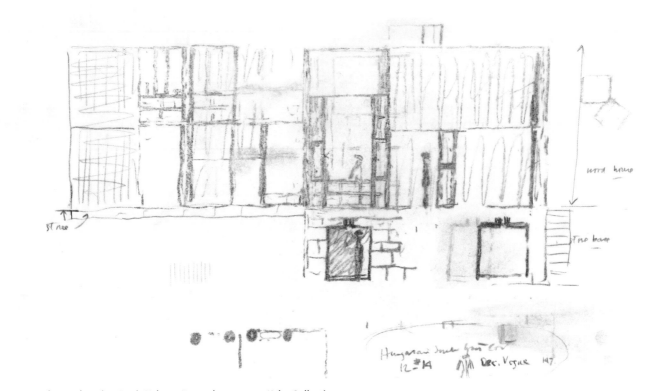

Fig. 209 Northeast elevation. Louis Kahn, c. December 20, 1963. Kahn Collection

angled to the first cube as well as to the street, are the bedrooms and baths (on two levels), and, along its northern edge, the entry hall.

With Kahn traveling much of the summer of 1963, progress again came to a standstill. By September 20, however, the Fishers had received a drafted set of plans, and following an intensive period of design development, a set of eight drawings was completed for presentation to the clients at a meeting held at Kahn's office on October 22.[13] With only minor changes needed to improve the layout of the bedroom areas, the drawings were submitted for cost estimation. The Fishers, who must by then have been very eager to move ahead, were in for a shock; the cost had ballooned to $250,000, over five times their budget.[14]

Kahn, who now also must have been embarrassed by the figures, quickly returned to the drafting room. A revision to the scheme, which Kahn hoped was the last, was sent to the Fishers on December 23, 1963, shortly after he departed for a three-week trip to the Indian subcontinent. Noting that he "must leave momentarily," Kahn hastily penciled: "We did all we could to meet the limit of $50,000. I reduced even more . . . so I believe [it] is good now. . . . Will keep in touch if I can at all."[15] A set of three drawings, folded up for mailing, was evidently the basis for a meeting after Kahn's return, on January 29, 1964.[16] In what Kahn now characterized as "a wood house on a stone plinth,"[17] the revised design reduced the floor area by 35 percent (the cubes were now of different dimensions, the one to the north, 28 feet, 6 inches by 23 feet, 6 inches, and that to the south, 25 feet, 6 inches square) and the expensive stone walls from three stories to one, the "stone plinth" (fig. 209). The inglenook was substantially reduced in size and scope but retained its essence as the center of family life. Kahn transformed it from stone enclosing walls into a freestanding stone mass; faceted at first and then refined as this scheme was developed, it took a semicircular form that was set obliquely within the interior, functionally

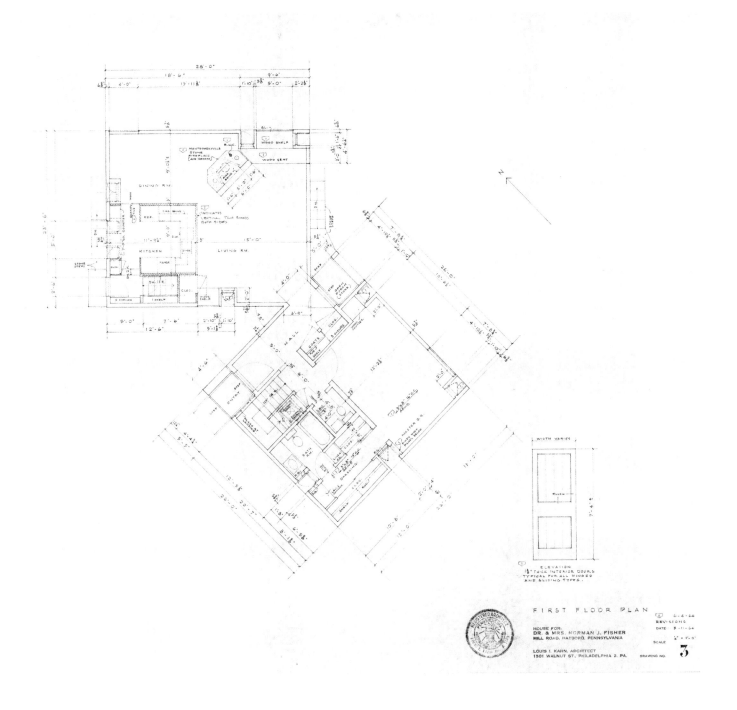

Fig. 210 First-floor plan (prior to revisions to shape and location of fireplace, and elimination of porch and inset window in kitchen). Albert J. Webb, dated June 4, 1964. Collection of Doris and Norman Fisher Family

FISHER HOUSE

housing the fireplace and flues for the mechanical systems (fig. 210; see fig. 87). For the first time since the initial sketches of September 1960, the fireplace was oriented to the living room. In a final set of gestures, Kahn fine-tuned the relationship between the fireplace and the built-in window seat while also extending the height of the stone mass above the rooftop to a height of 8 feet, 6 inches to emphasize the importance of this element by making it visible from the street. He also moved the connecting point of the two cubes 5 feet inward to incorporate a "porch" entry for direct access to a lower terrace area (this would eventually be eliminated). Kahn rejected a proposed use of vertical boards for the kitchen enclosure, saying he did not "want it to look like the exterior walls," and suggested, instead, "regular panels with stiles and rails." This too was revised due to cost, and the walls would be surfaced instead in plaster on both sides. With these changes the design had indeed taken its final form. The

Fig. 211 Louis Kahn with Carl Saldutti, masonry contractor. Photograph November 17, 1964. AAUP, by the gift of Norman and Doris Fisher

Fig. 212 Completed foundation. Photograph July 1965, showing stone lintels over porticos at far end (later removed). AAUP, by the gift of Norman and Doris Fisher

Fishers quickly approved the design, and working drawings were completed by early fall.[18]

Bids were taken in September, and a contract was signed with the builder, E. Arol Fesmire, on October 24, 1964. Construction began shortly thereafter.[19] Kahn chose local "Montgomeryville" stone, a reddish-brown sandstone that had been used throughout the area since the early eighteenth century and surely a familiar material for the masons. He specified that face stones would be laid in "units as large as possible (For two man setting)"[20] and that individual stones, following the pattern he established at the Weiss house, were "not to be dressed but ... [laid up] in a rough selected way. [The wall] must be rugged but not grotesque."[21] Mortar joints were to be deeply raked, so that each stone would stand alone, with every effort made to expose the weathered surface and to avoid the display of cut marks. Clearly Kahn had high expectations for this work, and he made at least five inspection trips to ensure proper execution, even demanding at one point that a section of stone wall be torn down and rebuilt as the layout had become too irregular (fig. 211).[22] Foundation work was completed by July 1965 (fig. 212), and following the initial purchase of lumber and millwork in September the house was framed up, with the sheathing and roofing work completed by the end of the year.[23] The detailing of the windows, comprising 6-by-6-inch jambs and 4-by-6-inch headers of cypress, required prefabrication and erection prior to wall framing to facilitate the proper alignment of interior and exterior finishes.

Several notable changes were made to the design on site, including the elimination of an inset window positioned to allow ventilation in the kitchen and dining area, which is shown partly installed, at bottom left, in a photograph taken by Norman Fisher (fig. 213). This was, apparently, one element too many in an already congested space. Difficulties in the sourcing and selection of materials required other changes, including the elimination of the stone lintels over openings on the northeast façade because of the "unpredictable splitting" of the Montgomeryville stone in the large sizes specified, 7 to 9 feet in length and 17 inches deep.[24] The resulting openings would have measured 5 feet wide by 6 feet high. More significant, perhaps, was the shortening of the chimney, contrary to Kahn's wishes, from a height of 8 feet, 6 inches above the roof to a height of approximately 18 inches, which made it largely invisible (fig. 214).[25] This decision was most likely

Fig. 213 Inset window frame from northwest, c. December 1965 (removed during construction). AAUP, by the gift of Norman and Doris Fisher

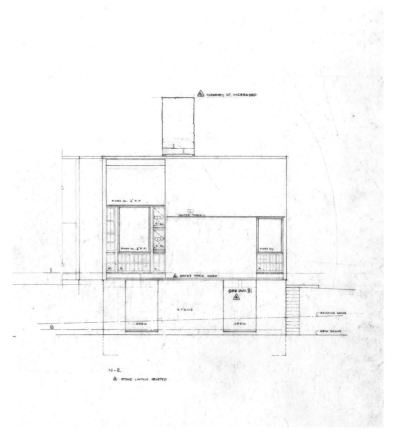

Fig. 214 Northeast elevation. Albert J. Webb, dated May 11, 1964, revised June 18, 1965, showing Kahn's preferred height for chimney. Kahn Collection

driven by cost concerns, but the change would blunt the sharp clarity between wood and stone and obscure the centrality of the chimney in the design.

With the house enclosed (fig. 215), electrical, plumbing, and the extensive environmental systems were installed through the winter and continued into the early summer of 1966, and insulation work was completed by June.[26] The distinctive rough wall surfaces of the interior, inspired by what Norman described as a "primitive plaster similar to what was seen in the earlier years of the country," took extensive trial and error to replicate.[27] In the end a cheap plastic trowel did the trick. The painstaking labor of the interior millwork and trim, detailed to follow traditional examples, occupied the contractors through the end of 1966, along with the completion of the kitchen cabinetry and bathrooms (with rift-sawn-oak base cabinets and clear black Pennsylvania slate tops in honed finish).[28] Fesmire's final billing, dated July 11, 1967, enumerated a contract price of $53,667.51 plus $6,399.61 in extras for a total construction cost of $60,067.12.[29]

Almost immediately after moving in, the Fishers realized that the dining area was not satisfactory and persuaded Kahn to replace the narrow, offset window there with a larger, 8-by-10-foot window, allowing a view of the creek and woodland beyond (figs. 216, 217). Kahn must have envisioned the family gathered around the dining table, focused inward in animated conversation, but his ideal broke down with reality, with the simple fact that on weekday afternoons, Doris often ate alone—an observation that architect and clients had both overlooked. In the end, Kahn was happy with the change.[30]

On arriving at the house, one sees the bedroom volume first, skewed at a 45-degree angle to the street (fig. 218). Deep reveals provide shelter for operable window units and, at the entry, a porch area (fig. 219). Horizontal string courses, aligned according to logic of the fenestration, protect the tongue-and-groove cypress siding and provide a solution to the clumsiness of the end-to-end joining of standard 8- to 10-foot stock lengths. Lead-coated copper forms the roof soffit as well as the drip pans at the bottom of the deep reveals. From the terrace below, which is accessed through a pair of openings in the monumental stone walls or from an exterior stairway, one can see the full material palette of the house, including the cypress siding and the Montgomeryville stone, as well as the cabinetlike quality of the woodwork (fig. 220). Beyond the kitchen, with its distinctive window unit, is a

Fig. 215 From northeast, showing coloration of unfinished cypress siding. Photograph February 1966. AAUP

Fig. 216 From northwest, prior to installation of large window in dining area. Photograph February 1966. AAUP

Fig. 217 From northeast, after installation of large window in dining area. Photograph 1990

Fig. 218 Bedroom block from southwest. Photograph 1990

Fig. 219 Entry, with front door open, from west. Photograph 1990

Fig. 221 Kitchen window from northwest. Photograph 1990

textures for natural light to strike upon, giving the interior a "beautiful patina."³² The set piece of the fireplace, window, and seat is among Kahn's most memorable accomplishments (see fig. 1), capturing, in the precision of the wood joinery, the power of the stonework and the delicacy of the light, a "structure" of transcendent quality. Kahn specified oak, a traditional and durable material, for the window seat, stairs, and floors (and for the built-in desks in the three bedrooms). The window seat, which provides an exciting series of vistas both inside and out, is cantilevered out on continuous 2⅝-inch-wide planks (fig. 226), detailed to incorporate an armrest on the left side.

Over the years that they lived in the house the Fishers confronted issues related to its long-term preservation. Kahn's preference for allowing the exterior wood siding to weather naturally, or silver, with age was thoughtfully reexamined. Beginning about 1980, the Fishers began to experiment with surface finishes, adding both preservatives and

small utility building designed to hide, within the inverted slope of the roof (suggested by the V-shaped water table), the air conditioning condenser and, on one of the sides, the utility meters (figs. 221, 222).³¹

Under the cover of the porch, a window offers a surprising view of the stair hall and oak balustrade within, an expression of Kahn's dictum that all rooms must have some natural light (fig. 223). Inside, as one passes through the skewed joining of the cubes, the duality of the plan is dramatically revealed (figs. 224, 225). The unusually narrow red-oak flooring (just 1½ inches wide) used throughout the house and the rough plasterwork provide richly varied surfaces and

Fig. 220 Living block from north. Photograph 1990

Fig. 222 Utility shed from northeast. Photograph 1990

Fig. 223   Interior staircase from entry portico. Photograph 1990

Fig. 224 Living room from entry hall. Photograph 1990

Fig. 225 Living room. Photograph September 1977

colorants to the exterior wood. The distinctive, warm coloration of the house, falsely associated by many as a hallmark of Kahn's residential designs, was the result of the Fishers' experiments, perhaps a necessity given the cabinetlike quality of the exterior woodwork.[33]

In 1998, Norman and Doris Fisher ensured the long-term preservation of the structure through restrictive easements. "Our original hope," the couple wrote, "was to build a special home for ourselves, not a museum or a monument. Living in a Kahn house you didn't have a choice. Because of that, we have given our home to the National Trust for Historic Preservation with the hope it will be preserved unchanged for future architectural students, architects and historians to study . . . [and] that others may share in the discoveries that abound here."[34] Norman died in 2007, and Doris left the house the following year, moving closer to her younger daughter. The house transferred to the National Trust in 2012, and with proper covenants in place, it was returned to private ownership.

Fig. 226 Window seat. Photograph July 2011

STEVEN AND TOBY
KORMAN HOUSE

WHITEMARSH TOWNSHIP
MONTGOMERY COUNTY
1971–73

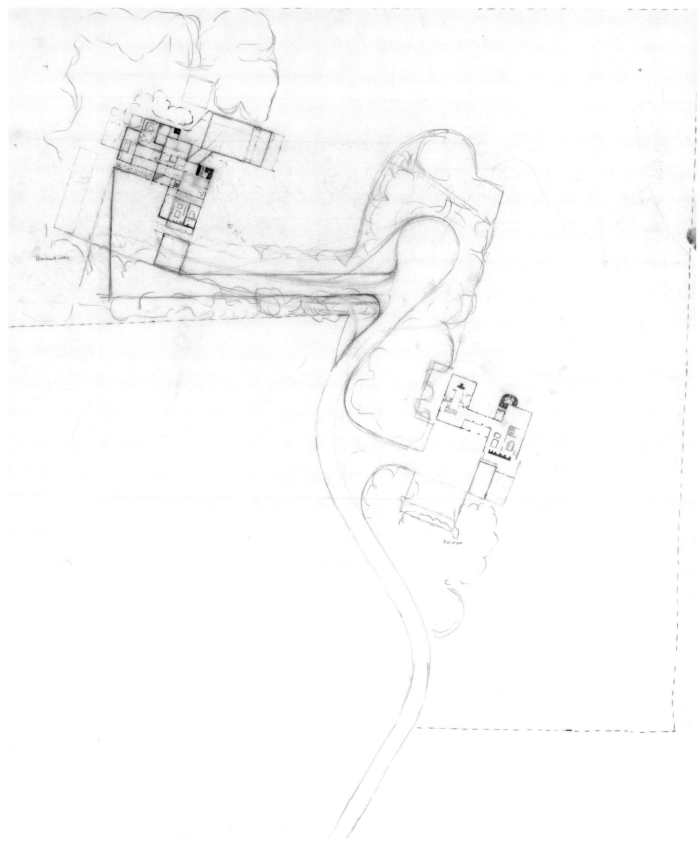

Fig. 228 Site plan. Dated July 30, 1971. Kahn Collection. Honickman house is at top left and Korman house at lower right

Fig. 227 Steven and Toby Korman House, Whitemarsh Township, 1971–73. From south. Photograph November 2011

The country house that Louis Kahn designed for Steven and Toby Korman in 1971–72 and completed in October 1973 was the last residential work he realized (fig. 227). Elegant and assured, the two-story brick and cypress structure was his largest house (with an area of over 6,500 square feet), and yet the design has all of the intimacy and surprise found in his more modest works. The house is situated on the flat open reaches of Whitemarsh Township, a landscape interlaced with pastures and wide bridle paths. Tucked into these rural surroundings are the estates of many old Philadelphia families and, as would be expected, some of the finest examples of residential design to be found in the region, including two that were formative to Kahn's approach: George Howe's Square Shadows (see fig. 32) and Kenneth Day's Philip Dechert house (1939–40). The Korman house extended and enriched this long tradition, and Kahn himself saw his design as "modern only in its attitude toward space."[1]

The Korman family had been in the residential construction business since 1909 and by the 1950s was competing against the legendary William Levitt in the great suburban expansion of that time.[2] By the late 1960s, when the third generation was assuming responsibilities for the business, its focus began to shift into a more diverse range of real-estate investments.[3] When the company's development proposal for a subdivision of luxury houses on the land was rejected by Whitemarsh Township, the family chose to create a compound for its own use, with each of the five Korman grandchildren receiving a property of approximately 4 acres.[4] Steven Korman and his sister Lynne Honickman chose adjoining properties at the end of the already built road while their cousins Berton Korman, Leonard Korman, and Judith Langsfeld selected plots along the drive (eventually, Judith chose not to build there). Berton and his brother Leonard were the first to build, choosing Hugh Newell Jacobson and Carl Massara as their architects.[5] Together, Lynne and Steven pursued Kahn to design their houses, with their first official meeting with him taking place on February 6, 1971; by May they had signed contracts with him.[6] The two houses were developed in parallel, with the two couples often meeting together with Kahn to review the designs as they evolved. Ultimately, however, the Honickmans decided not to proceed with their house, which had grown substantially larger in size and cost than its neighbor, although construction drawings were nearly completed at the time they pulled out in the spring of 1973. Steven, too, faced challenges; he recalled the "terrible fights" he had with Kahn over the architect's refined sense of detailing and his expectation that these elements would be assembled in a "flawless fit." In the end, however, he admitted that these were "two of the best and worst years of my life. . . . The simplicity was what made it so difficult."[7]

At Kahn's suggestion, the Kormans prepared a summary of their thinking on the project, which they titled, "The Korman Family: A New Home."[8] In its four pages they laid out what they had in mind for their house, providing details of their young family, consisting at the time of "three boys and a dog and a goldfish." They desired a house of glass, stone, and wood, materials that would give it a "light—bright—cheerful" feeling; ample storage so it would have an "uncluttered look"; and a master bedroom suite and a small den, "upstairs or down (for Steven's hideaway?)." They wanted "the boys' area to be clustered together" so that the parents could enjoy "privacy . . . away from the children." Summing up, the couple wrote, "We would love an easy-to-care-for, warm, hospitable, exciting, home to raise three boys." One additional requirement would prove significant: Steven's severe allergies demanded a contained air-handling system and limited the need for windows that opened.

Kahn presented his preliminary ideas on July 30, 1971, with a series of rough sketches on yellow tracing paper, including a site plan (fig. 228) that delineated the location of the existing road and cul-de-sac (at the center of the sheet) and the proposed locations and basic interior layout for the Honickman house (at top left) and the Korman house (at bottom right). For the Kormans, Kahn indicated that a grove of trees would be used to screen the approach to the house, culminating in a clearly defined forecourt. The program was contained within two principal volumes, with the children's areas located to the northwest and the living areas to the southeast. A sheltered entrance served as the connector between the two volumes, with a massive, semicircular, stone inglenook (indicated by the heavy poché drawing) anchoring the plan to the northeast, and a simpler, although equally massive, rectilinear chimney containing fireplaces for the dining area and master bedroom as well as grilling areas in the

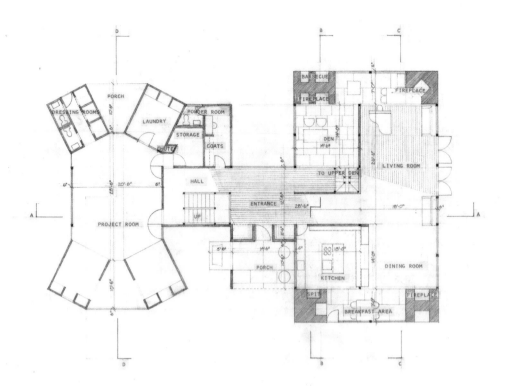

Fig. 229 First-floor plan. Dated March 11, 1972. Kahn Collection

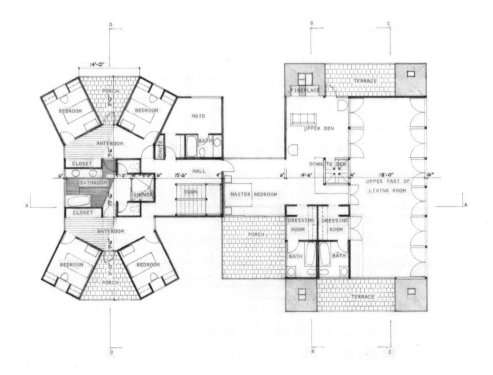

Fig. 230 Second-floor plan. Dated March 11, 1972. Kahn Collection

kitchen. The double-height living and dining area featured floor-to-ceiling glazing, oriented to the southeast to face a grove of proposed plantings.

This plan was refined over the next eight months, leading to a meeting on March 11, 1972, at Kahn's office, where the couple was presented with a set of twelve drawings for approval (figs. 229, 230).[9] While they were pleased with the progress, the Kormans rejected a number of elements of this scheme. What they mainly took issue with was the arrangement of the boys' rooms. Where Kahn saw clusters, the Kormans saw "factions,"[10] a revelation similar to Jonas Salk's realization that an early design for his institute in La Jolla, composed of two courts rather than one, would have a similar result.[11] Toby also had concerns over the location of the balcony openings on the upper den, seeing them as potential hazards given the playful roughhousing that father and sons frequently engaged in. An unexpressed concern, which was revealed only with the many revisions to come, was the orientation of the house. Large shutters, specified on the upper level of the living room windows, suggest this. The room's southeastern orientation would have resulted in excessive solar gain, which, compounded by the lack of ventilating windows, would have made the room uncomfortable during the summer months. (The final scheme would be oriented to the northeast.) Moreover, the suggested location of dressing rooms at the northwest corner of the house would have placed the swimming pool close to the cul-de-sac, raising issues of privacy.

By early June 1972, a new scheme was produced that addressed these concerns. At this moment Kahn brought in E. Arol Fesmire, the builder who had recently completed construction at the Fisher house, to consult on the matter of costs and construction, and he eventually became the general contractor for the job. Over the summer this scheme would be elaborated to include spacious walk-in closets and built-in study areas for each of the boy's rooms, as well as a double-height volume for the kitchen with an adjacent, spacious family dining room. Elevations were studied and refined, in particular that of the chimneys flanking the, now, northeast-facing façade, where large blocks of cut limestone were specified for the full height of 27 feet, 6 inches, but cost considerations would reduce much, if not all, of this elaboration (fig. 231). With that, the Kormans signed an agreement with Fesmire on October 12, 1972, and construction began shortly after.[12]

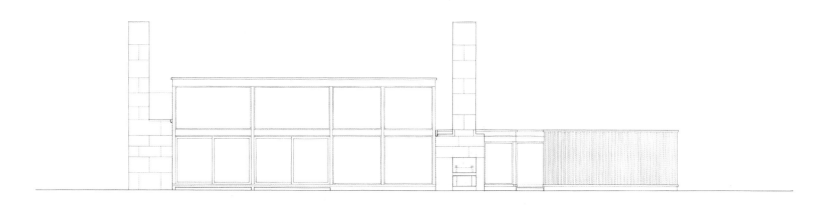

Fig. 231 Northeast elevation showing limestone chimneys. June 1972. Kahn Collection

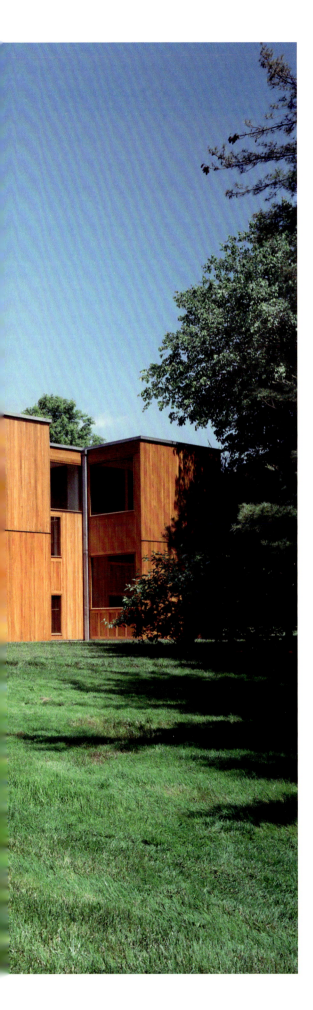

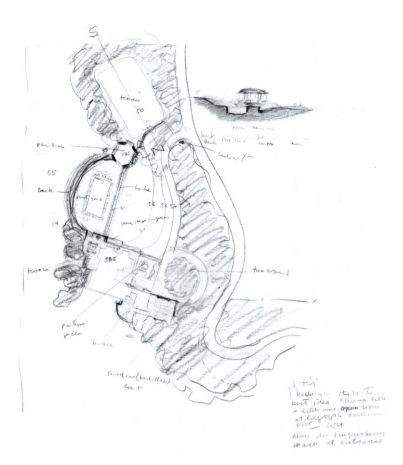

Fig. 232 Site plan study. Harriet Pattison, with notes by Louis Kahn, c. 1973. Kahn Collection

One approaches the house along a gently curving drive bound on one side by majestic pines and on the other by flowering cherry trees (fig. 232). Visitors arrive at a forecourt. Warm cypress siding and ample windows welcome visitors who, upon arrival, might see the family gathering for a meal in the prominent family dining room (fig. 233). A sheltered entry, as shown on the plans (figs. 234, 235), brings one to a pair of wood and glass doors that open into a generous entry hall. Turning to the left, one becomes aware of the principal living areas, walking past a mysterious oak-clad cabinet (containing a private staircase) into the living room. Here the view of the open landscape beyond is framed by columns of Douglas fir, affording a window of remarkably delicate elegance (fig. 236). The morning sun streams into this room, while in the evening the window above the dining area (screened by a partition wall) reveals the chimney ablaze with the light of the setting sun (fig. 237).

Fig. 233 From west. Photograph 2008

KORMAN HOUSE   227

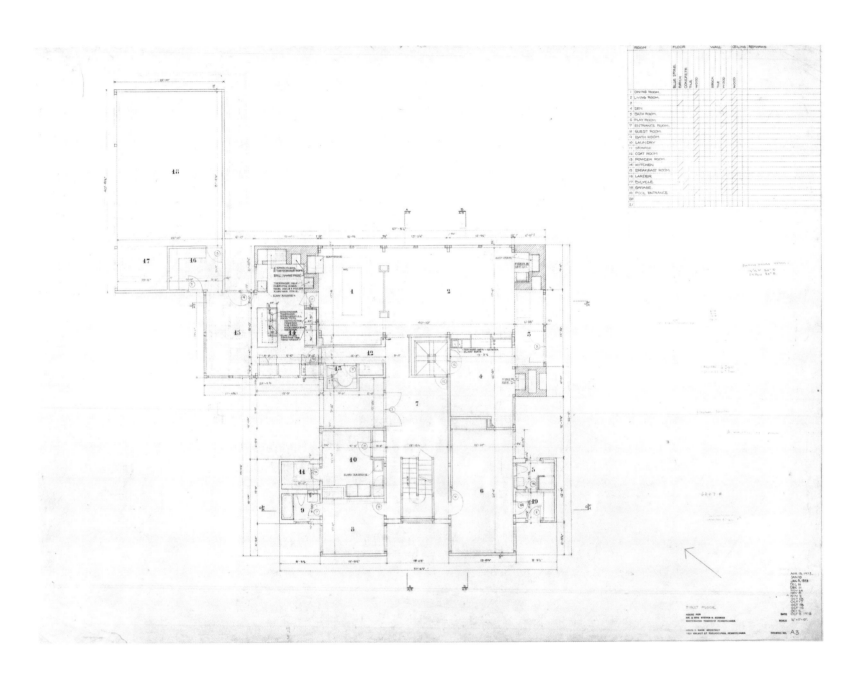

Fig. 234 First-floor plan. Dated October 3, 1972. Kahn Collection

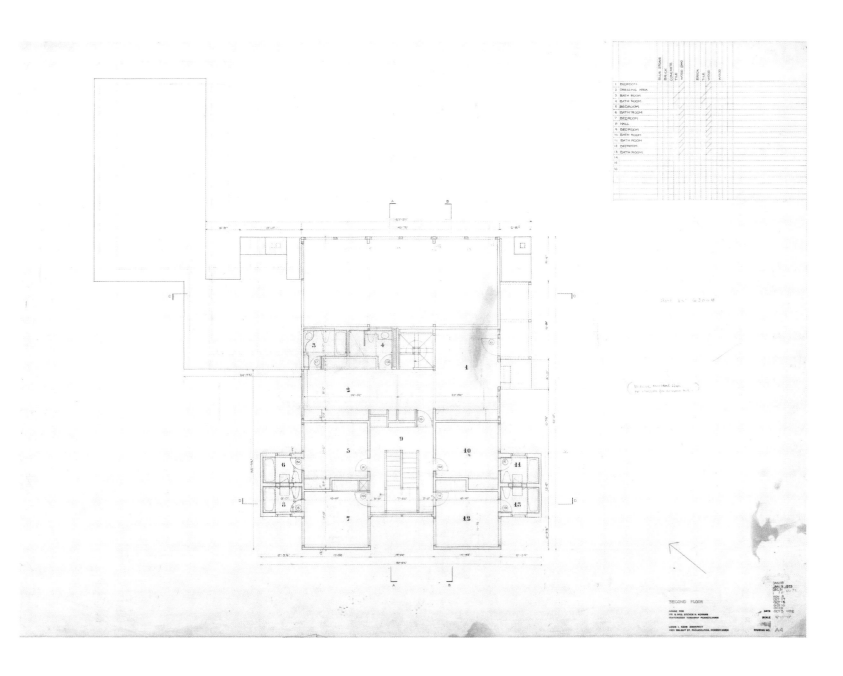

Fig. 235 Second-floor plan, dated October 3, 1972. Kahn Collection

KORMAN HOUSE　229

Fig. 236   Living room. Photograph 2008

Turning around to face the southeast one takes in the proportion of the room: 17 feet, 6 inches in both height and width, with three structural bays of 13 feet, 2½ inches each defining the room's length (fig. 238). The square proportions are further accented by the fireplace inglenook, which is offset to the left. A brick-paved loggia provides access to the exterior as well as to a secluded den (visible through cabinetry to the right). The inglenook and loggia area, itself 6 feet, 8 inches in width, is built of a brick that Kahn chose for its "very rich brown-red" color (fig. 239).[13] Alcoves provide places to sit by the fire and to store firewood, or perhaps to display a work of sculpture (fig. 240). Kahn specified that the mortar be raked with a grapevine joint, a pattern used extensively on Philadelphia's Colonial-period architecture. This technique, creating an indented line at the center of the joint, provides an irregular, somewhat rough line, which comes to life in changing light. The brick floor extends outside to the large terrace and is also used on the private terrace of the master bedroom above (fig. 241). On the exterior toward the pool and tennis court the clustered service areas of the bedrooms are revealed, with small windows, each surmounting a pair of shutters, the only ventilating windows in the house (fig. 242).

The entry hall includes a monumental staircase, which rises three stories from the basement (an area that included mechanical spaces and a small exercise room), to the first floor (with a playroom to the left and laundry and guest rooms to the right), to the second-floor bedrooms, the resulting hall eliminating any concern the family may have had about "factions" (figs. 243, 244). The detailing of the staircase and balustrades provided an opportunity for Kahn to study and reinterpret traditional woodwork. The four bedrooms, one for each of the boys and one guest room, measure a modest 11 by 13 feet, although built-in cabinets, large windows, and private baths more than make up for this in luxury. The substantial master suite, spanning the full width of the house, includes a fireplace, study area for Toby, his and hers bathrooms, extensive built-in closets, an outdoor terrace for sunbathing, as well as the hidden staircase, allowing Steven direct access to his study (figs. 245, 246).

Like the loggia, the kitchen and family dining room are floored in brick (fig. 247), with the family dining room situated at an important nexus of the plan (fig. 248). Cooking areas were incorporated into the volume of the chimney, and oak cabinets were specified throughout. A door from the kitchen returned one to the exterior, out onto the open meadow beyond. From the northeast, the view back to the house reveals the living areas flanked by the chimneys, each different, and each very powerful (figs. 249, 250).

The house became the home of the Kormans' oldest son, Larry, and his family in 1998. Since that time, great effort has been expended on preserving the house and bringing to fruition aspects of Kahn's design intent for the landscape and interior features that could not be realized earlier.

Fig. 237   Dining room. Photograph 2008

Fig. 238 Living room and inglenook. Photograph 2008

Fig. 239 Inglenook. Photograph November 2011

Fig. 240 Vestibule to garden. Photograph November 2011

Fig. 241 From southeast. Photograph 2008

Fig. 242 Bedroom wing from south. Photograph November 2011

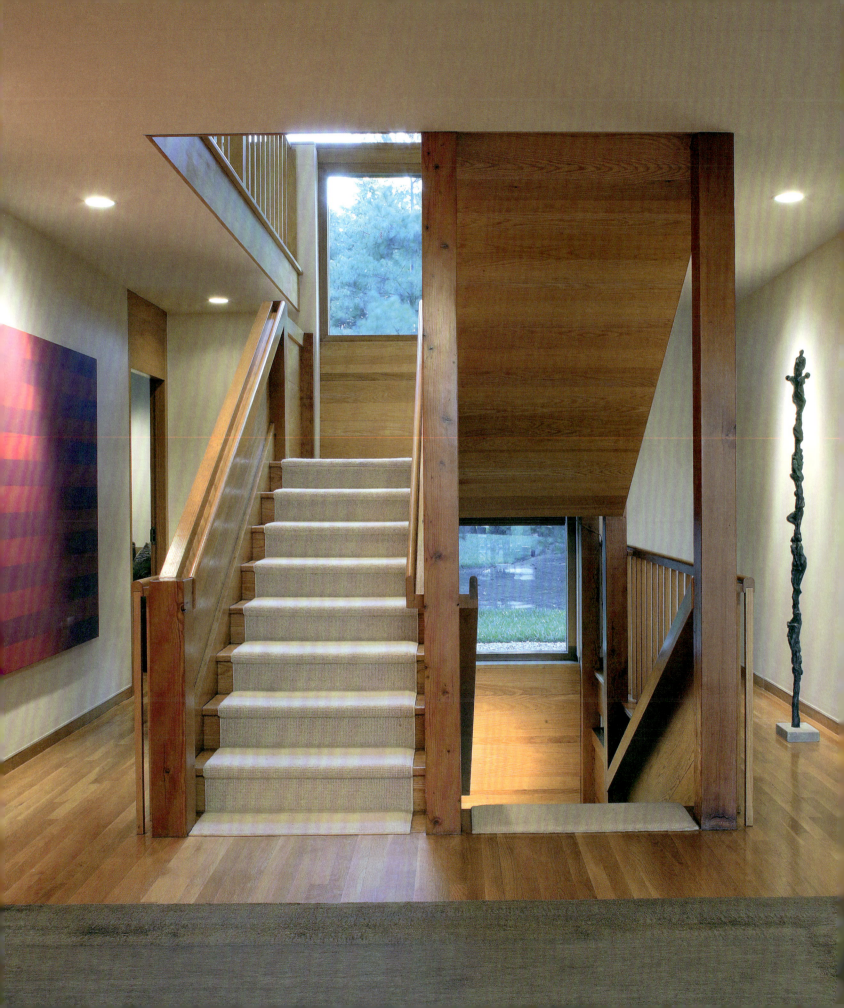

Fig. 243   Entry hall and staircase. Photograph 2008

Fig. 244 Second-floor hall. Photograph November 2011

Fig. 245 Master bedroom, with staircase to den. Photograph November 2011

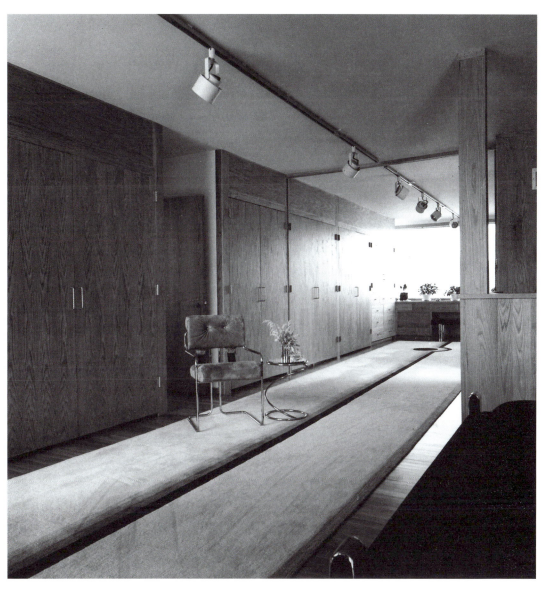

Fig. 246 Master bedroom dressing area. Photograph 1974. Kahn Collection

Fig. 247 Kitchen. Photograph 2008

Fig. 248 Family dining room. Photograph 1974. Kahn Collection

Fig. 250 From northeast. Photograph 1974. Kahn Collection

Fig. 249 From northeast. Photograph November 2011

NOTES

PROLOGUE
1. Scully, *Kahn,* 10.
2. David G. De Long, in Brownlee and De Long, *In the Realm,* 51–52.
3. Shanken, "Between Brotherhood and Bureaucracy," 150.
4. Inscription on medal, photograph, Kahn Collection, 030.IV.A. 960.1.
5. See Maniaque, "House, A House, Home"; Reed, "Louis I. Kahn"; Fisher, "Fisher House"; Saito, *Houses;* "Houses," *A + U.*
6. See Eisenman, "From Plaid Grid"; and Jarzombek, "Good-Life Modernism."
7. Brownlee and De Long, *In the Realm,* 304–417.
8. LIK, "Form and Design" [1960], in Twombly, *Essential Texts,* 64.

HOME
1. For a summary of the life of Louis Kahn (1901–1974), see Whitaker, "Chronology."
2. Kahn's romantic memories of the region were reinforced after spending a month there with his grandmother in July 1928, even though the Russian Revolution had brought hardship to the Baltic States; see "A Verbal Autobiography" [1973], in Wurman, *What Will Be,* 225, and Tyng, *Rome Letters,* 8, 15. Kahn's birthplace was identified by Susan Rose Behr, producer of the documentary *My Architect,* who located Leopold Kahn's Petition for Naturalization, dated January 29, 1915, in which the family name is Schmulowsky and the birthplace of his three children is listed as Pernow (Pernau), Leopold's last residence before emigration. Naturalization Petitions for the Eastern District of Pennsylvania, 1795–1930, M1522, 106 (roll 106), Petition No. 13973, National Archives, Washington, D.C. This was confirmed by Ingrid Mald-Villand of the Union of Estonian Architects, who found a record of Kahn's circumcision in the state archives of Latvia in 2006. This document also lists Kahn's birthplace as Pernow.
3. By the time of the family's arrival in Philadelphia on June 25, 1906, Leopold was already using Kahn as his surname, although it was misspelled as Kahan in the passenger manifest. The son is listed as Isidore in the manifest, but by the time he entered public school in 1907, he was known as Louis. Passenger Lists of Vessels Arriving at Philadelphia, Pennsylvania, 1883–1945, Micropublication T840, RG085, Rolls #1–181, National Archives, Washington, D.C.
4. LIK, Architects' Personal History and Professional Field Interview I, p. 1, Architect Assessment Project, summer 1958, Institute for Personality Assessment and Research, University of California, Berkeley (copy at AAUP). Records held in the archives of Philadelphia's Central High School, including his enrollment cards and transcripts, identify eleven addresses for the family from November 1907, when Kahn first enrolled in elementary school, to 1916, when he entered high school.
5. This was intended as an interim move because the couple hoped that after a year they would go abroad to study—Louis with Walter Gropius, and Esther, whose field was psychology, with Anna Freud; see EIK, interview [1982], in Latour, *L'Uomo,* 23.
6. City of Philadelphia, Department of Records, Deeds, EIK, July 11, 1963, D-2200–511. The deed is in Esther Kahn's name.
7. Kahn had a daughter, Sue Ann (born 1940), with his wife, Esther; a second daughter, Alexandra Tyng (born 1954), with Anne Tyng; and a son, Nathaniel Kahn (born 1962), with Harriet Pattison. Nathaniel Kahn dissected his father's unconventional family arrangements in his 2003 documentary *My Architect.* See also Tyng, *Rome Letters.*
8. Sue Ann Kahn, interview [1982], in Latour, *L'Uomo,* 31.
9. "Key Lecture, Symposium on the Education and Training of Architects" [1973], in Wurman, *What Will Be,* 249.
10. Lenore Weiss to LIK, letter, August 14 [1953], Kahn Collection, 030.II.A.32.57.
11. According to David Karp, son of Leon Karp, an artist and art director for the Philadelphia advertising firm N. W. Ayer, Kahn pumped his father—a longtime friend—for work. Karp brought Kahn commissions for alterations from three of his colleagues, artists Leo Lionni, Paul Darrow, and Dimitri Petrov. Interview with WW, March 21, 2011.
12. EIK thought that this project was never completed because the Shermans "really didn't want a modern house." Telephone interview with David B. Brownlee, October 25, 1990, David B. Brownlee Collection, AAUP, box 1, "Esther K."
13. EIK, ibid.
14. Citizens' Council on City Planning, *Annual Report,* 1952–53, p. 11, Kahn Collection, 030.II.A.65.7; and John C. Phillips, president, Citizens' Council on City Planning, to LIK, letter, January 4, 1952, Kahn Collection, 030.II.A.61.34.
15. Mrs. Arthur Hooper to LIK, letter, February 4 [1945], Kahn Collection, 030.II.A.68.14.
16. LIK to AGT, letter, February 9, 1954, in Tyng, *Rome Letters,* 100.
17. LIK, specification sheet for *Architectural Forum,* undated, p. 4, Kahn Collection, 030.II.A.33.35.
18. Fred E. Clever to Stewart Rauch, president, PSFS, letter, January 15, 1960, Tyng Collection, AAUP, 074.II.F.12.
19. Charles H. Woodward to Margaret Esherick, letter, April 29, 1960, Kahn Collection, 030.II.A.34.2. Charles H. Woodward to Robert Venturi, letter, June 18, 1962, in Schwartz, *Mother's House,* 6.
20. Wendy Oser, telephone interview with WW, February 21, 2011. The Osers arrived in Southampton, England, on the *Majestic,* July 7, 1933, in transit to Leningrad. National Archives, London, UK Incoming Passenger Lists, 1878–1960, records for Jesse Oser and Ruth Oser.
21. For Clever, see Obituary, Emerson Darnell, *Philadelphia Inquirer,* July 15, 1992; for Roche, see Obituary, *Philadelphia Bulletin,* July 31, 1966; for the Sterns, see *O Say Can You See "By Dawn's Urban Blight,"* rev. ed. (Washington, D.C.: Acropolis, 1968).
22. See Goldhagen, *Situated Modernism,* 38–40.
23. Alice Seiver to LIK, letter, July 27, 1959, Kahn Collection, 030.II.A.62.59;

and Alice Seiver to LIK, letter, December 2, 1959, Kahn Collection, 030.II.A.65.35.

24. Steven Korman described how he pursued Kahn in *House: The Korman Residence,* DVD.

25. Philip M. Stern to LIK, letter, November 25, 1966, Kahn Collection, 030.II.A.81.41.

26. Marty Adler to LIK, letter, March 31, 1955, Kahn Collection, 030.II.A.32.35.

27. See, for example, Tyng, *Rome Letters,* 202–4.

28. LIK to Mr. and Mrs. Lawrence Morris, letter, October 1, 1958, Kahn Collection, 030.II.A.32.37.

29. Salk "is just as much designer of this project as myself," Kahn admitted in *Louis Kahn, Architect,* videocassette (VHS).

30. LIK, quoted by Mary Harrington Hall, "Gift from the Sea," *San Diego,* February 1962, 44.

31. Fisher and Fisher, "Seven Years," 157.

32. Kahn and Fisher, "House Within a House," 50.

33. Philip M. Stern to LIK, letter, November 25, 1966, Kahn Collection, 030.II.A.81.41.

34. Ibid.; and Philip M. Stern and Helen Stern to LIK, letter, April 4, 1967, quoted in Ronner and Jhaveri, *Complete Work,* 33. (This letter is missing from the correspondence files of the Kahn Collection.) Philip M. Stern to LIK, letter, January 21, 1969, Kahn Collection, 030.II.A.81.41.

35. LIK, in Kahn and Fisher, "House Within a House," 52, 54.

36. Norma Shapiro, interview with the authors, January 7, 2011.

37. Ida Jaffe to LIK, undated letter [1954], Kahn Collection, 030.II.A.66.6.

38. Helen Stern to GHM, email, July 25, 2011.

39. Mitzi (Goldenberg) Marks to GHM, email, October 14, 2011.

40. LIK to A. Arthur Miller, letter, November 23, 1959, Kahn Collection, 030.II.A.80.51.

41. Jocelyn Roche in conversation with the current owner of the house, Caryl Wolf, in the early 1970s; recounted by Wolf in an interview with the authors, April 6, 2011.

42. The Kormans described their family and their needs in "The Korman Family: A New Home," undated typescript, Kahn Collection, 030.II.A.36.25.

43. LIK, in Kahn and Fisher, "House Within a House," 54.

44. Mrs. Paul Silver to LIK, letter, February 14, 1959; and LIK to Mrs. Paul Silver, letter, February 25, 1959, Kahn Collection, 030.II.A.65.37.

HOUSES

1. Solis Daniel Kopelan (originally Kaplan, 1902–1987) graduated from the University of Pennsylvania school of architecture in 1929 and probably went to work immediately as a draftsman and designer for Paul Cret. The partnership was short lived; the only known document from the firm alludes to a letter Kopelan wrote to Shell oil offering their skills for service-station design, which were not accepted; see D. G. Coombs, manager of operations, Shell Eastern Petroleum Products, to Kopelan, letter, December 4, 1930, Kahn Collection, 330.I.B.4.

2. See Hitchcock, *Modern Architecture,* 199–206.

3. For Lurçat, see Jean-Louis Cohen, *André Lurçat, 1894–1970* (Liège: Mardaga, 1995); for Mallet-Stevens, see *Robert Mallet-Stevens: L'Oeuvre complète* (Paris: Centre Pompidou, 2005).

4. Kahn used this term in his travel drawings and postcards home to describe the works he was seeing on his journey.

5. For Kahn's travels in Europe in 1928–29, see Whitaker, "Chronology," and Michael J. Lewis, "Louis Kahn's Art and His Architectural Thought," in Kries, Eisenbrand, and von Moos, *Power of Architecture,* 67–83.

6. Paul Philippe Cret, "Styles—Archaeology" [1909], in White, *Paul Philippe Cret,* 50.

7. LIK, in Hochstim, *Paintings and Sketches,* 26.

8. These files, including material that Cret himself must have clipped and brought with him from France, were expanded throughout his career, with tens of thousands of images housed in vertical files that were systematically organized by themes and types; the files are now with the Paul Cret Collection, AAUP.

9. "An English Garden Village: Silver End, Witham, Essex," *Architectural Record* 68 (October 1930): 312–17 (a clipping can be found in Cret's files under "Country and Suburban Houses, England," 275.359, Paul Cret Collection, AAUP). For Silver End, see Alan Powers, *Modern: The Modern Movement in Britain* (London: Merrell, 2005), 60–61. This project was well published; it had already appeared in *Baumeister* 28 (February 1930): 90; *L'Architecte* n.s. 7 (August 1930): pl. 47; and on the cover of *Architectural Forum* 53 (August 1930).

10. *L'Architecte,* September 1930, pl. 53. Two images of the Maison Planeix also appear with a discussion of the properties of glass in *Architectural Record* 68 (October 1930): 338, just a few pages from the Silver End illustrations. It is not known when Kahn first became aware of Le Corbusier's work, but it must have been before this publication arrived. Paul Cret included a lucid discussion of Le Corbusier in a lecture to a Philadelphia audience in 1927, while in August 1930, Kahn's longtime friend Norman N. Rice, fresh from a year in the architect's Paris atelier, saw the publication of the first in his series of articles and lectures on Le Corbusier ("The Minimal House: A Solution," *Architectural Record* 68 [August 1930]: 133–37). See Mardges Bacon, *Le Corbusier in America: Travels in the Land of the Timid* (Cambridge, Mass.: MIT Press, 2001), 5.

11. Hochstim, *Paintings and Sketches,* 206, no. 272. A small pencil sketch for a similar composition drawn on the same sheet as a landscape (119, no. 121) and a second, tightened, watercolor version in the collection of Nathaniel Kahn probably were done as Kahn revisited this theme in the fall. Two other interiors, an oil of an artist's studio (206, no. 273) and a watercolor of a living room (collection of Alexandra Tyng), are probably also from this later period, as is a greeting card with an image of an ancient architect confronting the model of a modern house. Hochstim, *Paintings and Sketches*, 231, no. 316.

12. LIK, in Hochstim, *Paintings and Sketches,* 26.

13. Wilhelm Kästner, "Bernhard Pfau, Düsseldorf," *Moderne Bauformen* 29 (March 1930): 133. For Pfau, see Julius Niederwöhrmeier, *Das Lebens des Düsseldorfer Architekten Bernhard Pfau, 1902–1989* (Stuttgart: Karl Krämer, 1997).

14. "Nursery Building, The Oak Lane Country Day School, Philadelphia, Howe and Lescaze, Architects," *Architectural Record* 67 (April 1930): 362.

15. This way of knowing reflects the impact of Progressive Era educators, such as J. Liberty Tadd, who shaped Kahn's early artistic education. See Burton, "Aesthetic Education."

16. "Value and Aim in Sketching" [1931], in Latour, *Writings,* 11. See also Paul Philippe Cret, "Ten Years of Modernism," *Architectural Forum* 59 (August 1933): 91–94, and LIK, "Architecture and the University" [1953], in Latour, *Writings,* 55–56. In the interview "How'm I Doing, Corbusier?" [1972)] (in Latour, *Writings,* 307), Kahn addressed the subject at length and elaborated the catalytic roles of Cret and Le Corbusier on his work: "Every man has . . . a figure in his work who he feels answerable to. I often say . . . to myself, 'How'm I doing, Corbusier?' You see, Corbusier was my teacher. I say, Paul Cret was my teacher and Corbusier was my teacher. . . . And I have learned not to *do* as they did . . . not to *imitate* . . . but to derive out of their spirit. . . . I don't want to say *what* was derived, because it hurts; *derive*—it's very strong, *derive* is powerful . . . *derive* is not the word, really—but *sense their spirit.*"

17. Vincent Scully noted Kahn's predatory nature in an interview [1982], in Latour, *L'Uomo,* 149.

18. C. Clark Zantzinger, secretary, Philadelphia Metropolitan District Housing Committee, to Robert D. Kohn, director of housing, Public Works Administration, letter, November 9, 1933. Sue Ann Kahn Collection, AAUP, 330.I.A.1. For a discussion of this project in the context of public housing, see Richard Pommer, "The Architecture of Urban Housing in the United States During the Early 1930s," *Journal of the Society of Architectural Historians* 37 (December 1978): 235–64.

19. The lasting influence of this project and Henry Wright's work on Kahn remains unexamined. For an analysis of Radburn as an enduring, if ideal, model for suburban development, see Eugenie L. Birch, "Radburn and the American Planning Movement," *Journal of the American Planning Association* 46 (October 1980): 424–31. For the overall impact of Wright and Stein, see Francesco Dal Co, "From the First World War to the New Deal: The Regional Planning Association of America," in Giorgio Ciucci et al., *The American City: From the Civil War to the New Deal* (Cambridge, Mass.: MIT Press, 1983), 221–60.

20. Henry Wright, "Shall We Community Plan?" *Journal of the American Institute of Architects* 9 (October 1921): 321; Henry Wright, "The Place of the Apartment in the Modern Community," *Architectural Record* 67 (March 1930): 222.

21. "St. Katherine's Village—Economic Report," undated, pp. 6, 4, Kahn Collection, 030.II.A.68.1. While this document relates to a different site, the Windmill design is unchanged. Kahn's handwritten annotations confirm that it is his voice that is describing the work.

22. "Pessac Housing Development," *Architectural Forum* 56 (March 1932): 281–82.

23. Kenneth Day, statement in James Ford and Katherine Morrow Ford, *The Modern House in America* (New York: Architectural Book Publishing, 1940), 124.

24. Day, who was the same age as Kahn, had also trained under Cret, but he had begun to practice architecture much earlier, in the late 1920s. He had had extensive experience, including the construction of a number of large country houses in a picturesque vernacular style. Day completed a series of notable modern residences in the later 1930s, and he was singled out by the Museum of Modern Art as one of the first American architects to embrace "natural traditional materials" in his buildings. John McAndrew, *Guide to Modern Architecture: Northeast States* (New York: Museum of Modern Art, 1940), 92.

25. Montgomery Schuyler, "Recent American Country Houses: An Introduction," *Architectural Record* 32 (October 1912): 273.

26. Charles Matlack Price, "The Pennsylvania Type: A Logical Development," *Architectural Record* 32 (October 1912): 307–27.

27. George H. Edgell, *American Architecture of To-day* (New York: Scribner's, 1928), 114.

28. For Howe, see Stern, *George Howe.*

29. For Mellor, Meigs & Howe, see *A Monograph of the Work of Mellor, Meigs & Howe* (New York: Architectural Book Publishing, 1923).

30. Paul P. Cret, "A Hillside House: The Property of George Howe, Esq., Chestnut Hill, Philadelphia," *Architectural Record* 48 (August 1920): 87–88.

31. For Howe and Lescaze, see William H. Jordy, "The American Acceptance of the International Style: George Howe & William Lescaze's Philadelphia Saving Fund Society Building," in *American Buildings and Their Architects,* vol. 5 (New York: Oxford University Press, 1972), 87–164.

32. See Scully, *Kahn,* 13.

33. For a discussion of the competition, see "Quaker Housing," *Architectural Forum* 68 (June 1938): 12.

34. Stern, *George Howe,* 179.

35. See LIK to Jury of Fellows, American Institute of Architects, letter, January 31, 1955, Kahn Collection, 030.II.A.62.63.43.

36. See Johnson and Lewis, *Drawn from the Source,* 51–59.

37. LIK, in Kahn and Fisher, "House Within a House," 54.

38. LIK to Jury of Fellows, American Institute of Architects, letter, January 31, 1955, Kahn Collection, 030.II.A.62.63.34. Kahn wrote three letters of support on the same day, for Alfred Bendiner, McAllister, and Stonorov. For Stonorov, see Frederick Gutheim, "Oskar Stonorov (1904–1970)," special issue, *Architettura: Cronache e storia* 18 (June 1972).

39. Le Corbusier and Pierre Jeanneret, *Oeuvre complète, 1910–1929,* ed. by W. Boesiger and O. Stonorov (Zurich: Editions d'Architecture, 1929).

40. LIK, undated notebook, n.p., Kahn Collection, 030.VII.4. Facsimile pages from this notebook are published in Wurman, *What Will Be,* n.p.

41. For a lucid discussion of Le Corbusier and the vernacular, see Francesco Passanti, "The Vernacular, Modernism, and Le Corbusier," in *Journal of the Society of Architectural Historians* 56 (December 1997): 438–51.

42. Kahn had a more direct hand in several of the firm's other residential additions, such as the Darrow, Finkelstein, and Hooper houses, but all remained unbuilt.

43. Simon, *Solar House.* The Pennsylvania house appears on pages 42–43.

44. The original text is in Kahn's own draft form, "A Solar House for Pennsylvania," September 19, 1946, p. 1, Kahn Collection, 030.II.A.59.56.

45. The term is defined by John M. Johansen in *John M. Johansen: A Life in* *the Continuum of Modern Architecture* (Milan: L'Arca, 1995), 19.

46. See Barry Bergdoll, "Encountering America: Marcel Breuer and the Discourses of the Vernacular from Budapest to Boston," in Alexander von Vegesack and Mathias Remmele, eds., *Marcel Breuer: Design and Architecture* (Weil am Rhein, Germany: Vitra Design Museum, 2003), 260–307.

47. AGT, telephone conversation with WW, June 17, 2011.

48. Vincent Scully, interview [1982], in Latour, *L'Uomo,* 155.

49. Vincent Joseph Scully, *The Cottage Style: An Organic Development in Later 19th Century Wooden Domestic Architecture in the Eastern United States* (Ph.D. diss., Yale University, 1949). This was later published as *The Shingle Style: Architectural Theory and Design from Richardson to the Origins of Wright* (New Haven: Yale University Press, 1955).

50. Scully, interview [1982], in Latour, *L'Uomo,* 155.

51. AGT, interview [1982], in ibid., 43.

52. Quoted in Barnes, "Architects' Prize-Winning Houses."

53. This was confirmed by Mansfield Bascomb, Esherick's son-in-law, interview with WW, September 25, 2011.

54. Kahn provided details of the masonry work at the Weiss house in a letter to Edward Knowles in the office of Abraham W. Geller, a New York architect. LIK to Knowles, letter, September 16, 1954, Kahn Collection, 030.II.A.66.6.

55. AGT, interview, [1982], in Latour, *L'Uomo,* 43.

56. Jarzombek, "Good-Life Modernism," 87.

57. LIK, undated notebook, n.p., Kahn Collection, 030.VII.4.

58. Jarzombek, "Good-Life Modernism," 87.

59. Although none of the surviving drawings for this project is dated, Kahn's initial design can be dated precisely. In a letter to Anne Tyng, dated March 16, 1954, Kahn recalled the design "as the one I did in the hospital" (Tyng, *Rome Letters,* 117). Evidence of gall bladder trouble, noted in a letter to his lawyer, David Zoob, dated April 25, 1952 (Kahn Collection, 030.II.A.60.10), along with time cards for the project showing billing for staff beginning the week of April 21, 1952, support the dating of initial sketches to mid-April 1952.

60. As he wrote on a preliminary drawing (not illustrated), Kahn Collection, 030.I.A.310.1.

61. Kahn considered several structural systems, including a steel frame, but by the time the Fruchters put the project on hold (they moved to Stamford, Connecticut, for business reasons) he seems to have settled on a timber-post system set on a 4-foot module.

62. Tyng submitted "2 photographs of a model and some descriptive text" for this project to the AIA Yearbook. See AGT to Vincent G. Kling, draft letter, February 26, 1952, Tyng Collection, AAUP, 074.II.A.2.

63. Archival records for this project are scant, consisting of a site survey and several pages of notes. Tyng's handwriting is apparent, as are her sketches, here; see Kahn Collection, 030.II.A.34.56.

64. See Tyng, *Rome Letters.*

65. Kahn reported meeting Mrs. Jaffe in a letter to Tyng, dated February 9, 1954 (in Tyng, *Rome Letters,* 100). Ida Jaffe followed up with a letter to Kahn detailing their needs, undated letter [1954], Kahn Collection, 030.II.A.66.6.

66. LIK to AGT, letter, March 16, 1954, in Tyng, *Rome Letters,* 117.

67. LIK, "How to Develop New Methods of Construction" [1954], in Latour, *Writings,* 57.

68. Kahn reported in a letter to Tyng, dated June 17, 1954, that he had started the designs of the Adler and DeVore houses (in Tyng, *Rome Letters,* 145). The Adlers departed for a vacation on June 14, returning in early August (see Kahn Collection, 030.II.A.32.35). Kahn's scheme for the DeVore house had been accepted by July 24, 1954. See LIK to AGT, letter, July 24, 1952, in Tyng, *Rome Letters,* 165–67.

69. "Two Houses" [1955], in Latour, *Writings,* 60.

70. Kahn's enthusiastic response can be found in a letter to Tyng, dated August 18, 1954 (in *Rome Letters,* 168). Tyng noted her own contributions in ibid., 194.

71. Marty Adler described their frustrations with the Dodge family, developers of the Cherokee subdivision, which "got so discouraging we felt we couldn't go on. . . . I still feel that at some later date in my life I will have a modern house and that you will do it, but in a place not so bound by strictures and subject to autocracy." Marty Adler to LIK, letter, March 13, 1955, Kahn Collection, 030.II.A.32.35.

72. LIK, undated notebook, n.p., Kahn Collection, 030.VII.4.

73. Tyng, *Rome Letters,* 192. Tyng's account of the creation of the plan was confirmed by Thomas R. Vreeland, who was present in the drafting room at the time. However, her recollection that the proposal for pyramidal roofs was made simultaneously with the plan is erroneous. Interview with WW, March 22, 2011.

74. Surviving time sheets document Tyng's work beginning during the week ending July 12, 1957, and continuing through November of that year. Following a four-month hiatus, Tyng spent about half her time on the design, completing a preliminary set of construction drawings by September 1958. Kahn Collection, 030.II.A.80.49.

75. Obituary, *New York Times,* March 15, 2005.

76. See Whitaker, "Chronology," 26. Gussman would donate a series of important paintings to the museum over the years.

77. The orientation of the plan was deduced by a comparison with the Gussmans' address in 1993 at 4644 South Zunis Avenue, Tulsa. The dimensions of the site conform exactly to Kahn's site plan.

78. Lawrence Morris to LIK, letter, March 14, 1958, Kahn Collection, 030.II.A.32.37.

79. See David De Long, in Brownlee and De Long, *In the Realm,* 64.

80. As recalled by David Reinhart, one of Kahn's assistants on the job, interview with WW, January 18, 2011.

81. LIK, "Order Is" [1955], in Latour, *Writings,* 59.

82. LIK, undated notebook, n.p., Kahn Collection, 030.VII.4.

83. See David B. Brownlee in Brownlee et al., *Out of the Ordinary: Robert Venturi, Denise Scott Brown and Associates, Architecture, Urbanism, Design* (Philadelphia: Philadelphia Museum of Art, 2001), 14.

84. "Program and Solution [Pearson House]," September 2, 1958, Venturi, Scott Brown Collection, AAUP, 225.RV.120.

85. Ibid.

86. Kahn ordered a detailed survey of the Fleishers' property at 8363

Fisher Road, Elkins Park, on March 19, 1959, LIK to George B. Mebus, letter, March 19, 1959, Kahn Collection, 030.II.A.9.2. Fleisher reported that he was not able to "work up sufficient enthusiasm" for the project, and suspended work, Robert Fleisher to LIK, letter, May 16, 1959, Kahn Collection, 030.II.A.34.14.

87. Kahn's words as recalled by Thomas R. Vreeland, interview with WW, March 22, 2011.

88. LIK, "Discussion in Kahn's Office" [1961], in Twombly, *Essential Texts,* 106.

89. William Huff, "Kahn and Yale" [1974], in Latour, *L'Uomo,* 345.

90. Thomas R. Vreeland, interview with WW, March 22, 2011.

91. Aldo Giurgola and Jaimini Mehta (in *Louis I. Kahn,* 246) suggest that Philadelphia's great diagonal, City Beautiful–inspired boulevard, the Benjamin Franklin Parkway, was a source of inspiration.

92. Scully, "Light, Form, and Power," 165.

93. George Woodward, Inc., to LIK, letter, July 22, 1959 [received July 24, 1959], Kahn Collection, 030.II.A.34.2.

94. Kahn Collection, 030.I.A.520.3, 030.I.A.520.12—030.I.A.520.14.

95. David G. De Long, in Brownlee and De Long, *In the Realm,* 68.

96. The authors are deeply indebted to Harriet Pattison for making available a series of letters that shed light on this moment.

97. LIK to Harriet Pattison, letter, September 15, 1959, collection of Harriet Pattison.

98. Le Corbusier, *Towards a New Architecture* [1927] (repr., New York: Dover, 1986), 17.

99. He would also have been struck by the craftsmanship of traditional woodwork, and the more recent interpretation of that tradition as expressed in concrete, work that was also superb and exquisite. The trip was of consequence to other of his works as well, most notably the Salk Institute, where sliding wooden shutters were designed for office spaces facing the ocean in a manner reminiscent of modern interpretations he had seen in Tokyo. Kahn's visit to Kiyonori Kikutake's Sky House was documented by the architect in "Sky House, Its Background and Significance," *GA Houses* 100 (August 2007): 81.

100. Kahn, who became aware of Noguchi's work in the 1930s, was in active collaboration with the sculptor by August 1961 on the design of the Levy Memorial Playground. Madokoro's work for Noguchi is documented in George O'Brien, "Factory into Home," *New York Times,* April 8, 1962.

101. See Soetsu Yanagi, *The Unknown Craftsman: A Japanese Insight into Beauty* (Tokyo: Kodansha, 1989).

102. See Brownlee et al., *Out of the Ordinary,* 18, n. 49.

103. A close parallel is seen in Edmund Wheelwright's Stedman House in Newcastle, New Hampshire (see Scully, *Shingle Style,* pls. 77, 78), although it may be more of a question of sensibility being put forward rather than a specific source being recalled.

104. *Louis I. Kahn: Conversations with Students* [1969], 2nd ed. (Houston: Architecture at Rice Publications, 1998), 189.

105. This observation was made by Jarzombek, "Good-Life Modernism," 87–89.

106. LIK, handwritten note on first-floor plan drawing, December 22, 1963 set, Collection of Doris and Norman Fisher Family.

107. William Huff, "Kahn and Yale" [1974], in Latour, *L'Uomo,* 419.

108. See Eisenbrand, "Between Grid and Pathway," 60–64.

109. LIK, interview, in John W. Cook and Heinrich Klotz, *Conversations with Architects* (New York: Praeger, 1973), 216.

110. LIK, "On the Colonial House," from "An Architect Speaks His Mind" [1972], in Latour, *Writings,* 293.

111. LIK, in Kahn and Fisher, "House Within a House," 52.

112. Pattison, a native of Chicago, trained in the office of Daniel Urban Kiley prior to completing a master's degree in landscape architecture at the University of Pennsylvania in 1967. She was the project landscape architect (for George E. Patton) on the design of Kahn's Kimbell Art Museum and independently collaborated with Kahn on the design of the Franklin Delano Roosevelt Four Freedoms Park and other projects.

113. Sue Ann Kahn, interview [1982], in Latour, *L'Uomo*, 31.

FURNISHINGS

1. LIK, in Kahn and Fisher, "House Within a House," 48.

2. Julie Oser McLeod, interview with WW, March 21, 2011.

3. The downstairs built-ins, as well as the bookshelves in the bedrooms, were fabricated by the contractor, Master Masons Construction Company, Kahn Collection, 030.II.A.33.33.

4. See Ross, *Gilbert Rohde,* 22–23, 244 n. 16, 245 n. 17.

5. Decorators' Cabinet Shop, Philadelphia, estimate, February 11, 1942, and invoice, June 9, 1942, collection of Wendy Oser.

6. Ibid., invoice, October 20, 1942, collection of Wendy Oser.

7. According to Sue Ann Kahn, these pieces fit the space exactly; interview with the authors, September 1, 2012.

8. Preliminary research on Kahn's freestanding furniture was undertaken by Jordan Pascucci in the 2008–2009 University of Pennsylvania Curatorial Seminar: Interiors and Furniture of Louis I. Kahn, led by GHM.

9. Rohde's influence on the modular furniture in the Organic Design exhibition was first suggested by Derek Ostergard and David A. Hanks, "Gilbert Rohde and the Evolution of Modern Design, 1927–1941," *Arts Magazine* 56 (October 1981): 107, fig. 26. In her preface to the Herman Miller 1940 catalogue reprint, Leslie Piña pointed out the strong similarities between many of Rohde's designs and those of his successor at Herman Miller, George Nelson, and of Nelson's associate there, Charles Eames. *Herman Miller 1940 Catalog & Supplement: Gilbert Rohde Modern Furniture Design* (Atglen, Pa.: Schiffer, 1998), 4.

10. See Noyes, *Organic Design,* 38, where the Raymond textiles are listed as designed by Noemi's husband, Antonin Raymond. See also Kurt G. F. Helfrich and William Whitaker, eds., *Crafting a Modern World: The Architecture and Design of Antonin and Noemi Raymond* (New York: Princeton Architectural Press, 2006), 18, 53.

11. See Whittier, "New Type of Furniture."

12. Noyes, *Organic Design*, 28.

13. See John Stuart Gordon, *A Modern World: American Design from the Yale University Art Gallery* (New Haven: Yale University Art Gallery, 2011), 359–61. The tambour doors in this group may have been the source for

the doors in Kahn's furniture proposal for the Equipment for Living program organized by Knoll Associates in 1944. The cabinets, made for sheet-metal fabrication, have a number of similarities to Kahn's own cabinets and those he designed for the Osers. Although "architectural planning and housing [were] not the objectives of this program," Kahn used them as excuses for extensive work on prefabrication, which he called the Parasol House Type, Kahn Collection, 0.30.I.A.155.1–19, 0.30.I.A.156.1–4. See H. G. Knoll Associates to LIK, letter and program, May 2, 1944, Kahn Collection, 0.30.II.A.60.23.

14. See New Furniture Incorporated catalogue, 1939, Paul Cret Collection, AAUP.275.431a; and Paul Makovsky, "Artek in America," *Metropolis* 30 (May 2011): 94–99.

15. "Furniture by Assembly Line," *Time,* July 15, 1940, 50.

16. Artek-Pascoe, Inc., catalogue (New York: Artek-Pascoe, 1941), 9. For Holtkamp, see Gordon, *Modern World,* 362. According to existing invoices, Kahn's office ordered the furniture on September 22 and October 28, 1941, to be shipped to the Osers at their apartment on Walnut Street (collection of Wendy Oser). The dining chairs were covered in a blue fabric, the Holtkamp chair had green webbing, and the top of the dining table was painted terracotta. Jesse Oser added Aalto stools in 1943, Artek-Pascoe, invoice, October 30, 1943, collection of Wendy Oser.

17. Decorators' Cabinet Shop, Philadelphia, invoice, April 13, 1942, collection of Wendy Oser.

18. LIK, "On the Colonial House," from "An Architect Speaks His Mind" [1972], in Latour, *Writings,* 293.

19. "Dining Room Cabinet Details," Genel residence, drawing 39A, September 8, 1950, rev. September 27, 1950, Kahn Collection, 030.I.C.315.1.

20. John A. Dubs of Philadelphia supplied the cabinetry; see estimate, May 19, 1949, and invoice, August 18, 1949, Kahn Collection, 030.II.A.32.22.

21. David B. Brownlee (in Brownlee and De Long, *In the Realm,* 39) sees evidence in the mural of "the profiles of the Egyptian pyramids Kahn had visited early in 1951," but given the already well-worked-out composition of 1950, this seems unlikely.

22. AGT, interview [1982], in Latour, *L'Uomo,* 43.

23. LIK, in Hochstim, *Paintings and Sketches,* 26.

24. AGT, interview with the authors, January 14, 2011, and Tyng, *Rome Letters,* 34.

25. Cabinet Work, September 11, 1949, Kahn Collection, 030.I.C. 310.2.

26. Schaffner, *Anne Tyng,* 100.

27. For Breuer's house, see Joachim Driller, *Breuer Houses* (London: Phaidon, 2000), 180–89.

28. See Norris, "Contemporary Home."

29. LIK, "On Color and Light," from "An Architect Speaks His Mind" [1972], in Latour, *Writings,* 295.

30. Norma Shapiro, interview with the authors, January 7, 2011.

31. "The Korman Family: A New Home," undated typescript, n.p., Kahn Collection, 030.II.A.36.25.

32. For the Exeter carrels, see Brownlee and De Long, *In the Realm,* 263, fig. 364.

33. Norma Shapiro, interview with the authors, January 7, 2011.

34. Ibid. Doris Fisher recalled that Kahn "decided it would be great fun to come along and pick out all the furniture." Interview with Peter Kirby, 1992, videotape, AAUP, MOCA Collection.

35. Suzanne Binswanger designed the interiors; see "Focus on Kahn," *Interior Design,* 129.

36. See Loud, *Art Museums,* 168, n. 134.

37. Steven Korman and Larry Korman, interviews with WW, January 21, 2013. For Kurtz's work, see Judith Stein, *The Painting of Elaine Kurtz* (New York: Martha Jackson Gallery, 1978). For the tapestries, see Brownlee and De Long, *In the Realm,* 200–201, fig. 301.

38. Norma Shapiro, interview with the authors, January 7, 2011.

39. LIK, in "Focus on Kahn," *Interior Design,* 134.

40. A design for a dining table, for example, is included among Kahn's drawings for the alterations of the Irving and Dorothy Shaw House in Philadelpha, Kahn Collection, 0.30.I.A.460.13.

41. See "Houses," *A + U,* 181–86.

42. EIK to LIK, letter, undated [1968], Kahn Collection, 030.II.A.34.24.

43. LIK, in Hochstim, *Paintings and Sketches,* 26.

44. See "Houses," *A + U,* 187–93.

45. Kahn Collection, 030.I.C.830.1–030.I.C.830.27.

46. LIK, "A Verbal Autobiography" [1973], in Wurman, *What Will Be,* 228.

47. LIK, "Talk at the Conclusion of the Otterlo Congress" [1959], in Twombly, *Essential Texts,* 47.

48. Kahn Collection, 030.I.C.830.21–030.I.C.830.26.

49. See Brownlee and De Long, *In the Realm,* 211–13, figs. 310–13.

50. The Kahn Collection has a schematic drawing for a chandelier 5 feet wide with a spherelike cluster of 8-inch globes (Kahn Collection, 030.I.C.830.001, unnumbered drawing) that is a refinement of the ones drawn in Kahn's own hand and is just about ready for fabrication, so why a chandelier was never installed in the house remains unclear.

EPILOGUE

1. See Loud, *Art Museums,* 245–46, 270 n. 8.

2. Simone Swithers Swan to LIK, letter, received November 13, 1973, Louis I. Kahn Collection, AAUP, box 147, "Swan House."

3. William Marlin to Marshall Meyer, office of LIK, letter, March 22, 1974, ibid.

4. Marlin, "Humble Titan."

5. See Simone Swithers Swan to LIK, letters, received November 13, 1973, and dated January 8, 1974, Louis I. Kahn Collection, AAUP, box 147, "Swan House."

6. Simone Swithers Kahn to William Laird, Kahn's assistant, letter, February 3, 1974, ibid.

7. Simone Swithers Kahn to William Laird, letter, February 14, 1974, ibid.

8. Calendar entry for March 29, 1974, Kahn Collection, 030.II.B.40. Swan canceled the project during that scheduled visit, office memorandum, March 29, 1974, ibid. She eventually asked Kahn's former student Charles Moore to design the house.

9. William Marlin to Marshall Meyer, March 22, 1974, Louis I. Kahn Collection, AAUP, box 147, "Swan House." This homage to Louis Kahn never appeared, for *Architectural Forum* ceased publication that very same month.

JESSE AND RUTH OSER HOUSE

1. EIK, telephone interview with David B. Brownlee, October 25, 1990, David B. Brownlee Collection, AAUP, box 1, "Esther K." Jesse Oser (1903–1990) and Ruth Levine (1907–1997) were married in 1930; Louis Kahn and Esther Israeli were married August 14, 1930.

2. Information about the family derives from interviews with the couple's daughters, Wendy Oser (telephone interview with WW, February 21, 2011) and Julie Oser McLeod (interview with WW, March 21, 2011), and subsequent telephone conversations and emails. Jesse never attended college but had a lifelong interest in the theater; in the early 1930s he studied with Jasper Deeter, actor/director at the famed Hedgerow Theatre in Rose Valley, Pennsylvania, where he acted in a handful of plays (and was also the printer of the theater's programs). He may well have introduced Kahn to the Hedgerow, where the architect took Esther on their first date; see EIK, interview [1982], in Latour, *L'Uomo,* 23.

3. The Osers purchased their lot from Maurice Heilveil, a real-estate developer, on February 6, 1941, Montgomery County (Pa.) Deed Book 1375, p. 198. They received an $18,000 mortgage from the Colonial Title Surety Company on June 23, 1941, Montgomery County (Pa.) Mortgage Book 1643, p. 418. Heilveil worked closely with Master Masons Construction Company on several projects in the Philadelphia area, including the Juniper Park development, and the company was the contractor of record for the Oser house.

4. Alexander, "Modern House in Rustic Setting."

5. "House in Melrose Park," *Architectural Forum*, 132.

6. "New and Different," *House and Garden,* 78; and "House in Melrose Park," *Architectural Forum.*

7. See, for example, advertisement for Lupton metal windows, *Architectural Forum* 85 (September 1946): 65.

8. Montgomery County (Pa.) Deed Book 1876, p. 474.

PHILIP AND JOCELYN ROCHE HOUSE

1. The transfers are recorded, respectively, in Montgomery County (Pa.) Deed Books 1563, p. 291, and 1905, p. 586. Philip Q. Roche (1902–1966) married the former Jocelyn H. Hibberd Bain (1912–1975) on February 25, 1944, City of Philadelphia, Marriage License Bureau, License 779633. Jocelyn had a daughter, Margaret, from her previous marriage to John McDonnel Bain, and another, Robin, with Roche. See also obituaries, *Philadelphia Bulletin,* July 31, 1966, *New York Times,* August 1, 1966, and *American Journal of Psychiatry* 123 (December 6, 1966).

2. Willie Sutton, with Edward Linn, *Where the Money Was* (New York: Viking, 1976).

3. Philip Q. Roche, *The Criminal Mind* (New York: Farrar, Straus and Cudahy, 1958).

4. Ronner and Baenziger, *Dokumentation Arbeitsprozesse,* n.p.

5. Photostat set of lost original presentation drawings, Kahn Collection, 030.IV.C.240.1.

6. Philadelphia's bid is documented in "U.N. Delegates Pleased Sites Are 'Close In,'" *Philadelphia Record,* November 19, 1946, and "U.N. Committee Enthusiastic Over Two Phila. Sites," *Philadelphia Inquirer,* November 20, 1946, Kahn Collection, 030.II.A.61.21.

7. Kahn Collection, 030.II.A.63.4.

8. LIK to Glenn E. Bennett, secretary, [U.N.] Headquarters Commission and Planning Staff, letter, November 29, 1946, ibid.

9. Quoted in George Barrett, "Philadelphia Site Impresses the U.N.," *New York Times,* November 20, 1946.

10. Philadelphia Committee for the United Nations Capital, Itinerary for Site Inspection Trips, November 19, 1946, Kahn Collection, 030.II.A.63.4.

11. The second site recommended was the Presidio in San Francisco. See United Nations General Assembly, Permanent Headquarters Committee: Sub-Committee 1, Recommendations, p. 23, Kahn Collection, 030.II.A.63.4. Philadelphia's loss is documented in James B. Reston, "One Day's Fast Work by Rockefellers Took U.N. Site Away from Philadelphia," *Philadelphia Record,* December 18, 1946, Kahn Collection, 030.II.A.61.21.

12. Roche house, construction drawings, sheet 20, "Cabinets in Dining Rm," LIK delineator, Kahn Collection, 030.I.C.240.1.

13. Montgomery County (Pa.) Deed Book 3723, p. 322.

MORTON AND LENORE WEISS HOUSE

1. LIK, quoted in Barnes, "Prize-Winning Houses."

2. Data sheet on house supplied to Mrs. James Ford, New York, in response to a request for information for a forthcoming book, June 26, 1951, Kahn Collection, 030.II.A.32.57.

3. Morton Weiss (1912–2004) and Lenore Mann (1917–2004). See Stephen O'Toole, "Art Paints a Life: Carver Center Given 'History,'" *Norristown (Pa.) Times Herald,* April 21, 2002.

4. LIK to Samuel Brenner (Harrisburg, Pa.), letter, August 23, 1945, American Heritage Center, University of Wyoming, Stonorov Collection, box 50, "Correspondence, July–September, 1945" (copy in David B. Brownlee Collection, AAUP, box 3, "Ahavath Israel Synagogue"). No further documentation of this project has been found.

5. Kahn Collection, 030.II.A.32.25.

6. Kahn taught studio at Yale during the first half of the fall 1947 semester. His responsibilities ended the last week of October, and a letter to Morton Weiss stating this suggests that he started work on the house in early November, LIK to Morton Weiss, letter, October 24, 1947, Kahn Collection, 030.II.A.32.20.

7. Data sheet on house, June 26, 1951, Kahn Collection, 030.II.A.32.57.

8. LIK to Mr. and Mrs. Morton Weiss, letter, September 25, 1950, Kahn Collection, 030.II.A.32.20.

9. Tyng, *Rome Letters,* 34.

10. AGT, interview with the authors, January 11, 2001.

11. Lenore Weiss to LIK, letter, August 14 [1953], Kahn Collection, 030.II.A.32.57.

12. EIK, telephone interview with David B. Brownlee, October 25, 1990, David B. Brownlee Collection, AAUP, box 1, "Esther K."

13. The 5 1/3-acre site was purchased on July 23, 1941, Montgomery County (Pa.) Deed Book 1408, p. 213. Wartime restrictions on residential construction delayed their need to select an architect until years later.
14. LIK, quoted in Platt, "Philadelphia's Traditional Countryside."
15. LIK, quoted in Barnes, "Prize-Winning Houses."
16. "Modern Space," *Architectural Forum,* 103. See also George H. Marcus, "Louis Kahn and the Architectural Barbecue," *Journal of Design History* (http://jdh.oxfordjournals.org; posted October 16, 2012).

SAMUEL AND RUTH GENEL HOUSE

1. Information about Samuel Genel (1910–1961) and Ruth Goodman Genel (1910–1955) and their family comes from their daughter Nancy Levanoni, email to GHM, December 20, 2010, and interview with WW, Poway, California, January 17, 2011; Esther Kahn, telephone interview with David B. Brownlee, October 25, 1990, David B. Brownlee Collection, AAUP, box 1, "Esther K"; and Samuel's obituary, *Philadelphia Inquirer,* August 6, 1961.
2. Miscellaneous bills and work summaries, Kahn Collection, 030.II.A.32.36.
3. Yale University, School of Fine Arts, Department of Architecture, Advanced Design—Problem II, Fall Term, 1948–49, A Suburban Residence, issued November 1, 1948; Kahn Collection, 030.II.A.61.27.
4. Samuel F. Hotchkin, *Rural Pennsylvania in the Vicinity of Philadelphia* (Philadelphia: George W. Jacobs, 1897), 34.
5. Montgomery County (Pa.) Deed Book 2732, p. 34; and LIK to Samuel Genel, invoice, July 1, 1948, Kahn Collection, 030.II.A.32.36.
6. Kahn Collection, 030.I.A.315.1–030.I.A.315.5 and 030.I.A.315.10. The seventh is reproduced in Ronner and Jhaveri, *Complete Work,* 56, fig. GEH.4.
7. Office memorandum, May 11, 1951, Kahn Collection, 030.II.A.32.36.
8. Tyng, *Rome Letters,* 100, 68.
9. Montgomery County (Pa.) Deed Book 3541, p. 965.

FRED AND ELAINE CLEVER HOUSE

1. Contract, September 23, 1957, Kahn Collection, 030.II.A.34.38. Urs Büttiker, who met the Clevers when he photographed their house in the early 1990s, states that after the Clevers had seen the Trenton Bathhouse they decided to ask Kahn to build them a house (*Light and Space,* 91). This was probably part of a tour that Kahn gave of a number of his buildings and like the one he would give the Shapiros before they hired him to design their house.
2. Clever house, time sheet summaries, 1957–58, Kahn Collection, 030.II.A.80.49; and AGT, interview with the authors, January 11, 2011.
3. Tyng, *Rome Letters,* 200.
4. John C. Phillips, president, Citizens' Council on City Planning, to LIK, letter, January 4, 1952, and Kahn's membership card with Clever's signature, Kahn Collection, 030.II.A.61.34. Information about Fred Clever (1922–2001) and Elaine Cox Clever (1922–2000) comes from an interview with the Clevers' daughter-in-law, Liliane Clever, with WW, May 9, 2011.
5. Obituary, Emerson Darnell, *Philadelphia Inquirer,* July 15, 1992.
6. "Clever Clever Combines Homelife and Homework," *Penn State Collegian,* August 3, 1945, http://digitalnewspapers.libraries.psu.edu/Repository/DCG/1945/08/03/036-DCG-1945-08-03-001-SINGLE.pdf
7. David Dillard, Reference Librarian, Temple University Libraries, to GHM, email, March 23, 2011.
8. Walter Cope to Fred Clever, proposal letter, March 12, 1959, Kahn Collection, 030.II.A.34.42. Construction drawings, sheets 1–7, are dated February 18, 1959, which prompted a billing for "professional services rendered" by the Kahn office for the completion of construction drawings, February 27, 1959, Kahn Collection, 030.II.A.80.49.
9. Fred E. Clever to Stewart Rauch, president, PSFS, letter, January 15, 1960, Tyng Collection, AAUP, 074.II.F.12.

BERNARD AND NORMA SHAPIRO HOUSE

1. The checklist by Bernard (1925–2007) and Norma Levy (born 1928) Shapiro is undated, but the age given for their son Finley (two weeks) puts it in early October 1958, Kahn Collection, 030.II.A.82.48. The contract date of October 17, 1956, is erroneous, a miswriting of 1958, Kahn Collection, 030.II.A.82.46. A letter from Kahn to the Shapiros enclosed with the contract is dated October 17, 1958. This was confirmed in the authors' interview with Norma Shapiro, January 7, 2011. This discussion is heavily indebted to her recollections of the project.
2. Norma's mother's sister Clara married Ben Oser, Jesse Oser's oldest brother.
3. Bernard Shapiro, Questions on Revised Plan, memorandum, undated, inscribed in another hand: "Re: Plans etc. of 2–4-60," Kahn Collection, 030.II.A.33.4.

MARGARET ESHERICK HOUSE

1. LIK, quoted in Hanson, "Chalice of Light."
2. Kahn received a site survey of "Sunrise Lane and the land around Pastorius Park, where Miss Margaret Esherick is interested in building a house," Charles H. Woodward to LIK, letter, July 22, 1959, Kahn Collection, 030.II.A.34.2. The contract with Kahn was dated October 1, 1959, according to an undated handwritten note from David Wisdom saying that the file copy of the contract had been sent to the law office of Zoob, Cohan & Matz, Kahn Collection, 030.II.A.80.11. The building contract is dated November 2, 1960, Agreement, Thomas J. Regan and Margaret Esherick, Kahn Collection, 030.II.A.139.
3. Margaret Esherick died April 6, 1962, *Chestnut Hill (Pa.) Herald,* April 12, 1962.
4. Esherick, "Architectural Practice," 327.
5. Margaret Esherick's letterhead shows that the shop had been established in 1926, Margaret Esherick to LIK, letter, December 22 [1960], Kahn Collection, 030.II.A.34.2.
6. The 1950 Philadelphia telephone directory lists Margaret Esherick at 8726 Germantown Avenue (the same address as her parents) and her bookstore at 8603 Germantown Avenue. The 1955 directory has the bookstore at 186 East Evergreen Avenue.
7. Esherick, "Architectural Practice," 419.
8. Ibid.
9. See Marc Treib, *Appropriate: The Houses of Joseph Esherick* (San Francisco: William Stout, 2008).

10. Joseph Esherick to LIK, letter, May 22, 1959, Kahn Collection, 030.II.A.34.12.

11. Joseph Esherick to Margaret Esherick, letter, April 5, 1961, Kahn Collection, 030.II.A.34.1.

12. LIK to Margaret Esherick, letter (typescript draft), March 16, 1960, Kahn Collection, 030.II.A.34.2.

13. David Contosta, *A Philadelphia Family: The Houstons and Woodwards of Chestnut Hill* (Philadelphia: University of Pennsylvania Press, 1988), 127.

14. Charles H. Woodward to Margaret Esherick, letter, April 29, 1960, Kahn Collection, 030.II.A.34.2.

15. Photograph of lost original perspective, c. May 1960, Eidgenoessische Technische Hochschule, Zurich, Archives, in Ronner and Jhaveri, *Complete Work,* 152–53.

16. Margaret Esherick House, construction drawings, sheet 1, Revisions, November 2, 1960, Kahn Collection, 030.I.C.520.001.

17. Nicholas Gianopulos, structural engineer, interview with WW, December 16, 2010.

18. Galen Schlosser, office of LIK, to T. J. Regan, March 6, 1961, Kahn Collection, 030.II.A.34.1.

19. Esherick, "Architectural Practice," 420.

20. Undated manuscript summarizing hours and expenses for the Esherick house in December 1961 and January 1962, Kahn Collection, 030.II.A.34.1.

21. Burnap Post, quoted in Kaye, "A Rare Kahn Residence," 55.

22. "Architectural Changes Forecast New Adventure in Living," *House and Garden,* October 1962, 158; and "Louis Kahn," *Architecture d'Aujourd'hui,* 25. Stoller photographed the house again in 1996; see "A Timeless Sense of Light," *House Beautiful.*

23. Robert Lautman to LIK, letter, January 15, 1963, Kahn Collection, 030.II.A.55.2. Prints of his photographs are in the Kahn Collection, 030.IV.A.520.2.

24. Scully, "Light, Form, and Power," 165.

NORMAN AND DORIS FISHER HOUSE

1. The Fishers purchased their lot on May 31, 1957, Montgomery County (Pa.) Deed Book 2789, p. 402. In 1982 the Fishers acquired an adjacent 1⅕-acre lot and an existing swimming pool, adding terracing and plantings the following year.

2. Nina Fisher, telephone conversation with WW, January 2, 2012. Norman Fisher (1925–2007) and Doris Meyers (born 1926) were married on June 28, 1953. Norman had trained as a family physician at Jefferson Medical College in Philadelphia.

3. Doris Fisher, interview with WW, September 2008.

4. Fisher and Fisher, "Seven Years," 149.

5. Collection of Doris and Norman Fisher Family, "Kahn" (copies at AAUP). The files include a handwritten receipt by Kahn, signed and dated September 14, 1960.

6. While none of the existing drawings is dated, a set of twelve photographs of Kahn at work in his office dated October 20, 1960, shows at least one drawing known to be associated with the earliest phase of the Fisher house in front of him, Pohl Collection, AAUP, photo shoot 39 w.

7. Calendar entries for March 25, 1961, "2:00 Dr. & Mrs. Fisher to office," Kahn Collection, 030.II.A.58.1, and box 121. Additional entries on February 26 and March 22, when the Fishers individually met with the architect, probably contributed to the initial development of this scheme. Numerous meetings are documented from May to September 1961, Kahn Collection, box 121, 030.II.A.9.27, and 030.II.A.58.1.

8. Doris and Norman Fisher, interview with Peter Kirby, video recording, May 29, 1992, AAUP, MOCA Collection. Norman Fisher's remarks were made in reference to the addition of a window in the dining room but can be taken as a basis for understanding Kahn's overall approach.

9. The calendar entry for January 14, 1962, noting "2:00 Fisher, Mr. Lorenzon to office," is the first of several meetings with the estimator; see also calendar entry for June 14, 1963, Kahn Collection, box 121.

10. Calendar entry for December 16, 1962, Kahn Collection, box 121.

11. The students never met the Fishers nor learned their names. The problem was assigned January 21, 1963, and the last class discussion was February 25, from master class notes (Louis I. Kahn), Notebook of David G. De Long, courtesy David G. De Long.

12. For this date, see calendar entry, Kahn Collection, box 121. The drawings show signs of tack marks at the corners, an indication that they were pinned up in the office for presentation.

13. Calendar entry, Kahn Collection, box 121, and 030.II.A.58.1.

14. This figure was recounted in Fisher and Fisher, "Seven Years," 151. No actual cost estimates survive in the Kahn Collection to verify this amount.

15. Handwritten note by Kahn on verso of second-floor plan drawing, December 22, 1963 set, Collection of Doris and Norman Fisher Family. For reference to his trip to India and Pakistan, see calendar entries in December 1963 and January 1964, Kahn Collection, box 121. According to his calendar, his flight departed on Sunday, December 22.

16. Calendar entries, Kahn Collection, box 121, and 030.II.A.58.1a.

17. LIK, handwritten note on first-floor plan drawing, December 22, 1963 set, Collection of Doris and Norman Fisher Family.

18. Meeting minutes, August 15, 1964, Collection of Doris and Norman Fisher Family, "Mill Rd 197 III" (copies at AAUP).

19. Owner/contractor agreement, signed and dated October 24, 1964, ibid. A series of 35 mm slides dated 11/64 show a bulldozer clearing the site, AAUP, Fisher Collection.

20. Outline specifications, dated May 11, 1964, with revisions June 4 and September 3, Collection of Doris and Norman Fisher Family, "Kahn" (copies at AAUP).

21. Meeting minutes, August 15, 1964, Collection of Doris and Norman Fisher Family, "Mill Rd. 197 III" (copies at AAUP).

22. Fisher and Fisher, "Seven Years," 157; see calendar entries for November 17 and December 28, 1964, and January 4, March 8, and April 17, 1965, Kahn Collection, box 121.

23. E. Arol Fesmire to Dr. Norman Fisher, invoices, October 7, 1965, November 10, 1965, December 3, 1965, and January 6, 1966, Collection of Doris and Norman Fisher Family, "Mill Road I" (copies at AAUP).

24. Kahn suggested alternative types of stone in a letter to Fesmire, dated May 20, 1965, noting that any substitutes "must not have a mica shine and ... must not be too light in color," Collection of Doris and Norman Fisher Family, "Kahn" (copies at AAUP). The lintels were deleted per revision on sheet 31 of the construction drawings, Kahn Collection, 030.I.C.570.1.

25. Kahn's preference is noted in a letter from David Wisdom to Fesmire, December 1, 1965: "Mr. Kahn still feels that [the chimney] should go to the height shown on drawing No. 8, revised 18 June 1965, that is 8' 6" above roof," Collection of Doris and Norman Fisher Family, "Mill Rd. 197 III" (copies at AAUP).

26. E. Arol Fesmire to Dr. Norman Fisher, invoices, February 4, 1966, April 7, 1966, and June 6, 1966, Collection of Doris and Norman Fisher Family, "Mill Road I" (copies at AAUP).

27. Norman and Doris Fisher, interview with Peter Kirby, video recording, May 29, 1992, AAUP, MOCA Collection.

28. See Booher, "Fisher House."

29. E. Arol Fesmire to Dr. Norman Fisher, invoice, July 11, 1967. Norman Fisher's undated handwritten tabulations detail a base cost of $38,450; revisions in 1964 costing $1,963; $800 for full basement under sleeping volume; $12,055 for mechanical systems; and $399.51 for bonding, totaling $53,677.51, Collection of Doris and Norman Fisher Family, "Mill Road I" (copies at AAUP).

30. Doris Fisher, interview with WW, September 2008.

31. In 1969, following the engagement of one of their daughters, the couple asked Kahn to design a timber bridge over the creek to provide access to a meadow area that was to be used for the wedding ceremony.

32. Norman Fisher, from Norman and Doris Fisher, interview with Peter Kirby, video recording, May 29, 1992, AAUP, MOCA Collection.

33. "We treat the exterior of the house almost like a piece of furniture. Through trial and error we came up with a regimen to bring out the beauty of the cypress. About every fourth year, when the wood is developing a little irregular graying, we wash and scrub the walls with sodium hypochlorite (Clorox). The formula is roughly four parts water with one part chemical. If there is much dirt we may add a little trisodium phosphate, as a detergent. When dry we use a colorless linseed oil, such as Cabots 3000. It requires a moderate amount of effort, but the results are well worth the work and the expense"; Fisher and Fisher, "Seven Years," 159.

34. Ibid., 161. See also Bruce Schoenfeld, "Cultural Icon: Preserving a Louis Kahn—Designed Home," *Sotheby's International Realty Domain* 2, no. 1 (1999): 37–41.

STEVEN AND TOBY KORMAN HOUSE

1. LIK, in "Focus on Kahn," *Interior Design,* 134.

2. Alan J. Heavens, "Master Builder for 80 Years," *Philadelphia Inquirer,* June 7, 1998.

3. See Henry J. Holcomb, "From a Mistake, an Industry Leader Emerged," *Philadelphia Inquirer,* February 9, 2004.

4. Survey of subdivision for Korman Communities, December 18, 1970, Kahn Collection, 030.I.C.845.4.

5. *House Beautiful* and *House and Garden* individually pursued Kahn to publish his design alongside those of the other two houses in the compound. Susan Lewin, design editor, *House Beautiful,* to LIK, letter, June 15, 1973; and Robert Lautman, photographer for *House and Garden,* telephone message, January 23, 1974, Kahn Collection, 030.II.A.36.28.

6. Calendar entry for February 6, 1971, "9:30 Lynne Honickman" and "4:00 Steve Korman," Kahn Collection, 030.II.A.52.29.

7. Steven Korman, quoted in Fleeson, "Kahn's Castle."

8. "The Korman Family: A New Home," undated typescript, n.p., Kahn Collection, 030.II.A.36.25.

9. Calendar entry, "11:30 Kormans," March 11, 1972, Kahn Collection, 030.II.A.50.30. For the preliminary design set, dated March 11, 1972, see Kahn Collection, 030.I.C.845.1.

10. Steven Korman, conversation with WW, c. 2005.

11. For a discussion of this, see David B. Brownlee, in Brownlee and De Long, *In the Realm,* 99.

12. Client/builder contract, Kahn Collection, 030.II.A.36.27. It was expected that construction would begin "approximately October 18."

13. LIK, in "Focus on Kahn," *Interior Design,* 134. Kahn's statements are excerpted from an audio recording from 1973 in the Kahn Collection.

BIBLIOGRAPHY

Alexander, A. H. "Modern House in Rustic Setting." *Philadelphia Inquirer,* October 12, 1947.

Barnes, Barbara. "Architects' Prize-Winning Houses Combine Best Features of Old and New." *Philadelphia Bulletin,* May 20, 1950.

Booher, Pierson William. "Louis I. Kahn's Fisher House: A Case Study on the Architectural Detail and Design Intent." Master's thesis, University of Pennsylvania, 2009.

Brownlee, David B. "Turning a Corner with Louis I. Kahn." In *The Building and the Town: Essays for Eduard F. Sekler,* ed. Wolfgag Böhm, 48–58. Vienna: Böhlau, 1994.

—— and David G. De Long. *Louis I. Kahn: In the Realm of Architecture.* Los Angeles: Museum of Contemporary Art, 1991.

Burton, Joseph A. "The Aesthetic Education of Louis I. Kahn, 1912–1924." *Perspecta* 28 (1997): 204–17.

Büttiker, Urs. *Louis I. Kahn: Light and Space.* Basel: Birkhäuser, 1993.

Eisenbrand, Jochen. "Between Grid and Pathway: The Houses of Louis Kahn." In Kries, Eisenbrand, and von Moos, *Power of Architecture,* 49–66.

Eisenman, Peter. "From Plaid Grid to Diachronic Space: Louis I. Kahn, Adler House, and DeVore House, 1954–55." In *Ten Canonical Buildings, 1950–2000,* 102–26. New York: Rizzoli, 2008.

Esherick, Joseph. "An Architectural Practice in the San Francisco Bay Area, 1938–1996." An oral history conducted in 1994–1996 by Suzanne B. Riess, Regional Oral History Office, Bancroft Library, University of California, Berkeley, 1996.

Fisher, Nina. "Fisher House." In "Visions of the Real, II: Modern Houses in the 20th Century," special issue, *A + U,* October 2000, 202–17.

Fisher, Norman, and Doris Fisher. "Seven Years with Louis I. Kahn." In Yukata Saito, *Louis I. Kahn Houses,* 149–61. Tokyo: TOTO Shuppan, 2003.

Fleeson, Lucinda. "Kahn's Castle." *Philadelphia Inquirer,* August 30, 1993.

"Focus on Kahn." *Interior Design* 45 (November 1974): 128–35.

Ford, Katherine Morrow, and Thomas H. Creighton. *The American House Today.* New York: Reinhold, 1951.

Frampton, Kenneth. "Louis I. Kahn and the French Connection." *Oppositions* 22 (Fall 1980): 20–53.

———. "Louis Kahn: Korman House." In *American Masterworks: The Twentieth-Century House,* 154–63. New York: Rizzoli, 1995.

Giurgola, Romaldo, and Jaimini Mehta. *Louis I. Kahn.* Boulder, Colo.: Westview, 1975.

Goldhagen, Sarah Williams. *Louis Kahn's Situated Modernism.* New Haven: Yale University Press, 2001.

Greenberg, Stephen. "Re-examining the House." *AJ,* March 1992, 22–25.

Hanson, Shirley. "Kahn House Called a Chalice of Light." *Chestnut Hill (Pa.) Local,* April 2, 1970.

Hitchcock, Henry Russell. *Modern Architecture: Romanticism and Reintegration.* New York: Payson and Clarke, 1929.

Hochstim, Jan. *The Paintings and Sketches of Louis I. Kahn.* New York: Rizzoli, 1991.

Holman, William G. *The Travel Sketches of Louis I. Kahn.* Philadelphia: The Academy, 1978.

"House in Melrose Park, Penn." *Architectural Forum* 83 (August 1945): 132–34.

House: The Korman Residence, Louis Kahn's Final Residential Commission. DVD. Directed by Glenn Holsten. Fort Washington, Pa., privately issued, 2008.

"Houses by Louis I. Kahn." Special issue, *A + U* 461 (February 2009).

Jarzombek, Mark. "'Good-Life Modernism' and Beyond: The American House in the 1950s and 1960s." *Cornell Journal of Architecture,* Fall 1990, 76–93, 208.

Johnson, Eugene J., and Michael J. Lewis. *Drawn from the Source: The Travel Sketches of Louis I. Kahn.* Cambridge, Mass.: MIT Press, 1996.

Kahn, Louis I., and Doris Fisher. "House Within a House." In "Houses by Louis I. Kahn," *A + U* 461 (February 2009): 48–54.

Kaye, Ellen. "A Rare Kahn Residence." *Today (Philadelphia Inquirer Magazine),* September 19, 1976, 54–55.

Kries, Mateo, Jochen Eisenbrand, and Stanislaus von Moos, eds. *Louis Kahn: The Power of Architecture.* Weil am Rhein, Germany: Vitra Design Museum, 2012.

Latour, Alessandra, ed. *Louis I. Kahn: L'Uomo, il maestro.* Rome: Kappa, 1986.

———. *Louis I. Kahn: Writings, Lectures, Interviews.* New York: Rizzoli, 1991.

Loud, Patricia Cummings. *The Art Museums of Louis I. Kahn.* Durham: Duke University Press, 1989.

Louis I. Kahn Archive. *Personal Drawings.* 7 vols. New York: Garland, 1987.

"Louis Kahn." *Architecture d'Aujourd'hui* 105 (December 1962–January 1963): 1–39.

Louis Kahn, Architect. Videocassette (VHS). Directed by Paul Falkenberg and Hans Namuth. New York: Museum at Large, 1972.

Maniaque, Caroline. "House, A House, Home." *GA Houses* 44 (December 1994): 12–33.

Marlin, William. "Louis Kahn: Humble Titan of World Architecture." *Christian Science Monitor,* May 8, 1974.

McCarter, Robert. *Louis I. Kahn.* London: Phaidon, 2005.

McHugh, Sharon. "Louis Kahn's Little Known Jewel." *Modern Magazine* 4 (Summer 2012): 42–46.

Mock, Elizabeth, ed. *Built in USA, 1932–1944.* New York: Museum of Modern Art, 1944.

"Modern Space Framed with Traditional Artistry." *Architectural Forum* 93 (September 1950): 100–105.

My Architect: A Son's Journey. DVD. Directed by Nathanial Kahn. New York: New Yorker Video, 2005.

"New and Different: The Home of Mr. Jesse Oser near Philadelphia." *House and Garden,* September 1944, 78–79.

Norris, Nancy. "Contemporary Home of Mr. and Mrs. Morton Weiss . . ." *Norristown (Pa.) Times Herald,* August 1, 1953.

Noyes, Eliot F. *Organic Design in Home Furnishings.* New York: Museum of Modern Art, 1941.

Platt, Polly. "Philadelphia's Traditional Countryside Is Changing." *Philadelphia Sunday Bulletin,* April 23, 1950.

Reed, Peter S. "Louis I. Kahn: Margaret Esherick House, Chestnut Hill, Pennsylvania, 1959–61; Norman Fisher House, Hatboro, Pennsylvania, 1960–67." Special issue, *GA* 76 (1996).

Ronner, Heinz, and Ralph Baenziger. *Louis Kahn: Dokumentation Arbeitsprozesse.* Zurich: Eidgenoessische Technische Hochschule, 1969.

Ronner, Heinz, and Sharad Jhaveri. *Louis I. Kahn: Complete Work, 1935–1974.* 2nd ed. Basel: Birkhäuser, 1987.

Ross, Phyllis. *Gilbert Rohde: Modern Design for Modern Living.* New Haven: Yale University Press, 2009.

Rowan, Jan C. "Wanting To Be . . . The Philadelphia School." *Progressive Architecture* 42 (April 1961): 131–63.

Saito, Yutaka. *Louis I. Kahn Houses.* Tokyo: TOTO Shuppan, 2003.

Schaffner, Ingrid, ed. *Anne Tyng: Inhabiting Geometry.* Philadelphia: Institute of Contemporary Art, 2012.

Schwartz, Frederic, ed. *Mother's House: The Evolution of Vanna Venturi's House in Chestnut Hill.* New York: Rizzoli, 1992.

Scully, Vincent. "Light, Form, and Power: The New Work of Louis Kahn." *Architectural Forum* 121 (August–September 1964): 162–70.

———. *Louis I. Kahn.* New York: Braziller, 1962.

———. *The Shingle Style Today, or, The Historian's Revenge.* New York: Braziller, 1974.

Shanken, Andrew M. "Between Brotherhood and Bureaucracy: Joseph Hudnut, Louis I. Kahn, and the American Society of Planners and Architects." *Planning Perspectives,* April 2005, 147–75.

Simon, Maron J., ed. *Your Solar House.* New York: Simon and Schuster, 1947.

Stern, Robert A. M. *George Howe: Toward a Modern American Architecture.* New Haven: Yale University Press, 1975.

"A Timeless Sense of Light and Space." *House Beautiful,* September 1966, 170–75.

Twombly, Robert, ed. *Louis Kahn: Essential Texts.* New York: Norton, 2003.

Tyng, Alexandra. *Beginnings: Louis I. Kahn's Philosophy of Architecture.* New York: Wiley, 1984.

Tyng, Anne Griswold, ed. *Louis Kahn to Anne Tyng: The Rome Letters, 1953–1954.* New York: Rizzoli, 1997.

Whitaker, William. "Chronology." In Kries, Eisenbrand, and von Moos, *Power of Architecture,* 21–28.

White, Theo B., ed. *Paul Philippe Cret, Architect and Teacher.* Philadelphia: Art Alliance, 1973.

Whittier, Roxane. "New Type of Furniture Created for Modern Living." *Philadelphia Record,* January 17, 1942.

Wurman, Richard Saul, ed. *What Will Be Has Always Been: The Words of Louis I. Kahn.* New York: Access, 1986.

INDEX

Page numbers in *italics* refer to illustrations.

Aalto, Alvar, 27, 80–81, 102
Adler, Marty, 7, 10
Adler House (unbuilt), 47n48–49, *50*
AIA. *See* American Institute of Architects (AIA)
alcoves
    in Esherick House, 177
    in Fisher House, 198, *199*
    in Genel House, 133–34
    in Korman House, 232
    in Roche House, 112
    in Shapiro House, 51
American Institute of Architects (AIA), 3, 33
American Society of Planners and Architects 3, 110
Architectural Forum (journal), 23, 85, 95, 99, 102, *103*, 120, 191
Architectural Record (journal), 19, 21, 23, 27, 190
Architectural Research Group, 22, 23
Artek-Pascoe catalogue, 81, *82*
artificial lighting, *90*, 91–*92*, *93*
Arts and Crafts Movement, 27, 69, 80
Avon Lea Farm, Charlestown, 33–34

balconies
    in Esherick House, 66, 177, *187*, *188*, *189*, 190
    in Korman House, 225
bedrooms. *See also* master bedroom
    in Esherick House, *191*
    in Fisher House, *212*
    in Genel House, *149*
    in Korman House, 232
    in Oser House, 76, 77–78, 80
    pavilion plans and, 43, 47, 48
Berlage, Hendrik, 18
Bernard, Bernard, 34
Bernard, Reba, 34
Bernard House, Kimberton (Stonorov & Kahn, architects), 34–35
bi-nuclear plan, 41, 43
birch, use of, 81, 82, 87, 112
blinds, *65*
Bobrowicz, Yvonne, 91
Bok, Curtis, 110

Breuer, Marcel, 36, *37*, 41, *86*, 87
Breuer House, Lincoln, Massachusetts (Gropius & Breuer, architects), *37*
Broudo, Louis, 7, 33
Broudo, Rae, 7, 33
Broudo House in Elkins Park (unbuilt), 7, *33*
Bryn Mawr College dormitory, 92
Bucks County, Pennsylvania, school (Tyng plan), *45*
buffet
    in Genel House, 87–89, *88*, 134
    in Oser House, 75, 76, 77
built-in furnishings, 75, 76, 82, 85, 87, 89, 134. *See also* window seat
"butterfly" roof, 120

cabinet pulls, 78–80, *79*
cabinetry, 80–81. *See also* buffet; furnishings; woodwork
    in Oser House, 75, *76*, 255n13
    in Weiss House, 82, *83*
California Arts and Architecture (magazine), *14*, 15
Carrara marble, 42
Carlihan, Elizabeth Ware, 36
cedar, use of, 29, 78, 99
ceilings, 51, 53, 60
    in Clever House, *157*
    in Esherick House, 174
    in Fisher House, 197
    in Genel House, 134
    in Shapiro House, 51
    in Weiss House, 120
chairs. *See* seating
chandelier designs, 92, *93*, 256n50
Cherry Hill, New Jersey. *See* Clever House
Chestnut Hill, Philadelphia. *See* Adler House; Esherick House; High Hollow; Pearson House
"Child's room, 1930" (Kahn watercolor), 20, *21*
Citizens' Council on City Planning, Philadelphia, 152
clerestory windows, 58, 60
Clever, Elaine, 152, 154
Clever, Fred, 7, 9, 152, 154

Clever House, 52, 150–57
    exterior views, *150–51*
    interior views, *156*, *157*
clients. *See also entries for specific clients*
    Kahn's relationships with, 10–13, 75, 95, 223
    lifestyles of, 7–9
    photographs of, *6*, *7*, *9*, *10*, *11*, *16*
Colonial style, 69
color, use of, 87, 89, 91
Congrès International d'Architecture Moderne (CIAM X), 61
construction drawings, 66, 110, 120, 186. *See also* elevations; floor plans; section drawings; site plans
cost considerations, 13
    Clever House and, 152, 154
    Fisher House and, 10, 66, 200, 201, 204, 206–8
    Korman House and, 225
Cret, Paul, 18–19, 28, 253n16
cypress, use of
    Fisher House and, 2, 69, 207, 208, *209*, 215, 218, 260n33
    Genel House and, 133
    Korman House and, 227
    Weiss House and, 120

Day, Kenneth Mackenzie, 27, 29, 112, 223, 252n24
Dechert House (Day, architect), 223
Decorator's Cabinet Shop, 78–80, *79*
De Long, David G., 2–3, 61, 200
Design for Postwar Living design, *14*, 15
DeVore House (unbuilt), 47–48, *49*
dining room, 131
    in Fisher House, 208, *210–11*
    in Genel House, *89*, 146–47, *148*
    in Korman House, 232, *233*, 247
    in later houses, 71
    in Oser House, *106*
    in Stern House, 13
    in Weiss House, *123*
dividers, 87–89, *88*. *See also* screens
drawings by Kahn, 15–17, 31, 81, *82*. *See also* elevations; floor plans; perspective drawings; section drawings; site plans; watercolors by Kahn

263

company logo and, *18,* 19
    sense of home in, *15, 17,* 81, *82*
Dudok, Willem, 18
Duhring, H. Louis, 27, 28

Eames, Charles, *80,* 87
Eames, Ray, 87
East Norriton Township. *See* Weiss House
Ebstel, John, 24
Edgell, George, 27
Eisenman, Peter, 3
elevations
    for Adler House, *50*
    for Broudo House, *33*
    for Esherick House, *61, 62, 65, 188*
    for Fisher House, *67, 198, 199, 200, 202, 204, 208*
    for Genel House, *132, 137, 145*
    for Jaffe House, *46*
    for Korman House, *225*
    for Morris House, *55*
    for Weiss House, *40, 83, 85, 121, 126*
Elkins Park. *See* Oser House
entry design
    in Esherick House, 61, 177, 188
    in Fisher House, 197, 198, 200, 206, 208, *213, 216, 217*
    in Genel House, 133, *138, 139, 142, 143*
    in Goldenberg House, 58
    in Honickman House, 71
    in Korman House, 227, 232, 240–41
    in Shapiro House, *51, 159,* 161, *163, 164–65*
Esherick, Margaret, *9,* 65, 91, 173, 174, 186, 190, 258n6
Esherick, Wharton, 41, 52, 61, 66, 91, 110, 174, 186, 190
Esherick House, *60–66,* 170–93. *See also under specific architectural elements and drawings*
    exterior views, *64, 170–71, 178–85*
    interior views, *186, 187, 189–91*
    natural light and, 60, 61, 63, 65–66
    railings in, 66, 177, *181,* 186, *188, 190*
    woodwork in, 66, 186–88, *187*
European modernism, 24–27

façade, 15, 58
    Esherick House and, 9, 61, 65, 174, 177, 207
    Fisher House and, 2
    Genel House and, 132–33
    Korman House and, 225

Shapiro House and, 161
Weiss House and, 41
Federal Housing Authority (FHA), 9
Fesmire, E. Arol, 207, 225
Finkelsteins, 7
fireplace, 206. *See also* inglenook
    in Esherick House, 61, 66
    in Fisher House, 66
    in Genel House, 133–34
    in Korman House, 232, *233, 234–35, 236*
    in Oser House, *26, 27,* 99, 102, *103, 104, 105*
    in Roche House, *38,* 39, 112
    in Stern House, 69
    in Weiss House, 41, 120, *123*
First Unitarian Church in Rochester, New York, 91
Fisher, Doris, *10,* 218, 259n2
Fisher, Norman, *10,* 218, 259n2
Fisher House, 2, 66–69, 194–215. *See also under specific architectural elements and drawings*
    construction of, 207–8
    design of, 10–11, 66–69, 194–207
    exterior views of, *195, 209–15*
    foundation of, *206,* 207
    furnishings in, 89, 91
    interior views of, *1, 216–19*
    plasterwork and, *1, 2,* 206, 208, 215
    stonework and, 66, 69, *206,* 207
    window seat in, *1,* 215, *217, 219*
    windows in, 207, 208, *209, 210–11,* 215
    woodwork in, *2,* 208, *214,* 215, *216,* 218
flat roofs, 52, 177
Fleisher, Janet, 56
Fleisher, Robert, 56, 254n86
Fleisher House in Elkins Park (unbuilt), *15,* 56–57
flexible screen, 81, *82*
flooring, 99, 161, 215, 232
floor plans
    for Clever House, *153*
    for Esherick House, *60, 62, 176*
    for Fisher House, *67, 68, 196, 199, 201, 203, 205*
    for Fleisher House, *56*
    for Genel House, *135*
    for Goldenberg House, *59*
    for Gussman House, *54*
    for Korman House, *224, 228, 229*
    for Morris House, *53, 55*
    for Oser House, 99, *102, 103*
    for Shapiro House, *162*
    for Swan House, *94,* 95
    for Venturi's Pearson House, *56*

"Form and Design" (Kahn essay), 3
Fortune Rock, Clara Fargo Thomas Mount Desert Island, Maine (George Howe, architect), *29,* 31
Fruchter, Barbara, 17
Fruchter, Leonard, 17
Fruchter House (unbuilt), *17,* 43–47, *44*
functional relationships, 27, 43, 48, 52, 71, 102
    Esherick House and, 177
    Goldenberg House and, 58
    Shapiro House and, 51
furnishings, 75–94, 256n15. *See also* buffet; cabinetry; seating; tables
    Anne Tyng and, 82, 87
    birch in, 81, 82, 87, 112
    built-ins and, 75, 76, 82, 85, 87, 89, 134
    in construction drawings, 75, *77,* 85, 89
    oak in, 76, 78, 79, 82, 208, 215, 227, 232
    open planning and, 81–82
    in Oser House, 75–82, *77, 78,* 102, 105–7, 255n13
    unit furniture and, 80, *81*
    walnut in, 78, 79, 80, 82, 85, 89, 134

Genel, Ruth, *7,* 131, 134
Genel, Samuel, *7 ,* 131, 134
Genel House, 41–43, 128–49. *See also under specific architectural elements and drawings*
    design studies for, 131–34
    dividers in, 87–89, *88*
    exterior views of, *128–29, 136, 138, 139, 140–41*
    furnishings in, *7,* 87–89, *88, 90,* 134, *146–48*
    interior views of, *42, 142–44, 146–47, 148–49*
geometrical ordering, 27, 63
    Anne Tyng and, 45, 47, 52
    Kahn's explorations of, 43, 47, 52, 57–58, 133
"giant pointillism," 85
Gilchrist, Edmund, 28
Glass House, New Canaan, Connecticut (Philip Johnson, architect), 43
Glenwood Low-Cost Housing Competition, 29
Goldenberg, Mitzi, 13
Goldenberg, Morton, 13
Goldenberg House (unbuilt), 57–60, *58, 59,* 69
Good-Life Modernism, 43
grapevine joint, 232
Gropius, Walter, 36, 37
Gropius House, Lincoln, Massachusetts (Gropius & Breuer, architects), 36–37
Gussman House (unbuilt), 52–53, *54*

264

"Harvard box," 36
Hatboro, Montgomery County. *See* Fisher House
Heilveil, Maurice, 257n3
Hejduk, John, 3
Herman Miller Furniture Company, 76, 77
hexagonal geometry, 52
hierarchy, concept of, 49, 51–53, 59
High Hollow (George Howe house, Chestnut Hill), *28,* 51
hip roofs, 49, 51, 52
Hochstim, Jan, 21
Holtkamp, Ewald, 81
home, Kahn's sense of, 5–7, 15–17, 71
Honickman, Harold, 69
Honickman, Lynne, 69, 223
Honickman House (unbuilt), *68, 71,* 223
House and Garden (magazine), 102
House in the Museum Garden (Breuer), *86,* 87
Houston, Henry H., 110
Howe, George
    houses by, *28, 29, 31,* 48, 51, 223
    influence on Kahn, 28–31, 33, 47
Howe & Lescaze, architects, *21,* 28, 29
Huff, William, 58, 69

idealized forms, 48–49, 55
inglenook. *See also* fireplace
    in Esherick House, *62,* 66
    in Fisher House, *2,* 66, 71, *197, 198,* 200, *204, 206*
    in Genel House, *42, 43, 144, 146–47*
    in Korman House, 223, 228, *229, 234–35, 236*
    in later houses, 71
    in Morris House, 53
    in Oser House, *26, 27,* 75, 99, 102, *103, 104, 105*
    in Roche House, 39, *114–15*
    as separate element, 66, 71
    in Shapiro House, 51, *166*
    traditional, 39, 58, 66
    in Weiss House, *40, 41, 83*
International Style, 33

Jacobson, Hugh Newell, 223
Jaffe, Ida, 7, 13
Jaffe House, *46,* 47
Jarzombek, Mark, 43
Jeanneret, Pierre, 23
Jersey Homesteads, Hightstown, New Jersey, *24,* 24–26

Jewish Community Center Bathhouse, Ewing Township, New Jersey, (Kahn, architect), *51–52, 58,* 152
John Burnett and Partners, architects, *19*
Johnson, Philip, 43, 57–58
Journal of the American Institute of Architects, 22, 23

Kahn, Esther, 7–8, 31, 91, 131, 251n7, 257n2
Kahn, Louis, *4, 87,* 206
    children of, 251n7
    early architectural influences on, 18–27
    essays by, 3, 23
    "Harvard box" and, 36
    location of Philadelphia-area houses by, *8*
    mass housing and, 23–24
    modernist houses and, 18–23
    patrons of, 7–13
    personality of, 10
    Philadelphia architects and, 27–36
    sense of home and, 5–7, 15–17, 71
    teaching assignments by, 84, 131, 200–201
    Tyng's design influence on, 36–37, *39*
Kahn, Nathaniel, 251n7
Kahn, Sue Ann, 5–6, 251n7
Kahn & Kopelan logo, *18–21*
Kastner, Alfred, 24
keypost, *188*
Kikutake, Kiyonori, 255n99
kitchen
    in Esherick House, *190*
    in Fisher House, *197, 198,* 208, *215*
    in Korman House, 232, *246*
    in Weiss House, 82, *83,* 126
Klumb, Henry, 15
Knoll, Florence, 87
Knoll furniture company, 87
Kopelan, Solis Daniel, 18, 252n1
Korman, Berton, 223
Korman, Larry, 232
Korman, Leonard, 223
Korman, Steven, 10, 69, 91, 223
Korman, Toby, 69, 223, 225
Korman family, 16
Korman House, *16, 68, 71,* 220–49. *See also under specific architectural elements and drawings*
    exterior views of, *72–73, 220, 226–27, 239, 248–49, 250*

    furnishings in, *89, 230–31, 233, 234–35*
    interior views of, *230–31, 233, 234–37, 240–47*
    plans for, *16, 222, 223–25, 224*
Kurtz, Elaine, 91

Lally columns, 29, 36
landscape. *See also* nature and place
    structural integration with, 36, 51, 71, 99
    windows onto, 21, 69, 71, 190, 197, 200, 227
Langsfield, Judith, 223
L'Architecte (journal), 19
Le Corbusier (Charles-Édouard Jeanneret), 19, 23–24, 33, 252n10, 253n16
    housing estate in Pessac (1925), 23–24
    Maison Planeix, Paris, *19*
    monastery of La Tourette, 61, *63*
Léger, Fernand, 27
Leidner, Bobette, 102
Leidner, Nelson, 102
Lemen quarry, 41
Lescaze, William, 28
Libbey-Owens-Ford, 36
lighting. *See* artificial lighting; natural light
linked-pavilion concept, 47. *See also* pavilion-plan concept
living room, 131
    in Clever House, *156*
    in Esherick House, *186, 187, 189*
    in Fisher House, *1, 2, 213, 217*
    in Genel House, *87, 88, 146–47*
    in Korman House, *89,* 227, *230–32*
    in Oser House, 77, *107*
    in Roche House, *114–15*
    in Shapiro House, *167*
    in Weiss House, *83, 85, 86, 124, 125*
loggia, in Genel House, *140–41*
Lurçat, André, 18

McAllister, Louis E., 31
McGlinn family, 131
McGoodwin, Robert Rhodes, 28
Mack, Arthur, 81

Madokoro, Yukio, 66
Magaziner, Louis, 15
Magaziner & Eberhard (architecture firm), 23
Maison Planeix, Paris, *19*
Mallet-Stevens, Robert, 18
Marlin, William, 95

Marshall Cole House, New Hope, *27*
masonry. *See* stonework
masonry piers, 53, *55*
Massara, Carl, 223
mass housing, 23–24, 31–33, *32*
master bedroom
    in Esherick House, *191*
    furnishings for, 76–80, *78, 79*
    in Gussman House, 53
    in Korman House, 223, *232, 238,* 244–45
    in Oser House, 76–80, *78, 79,* 99, *101*
materials, 24, 186, 188, 253n24. *See also* stonework; woodwork; *entries for specific types of wood*
    Fisher House and, 208, 215, 218
    Genel House and, *42, 43*
    Korman House and, 223, 232
    later houses and, 69, 71
    Weiss House and, 41
Mathsson, Bruno, 81
Meigs, Arthur I., 27
Mellor, Meigs & Howe (architecture firm), 28
Mellor, Walter, 27
Meyerson, Margy, 91–92
Meyerson, Martin, 91–92
Meyerson House renovation (Philadelphia), 91–*92, 93*
Moderne Bauformen (journal), *21*
modernism, 18–24, 81, 89
"Montgomeryville" stone, 207, 208
Moore, Charles, 3
Morris, Lawrence, 10
Morris, Ruth, 10
Morris House (unbuilt), 10, 52, 53, *55*
mural, 82, *84, 85,* 120, *125*
Museum of Modern Art, New York
    Aalto exhibition (1938), 81
    Breuer's exhibition house in (1949), 37, *86,* 87
    Kahn exhibition (1966), 69
    Organic Design in Home Furnishings exhibition, *80, 81*

Nakashima, George, 91
Narberth. *See* Shapiro House
National Assembly complex, Dhaka, Bangladesh, 91
natural light, 65, 87, 91
    Esherick House and, *60, 61, 63,* 65–66
    Fisher House and, 215
    Goldenberg House and, 58, *60*

    later houses and, 69, 71
    monastery of La Tourette and, 61
    Weiss House and, 120, *122*
nature and place, 1, 65, 69, 119–20. *See also* landscape; materials; natural light; site specificity
Nelson, George, 87
neo-Palladianism, 57–58
Noguchi, Isamu, 66

oak, use of
    in flooring, 99, 161, 215
    in furnishings, 76, 78, *79,* 82, 208, 215, 227, 232
    in woodwork, 186, *187, 188*
Oak Lane Country Day School classroom, Philadelphia (Howe & Lescaze, architects), *21*
open planning, 81–82
Organic Design in Home Furnishings exhibition, *80, 81*
Ösel (now Saaremaa), Baltic island, 5
Oser, Jesse, 98
Oser (McLeod), Julie, 75, 257n2
Oser, Ruth, 9
Oser, Wendy, 257n2
Oser House, 17, 96–107, *106*. *See also under specific architectural elements and drawings*
    exterior views of, *25,* 96–*97, 98, 99,* 100–*101*
    furnishings in, 75–82, *77, 78,* 102, 105–7, 255n13
    inglenook in, *26,* 27, 75, 99, 102, *103, 104, 105*
    interior views of, *76,* 104–7
    later residents of, 17, 102
    local building traditions and, 24–27, *25, 26*
    use of tile in, 99, 102, *104, 105*
Östberg, Ragner, 18

paintings, 91. *See also* mural; watercolors by Kahn
Palladio, Andrea, *57,* 58
Pascoe, Clifford, 81
Pattison, Harriet, 71, 251n7
pavilion-plan concept, 43, 45, 47–52, *48, 49, 50, 51*
Pearson, Forrest G., Jr., 56
Pearson House (Venturi), *56*
Pennsylvania Solar House, *36–37*
perspective drawings
    for Esherick House, *172, 174, 175*
    for Fruchter House, *17*
    for Jersey Homesteads, *24*
    for Oser House, *77,* 81, *103*

    for Pine Ford Acres, *31*
    for Silver End (English housing estate), *19*
    for Solar House, *36*
    for Windmill unit, *22*
Pfau, Bernard, 21
Philadelphia
    influence of local architects and, 27–36
    Kahn's own houses in, 5, 91
    local building traditions and, 27–29 (*see also* Howe, George; vernacular architecture)
    locations of Kahn houses in, 7–9, *8*
Philadelphia Housing Authority, 27, 29
Philadelphia Inquirer (newspaper), 99
Philadelphia Psychiatric Hospital, 131
Philadelphia Row House study (1951–53), *43*
Philadelphia Savings Fund Society (PSFS), 9
Philip Dechert House (Day, architect), 223
Phillips Exeter Academy library in New Hampshire, 89
Piña, Leslie, 255n9
Pine Ford Acres, Middletown, 31–33, *32*
plasterwork, *1, 2,* 161, 206, 208, 215
playroom, Düsseldorf, 1929 (Pfau drawing), *21*
prefabricated houses, *14, 15*
preservation, 215, 218
PSFS. *See* Philadelphia Savings Fund Society (PSFS)
PSFS building (Howe & Lescaze, architects), 28–29
pyramidal roofs, 154, 161, 254n73

Radburn, New Jersey, 23
railings, 66, 177, *181,* 186, *188, 190*
Raymond, Noemi, 80
restrictive easements, 218
Risom, Jens, 87, 89
Roberts, Ralph, 45, 47
Roche, Jocelyn, 13, 110
Roche, Philip Q., 9, 110
Roche House (Stonorov & Kahn, architects), 108–15. *See also under specific architectural elements and drawings*
    drawings for, 45, 110, *111, 112, 113*
    exterior views of, *108–9, 113*
    interior views of, *114–15*
    site for, *111–12*
Rockefeller, John D., Jr., 112
Rohde, Gilbert, 75–76, *77,* 80, 255n9

roof structure. *See also* flat roofs; hip roofs;
    pyramidal roofs
  Adler House and, 49, *50*
  Clever House and, 154
  Devore House and, 48
  Esherick House and, 174, 177
  Fisher House and, 198, 207
  Goldenberg House and, 58
  Morris House and, 52, *53*
  Pine Ford Acres and, *32*, 33
  Shapiro House and, *51*, 161
  Weiss House and, 41, 120, *121*
  Windmill house and, 23

Saaremaa (Ösel), Baltic island, 5
Saarinen, Eero, *80*, 87, 89
Saarinen, Eliel, 18
Sainte Marie de La Tourette, Eveux, Rhône-
    Alpes, France, 61, *63*, 65
Saldutti, Carl, *206*
Salk, Jonas, 10, 225
Salk Institute, 196, 255n99
Schumacher, Fritz, 18
Schuyler, Montgomery, 27
screens, 37, 65, 66, 81, *82*, 186, *188*. *See also* dividers
screen walls, 41, 48, 53, 56
Scully, Vincent, Jr., 2–3, 39, 60
seating
  in Fisher House, 69, 197
  in Genel House, 89, *133*
  in Goldenberg House, 58
  in Oser House, 81
  outdoor, *127*, 133
  in Weiss House, 82, 87, *124*, *127*
section drawings
  for Clever House, *155*
  for Fisher House, *197*
  for Genel House, *133*
  for Roche House, *112*
  for Shapiro House, *160*
Seiver, Alice, 10
"shadow joint" detail, 41
Shaker style, 69
Shanken, Andrew, 3
Shapiro, Bernard, 161
Shapiro, Norma, 13, 161
Shapiro House, 49, 158–69. *See also under specific*
    architectural elements and drawings
  exterior views of, *50*, *51*, *158–59*, *163*, *168–69*
  furnishings in, 89, 91, *166*, *167*
  interior views of, *164–67*

Sherman, Jay, 31
Sherman, Kit, 7, 31
Shingle Style, 39, 66
shutters, 63, 65, 69
  in Esherick House, *64*, 177, *186*, *189*, 190, *191*
  in Korman House, 225, 232
Salk Institute and, 255n99
Silver, Mrs. Paul, 17
Silver End Garden Village, Essex, England, *19*
Simpson, W. Percy, estate of, 131
site plans
  for Devore House, *49*
  for Esherick House, *173*, 174
  for Genel House, *130*
  for Jaffe House, *46*, 47
  for Korman House, *222*, *223*, *227*
  for Philadelphia Row House studies, *43*
  for Roche House, *111*, *112*, *113*
  for Solar House, *37*
  for Stern House, *12*
  for Weiss House, *118*
site specificity
  Goldenberg House and, 58, 60
  Howe's Square Shadows and, 29
  Oser House and, 99
Sky House (Kikutake, architect), 255n99
slate, 43, 133, 208
"society of rooms" concept, 69
Square Shadows, Whitemarsh Township
    (George Howe, architect), *28–29*, 48, 223
Staal, J. F., 18
staircases. *See also* railings
  in Fisher House, *216*
  in Korman House, 232, *240–41*, *242–43*, *244*
  in Shapiro House, *160*
stair screen, 186, *188*
Stein, Clarence, 23
Stern, Helen (Leni), 9, 10, *11*, 13, 69
Stern, Philip, 9, 10, *11*, 13, 69
Stern House (unbuilt), 9, 13, 69, *70*
Stetson, J. B., estate of, 98
Stonebridge, 17, 102. *See also* Oser House
stonework
  Fisher House and, 66, 69, 197, 198, *201*, *204*,
    206, *207*–8
  Genel House and, *132*
  Korman House and, 223
  Oser House and, 98
  Weiss House and, *40*, 41, 120
Stonorov, Oscar, 29, 33–34, *80*, *81*

Strand, Paul, 31
structural expression. *See also*
    pavilion-plan concept
  Genel House and, 41–43, 132
  ideal forms and, 55–56
  Jaffe House and, 47
  later houses and, 69, 71
  Weiss House and, 41
"Styles—Archaeology" (Cret paper), 18
supports. *See also* Lally columns
  Adler plan and, 48, 49
  Esherick House and, 186
  Weiss House and, 41
Sutton, Willie, 110
Swan, Eric, 95
Swan, Simone, 95
Swan House, Southold, New York (unbuilt), *94*, 95
Swastika Cottages (Henry Wright, architect), *22*

tables
  in Fisher House, 66
  in Genel House, *89*, 134
  in Weiss House, *85–87*, 86
Tait, Thomas S., 19
textiles, *76*, *78*, 91
Thomas, Clara Fargo, 29
tile, use of, 99, 102, *104*, *105*, 112, 134
timber framing, 29, 69, 120, 132, 161
trapezoidal plan, 36–37
Trenton Bathhouse. *See* Jewish Community
    Center Bathhouse, Ewing Township,
    New Jersey
Tulsa, Oklahoma. *See* Gussman House
Tyng, Alexandra, 251n7
Tyng, Anne Griswold, 85, *87*, 119, 134, 251n7
  influence on Kahn, 36–37, 39, 47, 52, 82, 87
  pavilion-plan concept and, 45, 47
  plans by, *45*, *113*, *121*, *135*, *155*, *160*, *162*

United Nations Headquarters siting, 110–12
unit furniture, 75–76, *79*, *80*, *81*
University of Pennsylvania
  Richards Medical Laboratories at, 53, 152
  teaching at, 200–202
utility spaces, 15, 120
  in Esherick House, 177
  in Fisher House, 66, 198, *215*
  in Genel House, 132
  in Goldenberg House, 58
  in Oser House, 99
  in Weiss House, 120

"The Value and Aim in Sketching" (Kahn essay), 23
Venturi, Robert, 9, 55–56
vernacular architecture, 27–34, 36–41
Versen, Kurt, 81
Villa Capra, "La Rotunda," *57, 58*
von Moltke, Willo, 80, *81*
Vreeland, Thomas R., 254n73

wall colors, 87
Wall Street Pastorale, 28
walnut, use of, 78, *79,* 80, 82, 85, 89, 134
Wasserman house. *See* Square Shadows
watercolors by Kahn
    of child's room (1930), *20, 21*
    of fishermen's houses, Percé, Quebec, *30, 31*
Weise, Frank. *See* Weiss, Frank
Weiss, Frank, 36
Weiss, Lenore, *6, 7,* 119
Weiss, Morton ("Bubby"), *6,* 119
Weiss House, 3, 39–41, 116–27. *See also under*
    specific architectural elements and drawings
    exterior views of, *39, 116–17, 127*
    furnishings in, 82–87, *83–86*
    interior views of, *86, 123–26, 126*
    mural in, 82, *84,* 85, 120, *125*
    music center in, 82, *83*
Wheelwright, Edmund, 255n103
Whitemarsh Township, Montgomery County.
    See Korman House; Roche House
Windmill plan, *22,* 23–24
windows. *See also* clerestory windows;
    natural light
    in Fisher House, *207,* 208, *209, 210–11, 215*
    floor-to-ceiling, 19, 71, 177, 225
    in Korman House, 227, *228–29*
    landscape view and, 21, 69, 71, 190, 197, 200, 227
    in Weiss House, *122*
window seat, *1,* 215, *217, 219*
Wissahickon schist, 98
Wogenscky, André, 61
wooden latching, *63,* 65
wood screen, 66, 186, *188*
wood siding, 27, 29, 41, 99, 132. *See also* cypress, use of
Woodward, Charles, 174, 177
Woodward, George, 174
Woodwards of Chestnut Hill, 9, 61, 110, 174

woodwork, 69, 91, *91,* 232, 255n99. *See also*
    entries for specific types of wood
    in Esherick House, 66, 186–88, *187*
    in Fisher House, 2, 208, *214, 215, 216,* 218
World Design Conference (Tokyo, 1960), 65
Wright, Frank Lloyd, 53
Wright, Henry, *22,* 23, 252n19
Wyndmoor. *See* DeVore House
Wynnefield, Philadelphia. *See* Fruchter House
Wynnewood, Lower Merion Township.
    See Genel House; Jaffe House

Yale Center for British Art, 91
Yale University, 39, 119, 257n6
    studio class problems at, 82, 131

ILLUSTRATION CREDITS

Jamie Ardiles-Arce, Kahn Collection: figs. 246, 248, 250

David B. Brownlee: fig. 31

Urs Büttiker: figs. 166, 169, 170

R. T. Dooner, AAUP: fig. 32

John Ebstel, Kahn Collection © Keith de Lellis Gallery: figs. 2, 28, 29, 123, 143, 144, 147, 148, 154, 156, 159, 161

Norman Fisher, AAUP: figs. 211–213

Edward Gallob, AAUP: fig. 52

Gottscho-Schleisner, Kahn Collection: figs. 93, 97, 124

Historic American Buildings Survey, Library of Congress Prints and Photographs Division: figs. 43, 195

Herman Miller: fig. 96

Courtland V. D. Hubbard, AAUP: fig. 38

Kahn Collection: figs. 48, 109, 137, 139, 225

Rollin R. LaFrance: fig. 46

© Robert C. Lautman Photography, National Building Museum, Washington, D.C.: fig. 82

Gottscho-Schleisner Collection, Library of Congress, Prints and Photographs Division: figs. 36, 130, 132

Ralph Lieberman: figs. 98–100

© Rene Burri, Magnum Photos: fig. 81

Marshall D. Meyers, AAUP: figs. 72, 74

Grant Mudford: frontispiece, figs. 1, 122, 125, 145, 186, 199, 217–224

John Nicolais, AAUP: figs. 215, 216

Anandaroop Roy: fig. 5

Yutaka Saito, AAUP: fig. 180

Ben Schnall, AAUP: fig. 33

© Ezra Stoller/ESTO: fig. 110

Lewis Tanner: fig. 3

© Matt Wargo: figs. 49, 61, 62, 91, 129, 131, 133, 138, 149, 157, 158, 160, 163–165, 171, 175–179, 185, 187, 188, 190, 191, 193, 194, 196–197, 227, 233, 235–245, 247, 249

Morton Weiss, AAUP: fig. 111

William Whitaker: figs. 118, 189, 198, 226